The Evasive Neutral

The Evasive Neutral

Germany, Britain and the Quest for a Turkish Alliance in the Second World War

Frank G. Weber

University of Missouri Press
Columbia & London, 1979

Library of Congress Cataloging in Publication Data
Weber, Frank G
    The evasive neutral.

    Bibliography: p. 221
    1. World War, 1939–1945—Diplomatic history.
2. Turkey—Neutrality. 3. Turkey—Foreign relations—
Germany. 4. Germany—Foreign relations—Turkey.
5. Turkey—Foreign relations—Great Britain. 6. Great
Britain—Foreign relations—Turkey. I. Title.
D754.T8W42   940.53′2   78-19641
ISBN 0-8262-0262-4

for Marie

Preface

The foreign policy of Turkey during the Second World War ought to have been determined by the alliance treaty the Turkish government signed with the British and the French in the autumn of 1939. Instead, the Turks did not live up to their pledge and followed an unforeseen course perplexing and infuriating to their allies. Only in 1944 did the Turks sever relations with Germany; a few months later, they timorously issued a declaration of war. But at no time were they active combatants for the allied coalition. Britain and later the United States scored Turkish diplomacy as one of unremitting bad faith. Turkish historians, and some foreign scholars, on the other hand, have defended it as the only reasonable course for a country with a small military establishment and a weak economy.

The Turkish archives are still closed to scholars, but official German and British correspondence that has been opened since the war suggests that Turkey's defenders are only partly correct. In 1938, the Turks would have preferred an alliance with Germany to the one they were to negotiate a year later with Britain and France. But at that time the Berlin foreign ministry was unwilling to accept a partnership with them. Some German statesmen valued an arrangement with the Arabs over an alliance with the Turks, while others strove for an untroubled relationship with Russia that would postpone the threat of war on the eastern front when fighting broke out in the West. They did not want to conspire with Turkey, Russia's ancient foe. Accordingly, Germany rebuffed the Turks and drove them to compound terms with Britain. When they finally sat down at the conference table, the Turks, whatever reservations they might have had, parleyed with keenness and enthusiasm. The Turkish negotiators said little about their country's military and economic debilities —the very debilities that some historians have cited as the justification for Turkish foreign policy decisions.

The Germans soon recognized that they had been wrong in rejecting Turkish help. As their relations with Whitehall and the Kremlin deteriorated in turn, the strategical attraction of a Turkish alliance grew proportionately. The Turks could have manned one arm of a giant German pincers. Moving up from the south, they could have helped to snare and annihilate the Red Army; descending from the north, they might have rolled over Britain's undermanned outposts in the Middle East. When, however, the blitzkrieg failed to subjugate the British, the Turks were no less eager for intervention but began to raise its price. They pressed the Germans to invade Iraq so that Turkey could acquire the oil of Mosul. In return for the prospect of an overland route to the Levant and Egypt, the Germans entered on this Iraqi gambit, though it was not part of their original timetable. Their preparations were skimpy, their plan of action unclear, and their defeat at Baghdad ignominious.

Germany's ejection from Iraq in 1941 cost her the trust of her Arab partisans and made her more vulnerable than ever to Turkish extortion. The Turks alone held the key to the overland route to the Suez Canal and the Persian Gulf, in short to those areas where Germany might best beat the British quickly and decisively. London had good reason to be grateful for Turkey's neutrality, which blocked Hitler's access to the Middle East. But, on the whole, the British government still considered the Anglo-Turkish alliance an unfruitful and humiliating relationship. Churchill wanted to open a Second Front in the Balkans, but Turkey's refusal to participate helped to frustrate his goal. He wanted to funnel more matériel to beleaguered Russia, but the Turks barred the Straits to this traffic. Lastly, the Turks threatened the integrity of the British Empire itself. They offered to come into the war in return for the cession of the Dodecanese islands, taken from the Turkish sultan by Italy in 1911. The Foreign Office might have conceded this demand had it not been aware that Turkey was ready to couple it with a claim to the British Crown Colony of Cyprus. Cyprus was legally Turkish until 1914, and a sizable Turkish minority still lived on the island. But no British government led by an imperialist like Churchill was prepared to negotiate on this basis, and in the end Whitehall, like the Wilhelmstrasse, was unable to bring Turkey into the war.

In this book, then, I investigate the diplomacy that kept Turkey intact and out of the fighting. But I also examine the aggressive alternatives that were considered by İsmet İnönü and his ministers. Rejection of these alternatives was often the outcome not of shrewd deliberation or fidelity to democratic principles, but rather of mere chance. Finally, the evidence suggests that Turkey was more responsible for Hitler's failure to win a stake in the Middle East than is generally realized. The Italians and the Vichy French were handicaps to the Führer, but it was the Turks who turned German diplomacy in the area limp, sterile, and sour.

I am happy to acknowledge the help of Mr. Robert Wolfe of the National Archives and Records Service. He gave me excellent advice for using the microfilmed German Foreign Ministry documents and furnished me with an inventory of the German Embassy Files, Ankara, before it was made generally available to scholars. Drs. Weinandy and Booms, directors respectively of the Politisches Archiv of the Foreign Ministry, Bonn, and the Bundesarchiv, Koblenz, kindly allowed me to transcribe additional German papers. Throughout two summers of research in London, J. R. Ede and his staff at the Public Record Office patiently delivered to me the British correspondence on Turkey and, in several cases, alerted me to other Middle Eastern material that elucidated the turns of Turkish diplomacy. They also introduced me to Mary Z. Pain, a seasoned research assistant without whom the work of transcription and abstraction would have taken much longer. Temple University gave me a generous research award, a semester's leave with salary, and the expert assistance of Edith Hampel and George Libbey, research librarians without peer in my experience. I was denied permission to use the Turkish archives, but Bulent Ogzuc of the University of Pennsylvania translated a number of useful Turkish political biographies. Finally, Louisa Barnes and Gertrude Jacobs typed the manuscript; I thank them both for their skill and forbearance.

F.G.W.
Philadelphia, Pa.
8 September 1978

Contents

Chapter 1

The Good Boy of Europe

"A piece of Europe is passing." The words were those of a colleague of Kemal Atatürk; the sentiment was shared by many observers of Turkish politics when Atatürk died on 10 November 1938. As president of Turkey, Atatürk had saved his country from partition and then reshaped it in his own image. Atatürk dethroned the sultan and abolished the caliphate. He forbade the men of Turkey to wear the fez and took the veil from the women. He taught his people to write in the Latin alphabet and substituted legal codes based on European practice for the old Koranic laws. And he reduced the frontiers of Turkey to the peninsula of Asia Minor, the city of Constantinople, which he renamed İstanbul, and to a defensible hinterland behind it.[1] He was a great revolutionary and a great statesman—many thought the greatest of his time.

But no revolutionary can completely break with his past. Nowhere did this become more apparent than in Turkish foreign policy in the last decade of Atatürk's life. Officially, as Atatürk many times declared, Turkey's foreign policy was peace, friendship, and trade with all nations. Turkey had no irredentist or territorial aims. She did not want to recover the former Balkan and Arab provinces of the old Ottoman Empire and counted it an asset that these had been struck away. It was a sound policy, but the Turks had to remind themselves constantly of its soundness, because necessity and not choice had dictated it.

The Great War left Turkey beaten and humiliated. During the fighting the British, French, Russians, and Italians drew up various plans to partition the Ottoman Empire. The British were to take Palestine and Mesopotamia; the French were assigned the Lebanon and Syria; İstanbul and the

1. John Patrick, Lord Kinross, *Atatürk: The Rebirth of a Nation*, p. 498. General accounts of Atatürk's social reforms are found in Donald E. Webster, *The Turkey of Atatürk: Social Process in the Turkish Reformation*, pp. 126–33; Henry E. Allen, *The Turkish Transformation: A Study in Social and Religious Development*, pp. 85–142; Roderic H. Davison, *Turkey*, pp. 141–43. For a German reminiscence of the reforming Atatürk, see Rudolph Rahn, *Ruheloses Leben: Aufzeichnungen und Erinnerungen*, p. 90.

Straits were reserved to Russia, until the Bolshevik revolution took her out of the war; and Italy was promised a portion of the southern coast of Anatolia, centering on the town of Antalya. Some of this land had been promised to Arab emirs and Zionist politicians on other occasions, but the Allies did not begin to worry about the contradictions until the territories disposed of by these secret treaties were actually in Allied hands at the end of the war. The Turkish Sultan Mehmed VI feebly protested against these arrangements, but Gen. Mustafa Kemal, then commander of the Turkish Army of Syria, struck a note of sharp defiance. As he told Gen. Otto Liman von Sanders, head of the German Military Mission that had helped direct Turkey's war effort, the fighting might be over for the Allies, but the Turks' struggle for independence was just beginning.[2]

Only a few patriots shared Kemal's conviction at first, but the landing of Greek troops in Smyrna (İzmir) in May 1919 roused almost all Turks against the Allies. The Greeks disembarked under cover of British, French, and American warships. But it was primarily the British who encouraged this operation, partly to protect Greek minority rights in the Smyrna area and partly to forestall an Italian landing there. The fighting was savage. Both Greeks and Turks committed atrocities. Meanwhile, the Allies occupied İstanbul in March 1920 and pressured the sultan's government into court-martialing Mustafa Kemal in absentia during the following May. But the Greeks were gradually demoralized by their slow advance into Anatolia, the dogged resistance of the Turks, and Communist infiltrators sapping morale in the ranks. In August 1921, at the Sakarya River, near Ankara, the Greeks were defeated in the bloodiest battle since their landing at Smyrna. Several months of military stalemate and diplomatic parleying followed the Battle of Sakarya, but after almost a year had elapsed, Kemal ordered a new offensive that forced the Greeks to evacuate Smyrna and all Anatolia in September 1922. On 20 November 1922, a peace conference convened in Lausanne with Gen. İsmet İnönü negotiating for the Turkish Republic. When it ended the follow-

2. Salahi Ramsdan Sonyel, *Turkish Diplomacy, 1918–1923: Mustafa Kemal and the Turkish National Movement*, pp. 1–11; Dagobert von Mikusch, *Mustapha Kemal: Between Europe and Asia*, pp. 188–98; Kinross, *Atatürk*, p. 130.

ing summer, the Allies conceded all Anatolia to the Turks, as well as Istanbul and a portion of Europe to the Maritza River, the frontier with Bulgaria. The Turks had canceled their capitulations early in the war; the treaty acknowledged this cancelation and swept away all reparations claims. But in return Turkey had to demilitarize the Straits and let through ships of all nations, unless she was herself at war. The Arab provinces were not returned, nor were the Dodecanese islands, captured by Italy in the war of 1911 but never previously acknowledged as lost by Turkey.[3]

Lausanne was a brilliant accomplishment for İsmet İnönü, who had only one previous experience as a negotiator. Nevertheless, many members of the Grand National Assembly, the Turkish legislature, criticized his conduct of affairs. These critics opposed any compromise and demanded full sovereignty over the Straits and a better frontier at the expense of neighboring Syria and Iraq. They insisted on recovery of Mosul and its oil fields from Iraq, but the British negotiators prevented it on the grounds that the population of Mosul was Arab and Kurdish, not Turkish as the Ankara government liked to claim. The Grand National Assembly finally ratified the Treaty of Lausanne in August 1923 by a vote of 213 to 14, but only after Mustafa Kemal had called new elections that defeated many of the critics of İnönü and his treaty. Thenceforth the deputies settled down to deal with internal rehabilitation, where there were problems enough in the 1920s.

Foreigners were aware of Turkish discontent over a censored press, arbitrary fines on dissident editors, limitations on the right to unionize and strike, and general stagnation in retail businesses, especially in the Black Sea coastal regions. The Republic strove for self-sufficiency in its early days, and shipping did not prosper. Above all, the peasants resented the high taxes levied to modernize industry and build railroads, even though the recent war with the Greeks had shown how desperately they were needed. Atatürk's answer to these problems was a dictatorship with parliamentary trappings. He skillfully played off his enemies against each other and, when this kind of management was insufficient, had recourse

3. The most recent detailed account of the Lausanne negotiations is in Sonyel, *Turkish Diplomacy*, pp. 185–229. For a brief account see Geoffrey Lewis, *Turkey*, pp. 75–76.

to courts-martial, prison terms, and a few executions. Many of the opponents he removed were former members of the old Committee of Union and Progress, the party that had brought Turkey into the World War and pushed an expansionist, Pan-Islamic, and Pan-Turanian foreign policy.[4]

The aging dictator always assured his colleagues that increasing political maturity would ease these party tensions and that negotiation would attain Turkey's foreign policy objectives. But the actions of Mussolini and Hitler began to suggest to the Turks that restraint and deliberation were not the only ways to full national recovery, especially since the responses of Britain and France had become so consistently feeble. Atatürk, remembering his experiences during the First World War, disliked Germans, but he admitted a certain grudging admiration for Mussolini. When one of his colleagues recommended that fascistic methods be applied to Turkey's problems, Atatürk did not deny that they might be effective but said that such things could be done when he was gone. He would leave it to his successor to imitate the European dictators if he wished. That successor, almost nobody doubted, would be İsmet İnönü, the prime minister, who transacted more and more of the actual business of government during Atatürk's last years.

The president and the prime minister were totally different in temperament. Atatürk had swagger, stage presence and, when he wished, a childlike charm. At the end of his life, he drank heavily, played poker obsessively, and kept irregular hours. İnönü was a shrewd, spartan soldier who did not like liquor or cards and preferred his family's company to Atatürk's wild all-night parties in the Ankara Palace Hotel. Both men could quarrel violently, but the ebullient Atatürk would forget a grudge faster than the taciturn İnönü. It was rumored that İnönü tried to turn Atatürk into a "Grand Old Man," titular head of the state but with no real power. Atatürk was supposed to have discovered this conspiracy and just before his death allegedly was planning to exile İnönü to London or Washington as an ambassador. How deep were the differences between the two men was

4. Sonyel, *Turkish Diplomacy*, pp. 211–25; Kinross, *Atatürk*, p. 410; Joseph C. Grew, *Turbulent Era: A Diplomatic Record of Forty Years, 1904–1945*, 2:824; Irfan Orga, *Phoenix Ascendant: The Rise of Modern Turkey*, pp. 164–67.

never reliably confirmed, but diplomats in Ankara were sure that Turkish foreign policy would change when power passed from one to the other.[5]

If İnönü was taciturn, his foreign minister, Tevfik Rüştü Aras, sometimes talked excessively. He could be disturbingly garrulous at diplomatic receptions. But both Sir Percy Loraine and Wilhelm von Keller, the British and German ambassadors, agreed that his conversation was interesting, his ideas provocative, and his influence with İnönü and Atatürk very important. Keller described him as a keen opportunist with an excellent sense of timing.[6] First among Aras's goals was the revision of the Treaty of Lausanne and the attainment of full Turkish sovereignty over the Straits. The Turks several times had put the matter on the League of Nations agenda but so far had gotten nothing by consultation.[7] Then, on 7 March 1936, the German army reoccupied the Rhineland and began its fortification. As Aras told Keller, there was now nothing the Powers could deny the Turks as long as the Powers condoned the treaty breaches of Adolf Hitler.[8]

In London some British foreign and military policymakers apparently agreed with the Turkish foreign minister. At Lausanne in 1923 the British deprived the Turks of control over the Straits so that their navy could, in the event of hostilities, pursue a Soviet fleet into the Black Sea and destroy the yards and arsenals on its shore. But in 1936 the British were far more alarmed about Hitler's introduction of conscription in Germany and Mussolini's aggression against Abyssinia than they were about the Soviet navy. Accordingly, the War Office and the Admiralty drafted a joint memorandum for submission to the Foreign Office. It urged the British government to conclude an alliance with Turkey and to prepare the way for it by sponsoring the restoration of Turkish regulatory control over the Straits. This memorandum advanced several arguments in favor of an Anglo-Turkish alliance. It would prevent Soviet expansion into the Medi-

5. Kinross, *Atatürk*, pp. 460, 485. There is an interesting appreciation of the Atatürk-İnönü combination in Loraine to Oliphant, 7 January 1939, P.R.O., F.O. 371/E547/132/44. (For list of abbreviations, see p. 221.)

6. Loraine to Oliphant, 7 January 1939, P.R.O., F.O. 371/E547/132/44. Keller to Foreign Ministry, 26 February 1936, A.A. 3199/404.

7. Rendel to Oliphant, 6 February 1936, P.R.O., F.O. 371/E681/26/44.

8. Keller to Foreign Ministry, 31 March 1936, A.A. 3199/703.

terranean and at the same time serve as a "counterpoise" against Italian aggression in the area. It would seal off Turkey from German economic penetration of the kind that had brought the Ottoman Empire into the First World War against Britain in 1914. Finally, an alliance would restrain Turkish intrigues for territorial expansion against Britain's client Iraq and eliminate the possibility that an enemy might use Turkish air bases to bomb the Suez Canal.

Foreign Secretary Anthony Eden and his Near Eastern experts discussed and minuted this memorandum at some length. They accepted all the strategical considerations raised by the military but rejected the recommendation for an Anglo-Turkish alliance. The Foreign Office felt that any unilateral approach to Turkey would be interpreted by the other Powers as conspiratorial. It was especially concerned about the reactions of the French government, which had objected strongly to being left out of the Anglo-German Naval Agreement of the previous year. Then, too, a British initiative in favor of the Turks might suggest to the other Powers that London was unsure of its defenses and felt compelled to cast about for support of any kind. Above all, in the words of one commentator, it would not do "to run after the Turks."[9]

Eden's decision of early 1936 was probably wrong. Within a few months the Turks recovered control of the Straits at the Montreux Conference without incurring any obligations to Britain. This diplomatic victory encouraged them to demand further treaty revisions to rectify their frontier with Syria. Indebted to none of the Great Powers, the Turks remained open to offers from all of them, a situation that they exploited against Britain until almost the end of the Second World War. The German ambassador, Keller, who seems to have known something about the deliberations in London, himself wondered why the British had not written a treaty with the Turks. In its favor he listed almost the same reasons as had the British army and navy planners and added one more. Keller commented that the Egyptian political scene was turning more uncertain for Britain. The Wafd, or Nationalist party, was demanding in crescendo that British

---

9. Phillips to Rendel, Most Secret, 13 January 1936; Rendel to Phillips, Admiralty, 17 January 1936; Oliphant to Loraine, 6 January 1936, P.R.O., F.O. 371/E269/26/44.

troops evacuate the country. The troops remained, but an Anglo-Egyptian treaty of 1936 restricted their stations and maneuvers to the Suez Canal Zone. The lifeline to India had not been cut but was distinctly frayed. Keller felt that the value of an overland route through Turkey to the Persian Gulf was correspondingly enhanced and that Foreign Minister Aras knew it.[10]

In the weeks immediately preceding the opening of the Montreux Conference on 22 June 1936, the Turkish government utilized this and other advantages to the fullest. Foremost among these was the support of Soviet Russia. Maxim Litvinov, the Soviet foreign minister, had been insisting that Turkey be allowed to resume her full military rights at the Straits so that in wartime she could exclude Russia's enemies from the Black Sea. For most of the sessions, Aras worked in such close accord with Litvinov that the British suspected that Turkish policy at the Straits originated in Moscow and that the Turkish foreign minister was little more than the toady of his Soviet counterpart. They rebuked Aras for his "subservience," but they shrank from provoking a quarrel.[11]

Aras boasted that the Turkish army was ready to meet any challenge or contingency if the Montreux Conference broke down, and he even threatened to send troops into the demilitarized zone before the Powers voted their approval. Sir Percy Loraine talked him out of this move by offering economic advantages in return for a more compliant attitude. However, Aras still reserved his right to use force if necessity compelled him, and he never tired of insisting that the necessity would come from Italy.[12] The Turkish government alleged that Mussolini was utterly opposed to any change in the Straits' regulation and was secretly preparing to land Italian troops at the Straits to deny the Turks their sovereign rights. In fact, as both the British and Germans knew, Il Duce was very sympathetic to Turkey's claims before the Montreux sessions opened and was prepared to approve them if Turkey would dissociate herself from the League

10. Keller to Foreign Ministry, 6 March 1936, A.A. 3199/461.

11. Rendel to Loraine, 3 September 1936, P.R.O., F.O. 371/E5115/26/44. Keller to Foreign Ministry, 24 June 1936, A.A. 919/1400. Max Beloff, *The Foreign Policy of Soviet Russia, 1929–1941*, 2:39–43.

12. Loraine to Eden, Very Confidential, 10 April 1936, P.R.O., F.O. 371/E2024/26/44; Loraine to Oliphant, Most Confidential, 25 April 1936, P.R.O., F.O. 371/E2407/26/44.

of Nations sanctions against Italian operations in Abyssinia. Mussolini told the Turkish ambassador in Rome that only events in the Red Sea interested him, not what happened in the Dardanelles.[13] But the Turks adhered to League policy, and Mussolini hardened his attitude. He sent no delegate to Montreux but only an observer, Bova Scoppa. Though he claimed irreconcilable differences with this Italian, Dr. Aras was nevertheless seen much in his company at Montreux.[14]

When the conference ended on 20 July 1936, Turkey had scored a complete victory and nullified the Treaty of Lausanne. In time of war, Turkey being neutral, belligerent ships could pass the Straits only to assist victims of aggression under the terms of the League of Nations Covenant. The right of unrestricted entry into the Black Sea, long a cardinal point of British foreign policy, was abolished, a victory not only for Turkey but also for Soviet Russia.[15] The British were dissatisfied with the result but admitted privately that they probably could not have changed the outcome. A Foreign Office official declared to the German chargé d'affaires in London that the Turkish army had always been strong enough to occupy the Straits whether the Great Powers consented or not. Another British spokesman, attempting to minimize his country's retreat at Montreux, stated to a Bulgarian diplomat that the development of air power had made land defenses at the Straits obsolete. But these British explanations did not convince the Bulgarians or their neighbors the Rumanians and Greeks. The governments in Sofia, Bucharest, and Athens all congratulated the Turks on their gains and then pleaded with Ankara to rest content with them. The Greek king remarked to the British ambassador that he had no other choice. His army was so badly equipped and trained that its maneuvers, which he was required to

13. Rendel, Geneva, to the Foreign Office, 13 May 1936, P.R.O., F.O. 371/E2737/26/44; Loraine to Foreign Office, Confidential, 20 May 1936, P.R.O., F.O. 371/E2895/26/44.

14. Hassell to Foreign Ministry, 3 July 1936, A.A. 919/3158. A few months after Montreux, Aras told Count Ciano, the Italian foreign minister, that if Ciano would take him into his confidence, he would work for League recognition of the Italian conquest of Abyssinia. Galeazzo Ciano, *Ciano's Diplomatic Papers*, ed. Malcolm Muggeridge, trans. Stuart Hood, p. 122.

15. Beloff, *Foreign Policy*, 2:46.

attend, had become a recurrent embarrassment to him.[16] The Polish foreign minister, Col. Joseph Beck, also praised Turkish diplomacy. Normally, Beck observed, the Turks were too far away to interest the Poles, but if they could push the British around, "they might deserve more attention in the future." Beck's reaction was rather cynical, but it seemed more reasonable after the British turned the bad bargain of Montreux into an abject one. The London press commended Turkey for using a conference where Hitler and Mussolini would have used cannon. But *The Times* for 22 June 1936 went further: it practically thanked the Turks for not simply tearing up the Treaty of Lausanne and then dubbed them the "good boy of Europe" for not doing so.[17]

If the British thought that flattery could be turned into forbearance, they did not know Tevfik Rüştü Aras. Back in Turkey, the foreign minister took every opportunity to surround himself with military men. He announced that his goal at Montreux had never been rearmament alone but also the emergence of Turkey as a Mediterranean factor whose friendship the Great Powers must cultivate. He warned Britain to be ready to negotiate the status of Mosul now that the question of the Straits was out of the way.[18] Attempting to repeat the tactics of intimidation that had served him so well at Montreux, Aras went to Milan in February 1937 to arrange an understanding with Mussolini and Count Galeazzo Ciano, the Italian foreign minister. He hoped to sign a political and economic agreement with Italy that the British would be frightened into matching. But Ciano was distinctly cool to his Turkish guest, and the Milan meeting had no result. Aras returned home empty-handed, but he informed the Turkish press that Ciano had agreed to visit Ankara and to authorize construction in Italian yards of several warships for the Turkish navy. Rome issued an immediate denial, the Italian ambassador remonstrated with

16. Eden to Newton, Berlin, Confidential, 18 July 1936, P.R.O., F.O. 371/E4547/26/44; Rendel to Foreign Office, 17 April 1936, P.R.O., F.O. 371/E2069/26/44; Waterlow, Athens, to Eden, 22 April 1936, P.R.O., F.O. 371/R2373/2373/19.

17. Moller to Foreign Ministry, 26 July 1936, A.A. 1002/no number; Bismarck to Foreign Ministry, 22 June 1936. A.A. 919/2540. For Eden's account of the Montreux Conference, see Anthony Eden, *Facing the Dictators: The Memoirs of Anthony Eden, Earl of Avon*, p. 472.

18. Keller to Foreign Ministry, 16 August 1936, A.A. 919/1327.

Aras in Ankara, and diplomats in the Turkish capital wondered aloud what the foreign minister's game was.[19] No one
was sure of the answer, but throughout 1937 the Turk showed
that he played for very big stakes.

The Alexandretta Affair

Though Tevfik Rüştü Aras had intimated that he was
preparing to challenge Anglo-Iraqi control of oil-rich Mosul,
he next turned his acquisitive attention to the Syrian port
of Alexandretta, under French mandatory jurisdiction since
the end of the First World War. Alexandretta was the best
Mediterranean harbor of the old Ottoman Empire. It was
also a vital communications hub through which passed one
of the main roads south into Syria and Palestine. Alexandretta could not be allowed to remain in France's possession
if the Turks hoped to recover their commerce and influence
in the Arab world. The Ankara government also charged
that the port was being used to smuggle arms and ammunition to the Kurdish and Armenian minorities within Turkey
who occasionally challenged Atatürk's regime.

Atatürk felt the loss of Alexandretta very keenly and, in
the earliest days of the fighting against the Greeks, declared
that the Turkish nationalists would never renounce the city.
But, during the War for Independence, he quickly perceived
that France did not wholeheartedly approve the aims of
Britain and her Greek client and would end hostilities
against Turkey for a price. The French demanded and Atatürk conceded recognition of their mandate in Syria, including Alexandretta within its northern frontier. As part of
an accord signed in March 1921, the French promised to give
special preference to the Turkish minority in the port and
its environs. Turkish would become an official language, on
a par with Arabic and French. Turks would enjoy job security, and their history and culture would be emphasized in
school programs.[20]

In line with his officially nonexpansionist foreign policy,
Atatürk said nothing more about the status of Alexandretta
until the last years of his life. From the beginning of the

19. Keller to Foreign Ministry, 10 February 1937, A.A. 3199/283, and
17 March 1937, A.A. 3199/554.
20. Erdmannsdorff to Ankara Embassy, 15 January 1937, A.A. 4719/49.

mandate, however, Syrian nationalists charged that France never adequately supplied those educational and vocational opportunities specified in international treaties. In 1936, a Popular Front government led by Leon Blum came to power in Paris and decided to solve the Syrian problem by liquidating the mandate and gradually turning over the administration to nationalist leaders in Damascus. In the name of the Turkish Republic, Dr. Aras at once objected that, while he had been willing to trust the welfare of the Turkish minority in Alexandretta to the benevolence of France, he would not continue to trust in their well-being if the government passed into the hands of half-educated and politically inexperienced Arabs. The foreign minister claimed that the Turks were a majority in the port city. When a League of Nations census contradicted him, counting 129,000 Arabs but only 71,000 Turks, he threatened to walk out of the League and draw closer to those recusants from it, Germany and Italy.[21]

Even before the Blum government had focused attention on the Alexandretta problem, the Turks had made diffident but clear bids for German support in Syria. They took their first soundings when the distinguished banker and Reich minister of economics, Dr. Hjalmar Schacht, flew to Near and Middle Eastern capitals in 1935. Schacht's aim was to stimulate business in the area for German contractors. He stopped in Ankara to write a contract for a German syndicate to build several blast furnaces in Turkey, but at the last minute Atatürk refused to close the deal. He did give Schacht, as the representative of the Krupp firm, a large order for artillery. The banker was told that the guns would be used to refortify the Straits but that some might be needed for action against the Syrians and French along Turkey's southern frontier.

Schacht later recalled that Atatürk was not very enthusiastic about placing orders with the Germans, but that Prime Minister İnönü intervened energetically to conclude the transaction with Krupp. Schacht summed up Atatürk's reception as courteous enough, but he thought that further German association with Turkey's territorial schemes was not necessarily the best way to increase the Reich's influence in the Near and Middle East. He pointed out that the Arabs

21. Keller to Foreign Ministry, 27 January 1937, A.A. 3199/188.

were more numerous, desperate, and prone to treaty revision because none of the Arab states was free from some form of Anglo-French control. The Turks, on the other hand, had long since expelled all foreign troops and had uprooted or severely circumscribed all foreign business interests. Proud of this achievement, the Ankara government would insist on being treated as an equal and would be less likely than some Arab regime to act as Germany's pawn. Schacht believed that German intrigue would be most fruitful in Egypt, not in Turkey. He recommended that steps be taken in Berlin to agitate against the British occupation of that country.[22] But the German foreign ministry ignored his suggestions and did nothing in 1936 to encourage either the Turks or the Arabs against the Anglo-French. German inactivity seems to have been due partly to the outcome of the Montreux Conference. The new convention set certain limitations of type and tonnage on ships navigating the Straits in peacetime. The German government believed these restrictions were specifically intended to exclude its pocket battleships from those waters. Despite reassurances from the British and other foreign ministries, the Wilhelmstrasse requested that the Turks have the restrictive sections of the convention deleted. However, the Turks refused and reminded Germany that she was not a Mediterranean power and consequently had no claims to preferential treatment.[23] The response caused a cooling of relations between Berlin and Ankara, but by the beginning of the next year it seemed to be forgotten.

In January 1937 the League of Nations proclaimed local autonomy for Alexandretta and its environs. City officials could now manage their affairs independently of Syrian authorities in Damascus. The Turkish inhabitants used this situation as an excuse to attack their Muslim and Christian Arab neighbors, killing so many that it seemed a Turkish majority might be the result. The Ankara government publicly deplored these crimes but secretly encouraged them by sending Kurdish tribesmen across the frontier to mutilate and murder Arabs in Alexandretta. Mosques and churches were desecrated indiscriminately. Meanwhile, the Turks made

22. Smend to the Secretary of State, 8 January 1937, A.A. 3199/70.
23. Eden to Newton, Berlin, Confidential, 18 July 1936, P.R.O., F.O. 371/E4547/26/44.

another appeal for German assistance. Groups of them interviewed Fritz Seiler, German consul in Beirut, requesting money and guns for their struggle with the Arab opposition. Though other consular personnel condemned the violence in Alexandretta, Seiler was sympathetic to the Turkish cause and cabled Berlin for permission to urge it on. He thought a Turkish occupation of Alexandretta was inevitable but that Ankara should not be allowed to score a unilateral victory. Instead, Germany should promote and participate in it, throwing a lien of obligation over Atatürk's government that might in time be developed into a formal Turco-German alliance. To this advice, the Wilhelmstrasse responded cautiously. It agreed to study the question of munitions delivery but forbade Seiler to subsidize the Turkish insurgents in Alexandretta. However, he was told to dissociate himself from any official Anglo-French condemnations of the violence.[24] If the Turks were not to be given any help, at least the Wilhelmstrasse did not intend to give them any offense.

Seiler might have persuaded his government to a more decisive line but for the difficulty of reconciling any German initiative with Italian policy in the Near East. Before the Wilhelmstrasse could make a final decision about supporting the Turkish party in Alexandretta, Rome appointed a new consul, Bivio Sbrana, to Syria. This man was a seasoned troublemaker, recently expelled from Morocco for anti-French intrigue there. His new assignment, he announced to Seiler, was to work for an Italian protectorate over all Syrian and Lebanese Christians. Sbrana expected French authority to be routed out not only of Alexandretta but of an area stretching considerably to the south of that city. The Italian government did not intend to permit either Turks or Arabs to administer the French mandate but would assume that function itself.

Seiler thought his Italian colleague obnoxious but admitted he was an excellent public-relations man. He gave parties and concerts and showed imported Italian movies, all of which the Syrians found quite enjoyable. The Italian foreign ministry paid most of his expenses but, according to Seiler, some of Sbrana's money came from the papal treasury. The Italian boasted that before he left Rome, Pope Pius XI had granted him an hour's audience and his personal en-

24. Seiler to Foreign Ministry, 2 February 1937, A.A. 4719/233.

couragement. Pope Pius, with the assistance of the Italian foreign ministry, was said to want to impose indivisible papal control over the numerous sects into which Syrian Christianity was divided. The Wilhelmstrasse was unable to verify any contact between Sbrana and the pope, but decided it would be unwise to offend either Pius or Mussolini. In May 1937 Hitler signed the Anti-Comintern Pact with Il Duce. The German government was determined that no subordinate questions, like the Arab-Turkish rivalry in Syria, would be allowed to undermine the pact. Seiler was instructed to continue to turn away his Turkish petitioners.[25]

They could not be discouraged. Although their approaches at the consular level had failed, the Turks decided to appeal next to the highest ministerial echelons in Berlin. In May 1937 Prime Minister İsmet İnönü represented Turkey at the coronation of King George VI in London. Ankara let it be known that İnönü would make a leisurely return through several European capitals and would be pleased to discuss Turco-German relations with the Berlin foreign ministry. The Wilhelmstrasse considered a conference with him but first solicited the opinion of Ambassador Keller in Ankara. Keller warned against a meeting. In view of Atatürk's declining health, he thought a power struggle for the Turkish presidency might soon erupt between İsmet İnönü and Foreign Minister Aras. Germany, in her ambassador's opinion, should not in any way appear to take sides prematurely.[26] Accordingly, the Wilhelmstrasse did not invite İnönü to visit Berlin, but, somewhat to Keller's surprise, the Turks did not allow themselves to take this snub too seriously.

On the contrary, in late July 1937 they sent a commercial mission to Germany led by Ali Çetinkaya, minister of public works. The foreign ministry wished to defer this mission until a later time but yielded to the solicitations of the Krupps, who lavishly entertained the Turkish delegation at Villa Hügel, the family seat. The Turkish minister opened his visit by granting Lufthansa a license to fly directly over Anatolia into Afghanistan, a privilege the Germans had long sought unsuccessfully. But the initial cordiality of the dis-

25. Seiler to Foreign Ministry, 2 March 1937, A.A. 4719/452, and 17 September 1937, A.A. 4719/1743.

26. Keller to Erdmannsdorff, 10 and 11 April 1937, A.A. 3199/no number.

cussions disappeared when Ali Çetinkaya tried to change the subject from trade to diplomacy. His German hosts refused to comment on the Alexandretta problem, the role of Italy in the eastern Mediterranean, or the long-range goals of Hitler's foreign policy. Nor would they agree to lend Ankara one hundred and fifty million marks unless the sum was made repayable in cash instead of kind—Turkish wool, cotton, mohair, and olive oil—as Ali Çetinkaya suggested. The Turk's rudimentary English and the deliberate rudeness of the younger members of his staff did not help matters, and, at the end of the talks, no decision had been made. Çetinkaya left Germany in a huff, but the Turkish foreign ministry sent the most fulsome thanks for the hospitality accorded him and indicated its willingness to let the Germans take more time to think about the terms of the credit.[27]

With the failure of Ali Çetinkaya's mission, the Germans had rejected Turkish overtures for friendship for the fourth time in two years. Yet the Turks accepted these setbacks uncomplainingly and almost cordially. For even if they had failed to clinch an entente with Berlin, they were fully aware that their rivals the Arabs had failed to do so, too. The tremors from the Alexandretta imbroglio reached far out into Transjordan, Saudi Arabia, and Iraq, whose governments determined to check what they called "Kemalist Imperialism." At first the Arabs sought a compromise with Turkey about their mutual territorial aims. In June 1937 King Abdullah of Transjordan met with Atatürk in Ankara and, in the name of the Arab states, offered to approve the cession of Alexandretta to Turkey if the Turks would support a union of Transjordan and Palestine as the nucleus of a larger Arab federation in the future. Atatürk returned the king a flat refusal.[28] Neither he nor Dr. Aras intended Turkey's expansionist drives to be contained behind any sort of Arab *cordon sanitaire.*

The Arabs turned next to Germany, at roughly the same time that the Turks were presenting their petitions. Arab contacts with the Reich were of both an official and a quasi-official nature. They made their first inquiries for aid to Dr. Fritz Grobba, the German minister to Baghdad, Iraq. Grobba was a squat, energetic veteran of diplomatic service in the

27. Memorandum by Reinhardt, 17 August 1937, A.A. 3286/1753.
28. Keller to Foreign Ministry, 3 June 1937, A.A. 4719/1106.

Middle East. In November 1937 Yussuf Yassin, private secretary of King ibn-Saud of Saudi Arabia, visited the German
minister and inquired whether the Reich was willing to accredit a minister to Jidda, the Saudi Arabian town where
foreign diplomatic personnel were required to live instead
of in the semisacred capital, Riyadh. Yussuf Yassin also asked
Grobba to undertake extended discussions about shipping
German guns and other war matériel to the Saudi Arabian
monarch. Grobba was informed that the weapons were to be
unloaded in a Syrian port where they could either be used
against the Turks threatening Alexandretta or reserved for
Saudi Arabian arsenals. When Grobba answered too eva-
sively, the Arab emissary remarked that Japanese businessmen had already visited Saudi Arabia and seemed anxious
to fill ibn-Saud's needs.[29]

That same November, Henry Kohn, an unofficial Arab
agent without formal diplomatic credentials, called at Gestapo headquarters in Berlin. Kohn was Persian by birth
but a German by virtue of his mother's second marriage with
a German citizen. He assured the Gestapo that ibn-Saud
regarded the opening of relations with Germany as urgent
in light of the Turkish threat to Alexandretta and Zionist
claims to Palestine. He asked for German war matériel to
be paid for by a five-year credit or, if the Germans insisted,
by eventual transfer to them of all British assets in Saudi
Arabia, especially oil wells and refineries. Kohn announced
that Prince Abdallah, brother of King ibn-Saud, was ready
to come to Berlin and confirm specific points of a contract if
the Germans would receive him.[30]

The Wilhelmstrasse deferred any action on these proposals until well into 1938. The newly appointed foreign
minister, Joachim von Ribbentrop, then convened a committee of permanent under secretaries and regional experts
to study relations with the Arab countries. Ribbentrop
sought advice from Fritz Grobba, German minister to Iraq;
Werner von Hentig, leader of the foreign ministry's Near
Eastern department; and Admiral Wilhelm Canaris, head

29. Grobba to Foreign Ministry, 9 November 1937, A.A. 4364/2633,
and 4 July 1938, A.A. 4364/1687. The document dated 9 November is
found in English translation in *DGFP*, 5:769–72. Łukasz Hirszowicz, *The
Third Reich and the Arab East*, p. 35.

30. Groscurth to Foreign Ministry, 22 December 1937, A.A. 4364/
1366.

of German counterintelligence. Of these three men, Fritz Grobba was the most favorable to the Arabs' proposals. He preferred them to the Turks, whom he described as too pro-Western and pro-British to be of any use to the Germans, and recommended that a German minister be sent to Jidda, where, unlike Britain, France, and Italy, the Reich was not yet represented. Grobba also approved delivery of German weapons.

Yet even he pointed out certain negative aspects of doing business with ibn-Saud. The king, according to Grobba, was ultimately striving for industrial self-sufficiency. Yussuf Yassin had requested that industrial dies and machinery as well as guns be furnished Saudi Arabia. In time, Grobba speculated, Saudi Arabia could become Germany's commercial rival in the Middle East, not merely her client. Moreover, though ibn-Saud opposed the Turks, the British and French mandate authorities, and the Zionists, he also bitterly hated the rulers of Bahrain, Kuwait, and Qatar, against whom he might waste the German weapons consignments. These tribal squabbles, Grobba concluded, were of no importance to German diplomacy.[31]

Hentig and Canaris were even more guarded in their appraisal of Arab affairs. Neither man objected to sending a German mission to Jidda, and Canaris would have made a token delivery of obsolete weapons to ibn-Saud as a polite gesture. But Hentig thought long-term credits to the Arabs too risky an investment, and he predicted that independent Arab governments would destroy all German cultural and commercial foundations in the Middle East. In his opinion, the Arabs were xenophobic whereas the Turks, accustomed to European contacts for several centuries, were tolerant of and even welcomed Western ways. Ribbentrop adopted Hentig's view, adding that the Arabs' militant anti-Zionism was an embarrassment to Germany at that time. Hitler's policy was still to expel Jews from the Reich. A special agency called *Haavara*, the Hebrew word for "transfer," was set up in Berlin to visa the Jews' departure for Palestine after they had been deprived of most of their goods. Ribbentrop feared that Arab control of Palestine would mean the end of Jewish resettlement in the Middle East. For this reason and the

31. Grobba to Foreign Ministry, 4 July 1938, A.A. 4364/1687; Woermann to Malletke, 29 September 1938, A.A. 4364/8027 (*DGFP*, 5:793).

others advanced by his advisers, the Nazi foreign minister decided against aiding the Arabs. Instead he defined Reich policy toward both Arabs and Turks as one of courtesy and noncommitment.[32]

Ribbentrop does not seem to have known it, but he had for the time being avoided an insoluble quandary confronting German diplomacy. As he would soon find out, it was impossible to work successfully with both Turks and Arabs. Their political and territorial aspirations were irreconcilable. Short of a signed accord with Germany, however, Ribbentrop's decision could not have been much more favorable to the policy of Tevfik Rüştü Aras. He steadily raised his demands on Alexandretta. Having gained the Alexandretta Turks internal liberties, he demanded of France that the Turkish army occupy the city to ensure these liberties. Paris was willing to negotiate the matter but wanted a codicil added to any agreement renouncing further Turkish expansion in Syria. Aras refused it.[33] German, British, French, and Greek diplomatic observers all feared that he had his eye on Aleppo, Mosul, Tripoli, and even more. The French charged that Aras would not stop until the Turkish frontier stood at Haifa.[34] Foreign Secretary Eden told some Foreign Office colleagues that Ankara was veering toward the Axis, though he did not know of any definite agreements between the Turkish government and Berlin.[35]

In fact, there were none. But fear that such agreements might be impending led the beleaguered French to allow the Turkish army to march into Alexandretta on 5 July 1938. A year later, the city and its environs, renamed "Hatay" by the Turks, were annexed by Ankara. Some French newspapers argued that the concession of Alexandretta was the kind of adroit move that, had it been made before the First World War, would have prevented Turkey from falling into the German coalition. Aras, however, did not permit such delusions to flourish. He declared that Turkey was not obligated

32. Memoranda on the Palestine Question by Rosenberg, 14 August 1938, A.A. 1830/92.

33. Keller to Foreign Ministry, 10 July 1938, A.A. 913/118, and 11 July 1938, A.A. 913/142.

34. Minutes by Eden and Bowker on Scrivener to Foreign Office, 10 January 1938, P.R.O., F.O. 371/E223/135/44.

35. Minutes by Eden on Waterlow, Athens, to Foreign Office, 8 January 1938, P.R.O., F.O. 371/E135/135/44.

to anyone and could throw her weight to whomever she wished.[36] France, Britain, and Germany vied with each other for her favor. France signed a friendship treaty with Ankara, Britain extended a credit of sixteen million pounds sterling, and Walter Funk, Reich minister for economics, flew to Ankara to conclude the trade agreement that Ali Çetinkaya had attempted unsuccessfully to negotiate the year before. Germany loaned Turkey one hundred and fifty million marks repayable in goods over a ten-year period. Though German businessmen did not want Turkish merchandise, Berlin paid them a subsidy to deal in it. The Turks initialed this agreement in Berlin just a week before Atatürk died.[37]

36. Keller to Foreign Ministry, 22 August 1938, A.A. 913/1702. For more on Turkish reactions to the incorporation of Hatay, see Süleyman Külçe, *Mareşal Fevzi Çakmak*, p. 287.

37. Keller to Foreign Ministry, 3 November 1938, A.A. 1379/207.

Chapter 2

An Old Comrade Returns:
The Mission of Franz von Papen

The solution of the Alexandretta problem did not end Turkish territorial demands. The British and French privately admitted that as long as they were encumbered by threats from Hitler and Mussolini, the Turks would exploit their encumbrance wherever they could.[1] Dr. Aras liked to compare the Turkish annexation of Alexandretta to the German occupation of Austria.[2] Regarding Czechoslovakia, against which Hitler's demands for the Sudetenland were becoming more and more strident, the Turkish foreign minister said the country was not worth a war and should be partitioned by Germany and Poland as the basis of an alliance between them directed against the Soviet Union.[3] In October 1938, Ambassador Percy Loraine elicited an even more startling response when he queried Aras about Turkey's position in the event a European war should break out. Although he avoided using precise language, the Turk strongly hinted that Ankara would fight in alliance with whichever belligerent offered the biggest inducement. He suggested to Loraine that the Turkish army be allowed to garrison Egypt if the British forces in that country had to be withdrawn for service against Hitler. He added:

> Today a nation cannot be expected to put its heart and its full will-power into a war unless satisfied of the justice of the cause for which it is fighting. To have fought, for instance, in order to maintain three and a half million persons of German race under Czech domination would not have been a good cause.

Loraine found Aras's Egyptian proposals of "first-class importance" and "distinctly interesting," but they affronted the Foreign Office, because they were completely unsolicited

1. Loraine to Foreign Office, 31 December 1938, P.R.O., F.O. 371/E149/149/89. (For list of abbreviations, see p. 221.)
2. Fabricius to Foreign Ministry, 27 July 1938, A.A. 913/2632.
3. Loraine to Foreign Office, Confidential, 14 March 1938, P.R.O., F.O. 371/C1829/132/18.

and because they frightened Egyptians of all political parties. In Alexandria and Cairo, Aras's remarks were interpreted as the beginning of an attempt to restore Turkish jurisdiction over Egypt, where it had not existed de facto since the early nineteenth century and not de jure since 1914, when the British proclaimed their protectorate.[4] Aware of this unfavorable reaction, Dr. Aras modified his proposal to suggest that Turkish army officers merely assist in training Egyptian troops. But, during the Second World War, Ankara revived the original project of a Turkish occupation of Egypt several times, always with the same disturbed reactions resulting in London and Cairo.

The British were also puzzled by Turkish intentions toward Bulgaria. With the other states of the Balkan Peninsula—Yugoslavia, Greece, and Rumania—Turkey was affiliated in the famous Balkan Pact, signed in February 1934. The pact committed the members to nonaggression, arbitration of all difficulties, and recognition of their current frontiers. Bulgaria, however, did not adhere to the Balkan Pact because the Allies, after Bulgaria's defeat in the First World War, severed Dobruja, one of her richest agricultural provinces, from her and awarded it to neighboring Rumania. Bulgaria never acknowledged this loss, coveted the return of Dobruja, and maintained generally cool relations with Bucharest during the interwar period. Bulgarian relations with Ankara were not much better. Turkey's frontier in Europe, which followed the channel of the Maritza River, was simply too near Edirne and İstanbul. In case of an attack on the Straits from the land side, the Turks would hardly have room enough to stem a retreat and regroup their forces in front of İstanbul. For security reasons, the Turks wanted to redraw their frontier farther west at Bulgaria's expense. In autumn 1938 Ankara ominously began to concentrate many army units along the Bulgarian frontier. The Foreign Office asked the Turks' intentions and advised that these forces would be better held in readiness for an attack from Hitler and Mussolini, but officials in Ankara refused to withdraw the troops.[5]

4. Loraine to Halifax, Most Confidential, 28 October 1938, P.R.O., F.O. 371/E6800/135/44.

5. Loraine to Foreign Office, 16 November 1938, P.R.O., F.O. 371/R9358/4/7.

When Atatürk died on 10 November 1938, the Foreign Office briefly expected that Turkish foreign policy would turn unequivocally in favor of Britain and France. Foreign observers believed that İsmet İnönü, his successor, was the choice of the Turkish army leadership, particularly of the pro-German Gen. Fevzi Çakmak. On the other hand, İnönü attempted to reduce military influence in the new administration by reorganizing the government ministries and substituting young lawyers and civilian technicians of liberal leanings for the old army crowd favored by Atatürk.[6] These new men had come to maturity after the First World War and had not been involved in Turco-German collaboration of that period. Despite these changes, however, İnönü was scarcely installed in office when he permitted and even encouraged a serious outbreak of Turkish anti-Semitism.

The position of the Jews was precarious under both the Ottoman Empire and the Republic. Although some Jewish families were longtime converts to Islam and occasionally held high office under the sultans, most Jews observed their ancient faith and aroused the hatred of the Turks as infidels —and even more as commercial competitors. Jewish merchants often adopted foreign citizenship to obtain European consular protection in their business transactions and, until the defeat of the Dual Monarchy in the First World War, held Austro-Hungarian passports instead of Turkish ones. After the armistice they switched their allegiance to Italy, even though she was involved in the Allied attempt to carve up the Ottoman Empire. According to their enemies, the Jews avoided military service during the War of Liberation and made high profits supplying the Turkish armies fighting the Greeks.

Atatürk officially dissociated himself from these allegations and, mindful of international opinion, was careful to avoid even the slightest taint of anti-Semitism. But he had all Jews forcibly deported from the strategically sensitive zones of Edirne and the Straits and would not permit the immigration into Turkey of central European Jews whose futures were endangered by the rising tide of Hitler's own anti-Semitism. In some cases, his government contemplated deporting Jews back to central Europe, even though they had

6. Kroll to Foreign Ministry, 29 November 1938, A.A. 4364/2205; Frederick W. Frey, *The Turkish Political Elite*, pp. 275–82.

been domiciled in Turkey for years. The Turks never carried out these expulsions, but İnönü, when he came to power, absolutely refused to alter Atatürk's restrictions on Jewish immigration. Even when Chaim Weizmann, the Zionist leader, promised that each Jewish immigrant would bring a capital of three thousand pounds sterling, the new president would not change his mind. Instead, he allowed the Turkish press to circulate wild rumors about the Jews, who were accused, among other things, of selling olive oil adulterated with machine oil to the simple Turkish consumers. İnönü cited Hitler's anti-Semitism in support of his own and announced that one of the goals of his new government would be the elimination of the Jewish middleman from the Turkish economy.[7]

Among those whom İsmet İnönü omitted from his government was the foreign minister, Tevfik Rüştü Aras. His dismissal surprised the diplomatic community and suggested at first that İnönü would repudiate Aras's rather pro-Axis policy. Aras's successor as foreign minister was Şükrü Saracoğlu. The day-to-day work of the ministry, however, was directed by Numan Menemencioğlu, the permanent under secretary who had had most to do with drafting the Turkish proposals at the Montreux Conference. The Germans knew Menemencioğlu well from his recent visits to Berlin in connection with the conclusion of the 150 million marks credit arrangement, and they had no reason to be dissatisfied with his new importance.[8] In July 1938, during the credit talks, Foreign Minister Ribbentrop asked Menemencioğlu how Turkey would apply the articles of the Montreux Convention in case of war between Germany and Poland and whether the Turks would be willing to sign a nonaggression pact with the German government. Ribbentrop was concerned that the British and French could ship war matériel to the Poles through the Straits and then north along various Balkan routes. Menemencioğlu, to Ribbentrop's relief, promised that Turkey would prohibit any such traffic, though he knew

7. Kroll to Foreign Ministry, 23 January 1939, A.A. 4720/106, and 13 December 1938, A.A. 4720/2292.

8. Loraine to Foreign Office, 19 November 1938, P.R.O., F.O. 371/E6881/69/44. Memorandum by Ribbentrop, 1 July 1938, A.A. 96/244. There are biographical details on Menemencioğlu's education and cultural tastes in Nimet Arzık, *Bitmeyen Kavga: İsmet İnönü*, pp. 17, 69, 73–77.

the Poles would be at a tremendous material disadvantage in any conflict. As to nonaggression pacts, Menemencioğlu stated that Turkey signed them only with neighboring states, such as the Soviet Union or France, a "neighbor" by virtue of her Syrian possessions. Even with Britain, he continued, Turkey would not consider such a treaty, because no part of the British Empire bordered Turkey. Ankara would, however, study the value of a full-scale alliance with the Reich if the Wilhelmstrasse wished to encourage it.[9]

The motives behind Menemencioğlu's remarks were probably territorial. Turkey was dissatisfied with her Bulgarian frontier for security reasons and could profit from foreign help to rectify it. The Turkish under secretary alluded to Bulgaria in July and returned to the subject in March 1939 in a conversation with Hans Kroll, chargé d'affaires of the German embassy in Ankara. On this occasion, Menemencioğlu argued that Turkish hegemony over the Balkan Peninsula would stimulate German export trade in that area.[10] Turkey had an irredentist grudge against Iraq, too. She still hoped to acquire the oil fields of Mosul. For that reason, İnönü's government refused to proclaim its sympathy for a union of Arab states when King Abdullah of Transjordan again asked it to do so in December 1938.[11] In April 1939 the Turkish ministers rebuffed an Iraqi delegation in Ankara that proposed that Turks and Arabs forget old animosities and plan a common defense against possible Axis aggression in the Middle East.[12]

Ribbentrop pondered these considerations during the remainder of 1938, but he was careful to send Menemencioğlu back to Ankara in a good mood. The day before the Turk left Berlin, he was invited to an unscheduled party at Ribbentrop's country house. Menemencioğlu, who enjoyed fine dining and nightclub entertainment, had a thoroughly good time. Members of the Krupp family who were present gave several of their newest tanks and long-range guns to the Turkish government as gifts. Menemencioğlu rather

9. Memorandum by Ribbentrop, 7 July 1938, A.A. 96/no number (*DGFP*, 5:730–32).

10. Kroll to Foreign Ministry, 18 March 1939, A.A. 96/53.

11. Loraine to Foreign Office, 2 December 1938, P.R.O., F.O. 371/ E7418/69/44.

12. Houstoun-Boswall, Baghdad, to Foreign Office, 19 April 1939, P.R.O., F.O. 371/E3007/297/44.

rudely observed that the Turks had found some of their recent heavy armaments imports not up to the highest technical standard, but his hosts took no umbrage, and Ribbentrop suggested that Turkish technical experts might like to observe and supervise German manufacturing processes so that quality of output might be improved.[13]

All armaments allocations to Turkey had to be approved by the Army High Command as well as by the foreign ministry, and Ribbentrop invited the General Staff to appraise the military potential of a Turco-German alliance after Menemencioğlu left Berlin. The military leadership, as it turned out, proved much more eager to include Turkey in the Axis than were the diplomats. It decided to raise from twelve to twenty-four the number of German officers serving in the Turkish army as technical instructors, and it invited two distinguished Turkish generals, Izzedin Calislar, inspector general of the Turkish army, and Ali Fuad Erden, commandant of the Turkish war college, to attend the next autumn maneuvers at Königsberg.[14] Meanwhile, Col. Hans Rohde, military attaché of the German embassy in Ankara, was ordered to make an extensive reconnaissance trip to the Middle East. Rohde was to estimate the quality of Turkish army and air-force personnel and bases throughout Anatolia; next, the strength of the fortifications along the Syrian and Iraqi frontiers; and last, the serviceability of the railroads, especially those leading into the Soviet Union. After finishing in Turkey, the colonel was scheduled to move on to Damascus and Baghdad for the very delicate and challenging assignment of sounding out sentiment about Turkey in both capitals. In Iraq, he was also to find out whether Britain had any real control over the Iraqi army and whether that army could resist a Turkish invasion. Rohde's trip ended in Iran, where he gathered information about that country's ability to wage war with Russia.[15]

Rohde's findings were positive for Turkey on almost all counts. The colonel held that not merely her neutrality, but her active cooperation was necessary for Germany at war. The war, Rohde argued, would not be won on the Suez Canal or in the eastern Mediterranean theater. Even if the Germans

13. Memorandum by Weizsäcker, 18 July 1938, A.A. 96/no number.
14. Marschall to Keller, 2 September 1938, A.A. 1399/1767.
15. Memorandum by Rohde, 9 January 1939, A.A. 1399/2.

defeated and drove the British out of Egypt, they could still fall back to the Persian Gulf and India and hold out long enough to wear Germany down. However, if Turkey were allied with the Reich, Rohde continued, the Turks could make havoc of Britain's land bridge to India through Transjordan and Iraq, demolish refineries and choke off Britain's fuel, and curtail the passage of Indian army relief units to the western front. He allowed that British forces might defeat the Turks in individual battles, but he did not believe they would pursue them into Anatolia. The Anatolian terrain was too rugged and exhausting to encourage a sustained British offensive, nor would the terrain make it easy for the Russians to strike back, should the Turks choose to invade the Soviet Union as Germany's ally. In short, Rohde emphatically recommended that the Reich and Turkey resuscitate their old brotherhood-in-arms.[16]

The diplomatic configuration certainly seemed to favor a Turco-German alliance. Hitler was fresh from his triumph at the Munich Conference of 30 September 1938, which he thought was a continuation, rather than the culmination, of Anglo-French appeasement. In Spain, the pro-Axis Francisco Franco had all but liquidated the Spanish Republic after the long bloodletting of the Civil War. Stalin's purges were rumored to have made a shambles of the Soviet army, and the dictator was not likely to do more than protest a new understanding between Berlin and Ankara. Even Mussolini and the Italians, who had long trumpeted their claims to the Mediterranean as "our sea," now seemed to admit that they had not the means to make good their alleged title. More than Rohde's enthusiastic endorsement of a Turkish alliance, it was Il Duce's apparent withdrawal of his pretensions to Mediterranean primacy that induced the Wilhelmstrasse to work for a compact with Ankara. The first indications that Rome would approve such a compact seemed to have been given in Jidda, Saudi Arabia. After repeated requests from King ibn-Saud, the German foreign ministry had finally decided to accredit Dr. Fritz Grobba, its envoy to Iraq, as part-time minister to Saudi Arabia. When Grobba arrived to open his legation in Jidda, he made the acquaintance of the Italian minister, Luigi Sillitti. Though Sillitti had recently presented ibn-Saud with a sizable gift of Italian arms in Musso-

16. Memorandum by Rohde, 24 January 1939, A.A. 1399/4.

lini's name, the Italian diplomat now told Grobba that only Germany could fully develop Axis influence in the Middle East because of her larger industrial plant, more abundant natural resources, and more advanced technical management. In the last analysis, Sillitti declared, Saudi Arabia needed imported foodstuffs, which Britain customarily supplied, even more than she needed heavy equipment. Unless Italy could become the granary of much of the Middle East, which Sillitti stated she could not do, Rome had no choice but to follow Germany's lead in cutting the area's traditional links to Great Britain.[17]

Grobba agreed and forwarded an elaborate projection of German Middle Eastern strategy in the event of war to Berlin. Like Colonel Rohde, he emphasized the threat that had to be posed to Britain's communications with India over the land bridge through Transjordan and Iraq. Unlike the military attaché, Grobba preferred that Arab instead of Turkish troops be used to do the major share of the fighting. Saudi Arabia, he noted, could also furnish the Germans with navy bases on the Red Sea from which the Bab el Mandeb, the narrow straits at the southern extremity of the Red Sea, could be blocked to prevent the arrival of British reinforcements traveling by water from India. Furthermore, he suggested that Germany consider supporting the proclamation of King ibn-Saud as caliph of all Islam so that the king could declare a *jihād* ("holy war") against the Anglo-French. Before the First World War, the office of the caliphate had belonged to the Ottoman Imperial House, but it was abolished by Atatürk and the Grand National Assembly in 1924. Any attempt to resurrect the caliphate could surely have been expected to insult the Turks and provoke their opposition, yet in this and several other points of his discussion, Fritz Grobba blandly assumed Turkish cooperation. He also forgot, or, more likely, willfully ignored, the old irredentist feuds between Turkey and the Arab world that made their smooth collaboration unlikely. However, his worst mistake was to sanction the reception in Berlin of a Saudi Arabian emissary, Halid Alhud, ibn-Saud's principal counselor of state, to sign a contract for the delivery of German arms to the Arab kingdom. Grobba suspected that the Turks would

17. Grobba to Foreign Ministry, 27 January 1939, A.A. 4364/9. Łukasz Hirszowicz, *The Third Reich and the Arab East*, p. 51.

react violently if Ankara found out about the transaction, but he and ibn-Saud hoped the strictest secrecy could be maintained concerning it.[18] However, the Turks did find out about the arms deal, and its discovery cost Berlin the entente with Ankara that so many other circumstances seemed to favor.

The Wilhelmstrasse had taken a long time deciding to bring Turkey into its alliance system, but it now made up for the delay by posting one of its most distinguished diplomats to Ankara to undertake the negotiations. Wilhelm Keller was replaced because of his age, and Franz von Papen named as his successor. Papen was a somtime chancellor of Germany and, most recently, the Reich's ambassador to the Austrian Republic before the Anschluss, but neither in those earlier positions nor in his Turkish assignment is it easy to estimate the man's integrity and influence. His memoirs are occasionally useful but filled with suave evasions and simplistic understatements. His biography depicts him as a creature of unrelieved mendacity and guile, largely responsible for the subversion of Austrian independence and for the German occupation in March 1938.[19] Yet according to Papen's own version, which is substantially confirmed by British diplomatic documents, whatever role he played in Vienna was not adroit enough to satisfy all the Nazi leadership. A young member of Papen's Vienna staff had been assassinated by Heinrich Himmler's secret police, and only a direct appeal to Hermann Göring saved Papen's own life.[20]

After his arrival in Ankara, in April 1939, the British Foreign Office asked Dr. Heinrich Brüning, himself a former German chancellor and then a political refugee in London, to write an appraisal of Papen's importance in Nazi Germany. Brüning stated that Goebbels hated Papen and that Foreign Minister Ribbentrop, his chief, disliked him. But the ambassador had the powerful backing of Göring, the Roman Catholic Church hierarchy, German conserva-

18. Grobba to Foreign Ministry, 18 February 1939, A.A. 4364/44 (*DGFP*, 5:800–807); Woermann to Weizsäcker, 11 May 1939, A.A. 4364/785.

19. Tibor Koeves, *Satan in Top Hat: The Biography of Franz von Papen*, pp. 294ff.

20. Franz von Papen, *Memoirs*, trans. Brian Connell, pp. 433–37, 441.

tive opinion, and Adolf Hitler himself. According to Brüning, Hitler loathed all the old German aristocracy but had
an odd kind of loyalty to the aristocrat Papen, who had
helped the Führer gain power in 1933.[21] Sir Nevile Henderson, the British ambassador to Germany, had information
connecting Papen with Ulrich von Hassell, former German
ambassador to Italy, and with other prominent officials who
were reported to be plotting Hitler's removal from power.[22]
The British ambassador to Turkey, Sir Hughe Knatchbull-
Hugessen, who replaced Percy Loraine just before Papen
arrived in Ankara, at first found the new German envoy
frank, friendly, and well informed. Only when the Foreign
Office warned its man that too many meetings with Papen
might seem like collusion to the Turks did Knatchbull-
Hugessen reduce his encounters to what mere politeness required.[23] After war broke out, the two men never met at all.

Papen and his wife did not remain long in the German
embassy where Keller had lived. They moved into the more
intimate former Czech legation, which had become German
property when Hitler, violating the Munich Pact, occupied
Prague on 15 March 1939. Here Papen could work with a
minimal personal staff and reduce the Gestapo's opportunity
for spying on him.[24] His ultimate goal was to turn the Axis
into a triangle, with its three points at Berlin, Rome, and
Ankara; his immediate task was to keep Turkey out of the
Anglo-French alliance system. On 31 March 1939 the British
government, shocked at Hitler's betrayal in Prague, gave a
guarantee of independence to Poland and followed it on
13 April by similar pledges to Rumania and Greece. When
Papen arrived in Ankara, negotiations to make Turkey a link
in what the Germans called a chain of encirclement were already under way. These negotiations were reported to the
Wilhelmstrasse by Chargé Hans Kroll and confirmed by the
German embassies in Moscow and Tokyo.

In his first interview with Foreign Minister Saracoğlu,

21. Foreign Office Minute by Young, 24 May 1939, P.R.O., F.O. 371/
C8027/53/18.
22. Henderson to Foreign Office, 17 August 1939, P.R.O., F.O. 371/
C11637/16/18.
23. Knatchbull-Hugessen to Sargent, 5 August 1939, P.R.O., F.O.
371/C11143/16/18.
24. Hughe Knatchbull-Hugessen, "Ambassador in Turkey," p. 234.

after the usual amenities, Papen reverted to speculation about a rapprochement between Turkey and Britain and France. Saracoğlu described his talks with the British and French ambassadors as only "feelers" with nothing yet agreed in writing. Whatever London and Paris might insist, Ankara intended to abstain from the guarantee to Greece. Still less, Saracoğlu continued, were the Turks inclined to associate themselves with the Poles. The foreign minister claimed he personally preferred strict neutrality for his country but was forced to at least some reconsideration of this policy by the Italian invasion of Albania on Good Friday, 7 April 1939.[25] Papen was instructed to allay Turkish qualms about Il Duce's Albanian operation, although, as will be seen, the campaign was something of a false issue raised by the Turks to improve their negotiating posture.

Two days later, on 29 April, Papen made his first call on the Turkish president. İsmet İnönü received Papen, who had served on the Turkish front in the First World War, like an old comrade returned and talked, in the ambassador's description, as one soldier to another. İnönü made some objections about Mussolini's campaign in Albania but was very free in his enthusiasm for Hitler, surprising Papen, who had heard that Atatürk always referred to the German dictator cuttingly. Papen then suggested that the Balkan Peninsula could best be guaranteed against further Italian encroachment by associating all the Balkan Pact countries as adjunct members in the Rome-Berlin Axis. İnönü made no demur and ended the meeting in an atmosphere of friendliness well exceeding what diplomatic protocol required.[26] Papen's dispatch is undoubtedly exaggerated, but it basically tallies with Sir Percy Loraine's impressions of İsmet İnönü. In his account of one of his last interviews with the Turkish president, Loraine described him as a calculating individual resolved that his country would survive, or even profit from, Fascist aggression in Europe. He heard from reliable sources that İnönü had authorized the sale of some Turkish aircraft to Francisco Franco during the closing weeks of the Spanish Civil War. When he asked Saracoğlu for further information

25. Kroll to Foreign Ministry, 26 April 1939, A.A. 96/133; Papen to Foreign Ministry, 27 April 1939, A.A. 96/135.
26. Papen to Foreign Ministry, 29 April 1939, A.A. 4364/824.

about this incident, the Turkish foreign minister only smiled enigmatically.[27]

Back in his embassy after his conferences with Saracoğlu and İnönü, Papen warned officials in Berlin to shackle the Italian Mars in Albania as quickly as possible, or Turkey, despite the amiable mood of her president, might yet accept an Anglo-French guarantee. Taking the Turkish objections about Albania at face value, Papen pointed out that Italy had conquered the country with only twenty thousand troops but had raised her occupation forces to seventy-two thousand men since April. Another one hundred thousand Italians were scheduled to sail across the Strait of Otranto from Bari and Brindisi. Before it was too late, he urged Ribbentrop, Mussolini must be convinced that their departure was unnecessary. Il Duce must even be persuaded to evacuate some of his troops already billeted in Albania. A solemn declaration of that intent from Mussolini, Papen believed, would induce Turkey to reject an Anglo-French territorial guarantee and give the Germans more time to make the Turks their ally. Papen's dispatch was referred to Ernst von Weizsäcker, state secretary of the German foreign ministry and the actual work executant for the often peripatetic Ribbentrop. Weizsäcker thought the Turks were sly and incorrigibly Anglophile and that therefore an appeal to Mussolini was pointless. Moreover, it would probably turn Il Duce noisy and resentful. Nevertheless, Weizsäcker sent on a warning to curtail troop increases in Albania to Ciano, who at first heatedly refused any action. But within two days, the Italian foreign minister calmed down, completely reversed himself, and invited the Turkish ambassador to his offices in the Palazzo Chigi. He assured him that Albania was the last Balkan outpost of Mussolini's new Roman Empire and that Italian forces would not advance from the Albanian frontier. It was reported to Berlin that the Turkish ambassador was unimpressed and seemed preoccupied by some other problem.[28]

27. Loraine to Oliphant, 7 January 1939, P.R.O., F.O. 371/E547/132/44; Loraine to Foreign Office, 25 January 1939, P.R.O., F.O. 371/E657/132/44.

28. Weizsäcker to Papen, 2 May 1939, A.A. 96/101; Papen to Foreign Ministry, 3 May 1939, A.A. 96/142 (*DGFP*, 6:408–9); Mackensen to Foreign Ministry, 3 May 1939, A.A. 96/175.

The day after Count Ciano delivered his pledge to the Turkish ambassador in Rome, German intelligence in Ankara received the first indication that the pledge had come too late. The Turks were reported as agreeing to associate themselves with the Anglo-French defense system, though the accord, which was published on 12 May 1939, was not a military alliance, for which London and Paris hoped and which Berlin feared, but only a treaty of friendship and mutual assistance.[29] The Anglo-French on one hand and Turkey on the other agreed to cooperate if a war started by the Axis spread to the Mediterranean and involved Italy. The same obligations were exchanged if the Axis attacked the Balkan Peninsula. But nothing was agreed about unity of command, liaison between the Anglo-French and Ankara, supply of war material, air-force assistance, deployment of combined forces, or the possibly menacing reaction of the Soviet Union. The Turks refused to proceed to a full-scale military alliance until London and Paris had associated Moscow with it. They had already objected to using their troops to defend Greece if Italy invaded that country from Albania. Moreover, any Turkish collaboration was premised upon delivery to Turkey of a large but still to be precisely determined quantity of new weapons. The British and French promised to make delivery in principle but in private wondered where they would find enough surplus arms to do so.[30]

Even more demoralizing to the British and French was the nagging realization that Turkish interest in the Friendship Declaration had nothing to do with fidelity to democratic principles, genuine attachment to Britain and France, or concern for the potential victims of Fascist aggression in Europe. Foreign Minister Saracoğlu had announced that Turkey would not fight "for the blue eyes of Poland."[31] If Britain and France managed to deliver the requisite weaponry to the Turks, it was quite likely that they would use it, not in Europe, but to settle old scores with the Arab states. The Turks were again making demands for additional Syrian territory around Aleppo and for Iraqi land around

29. Papen to Foreign Ministry, 4 May 1939, A.A. 96/145.

30. Knatchbull-Hugessen to Foreign Office, 27 April 1939, P.R.O., F.O. 371/E3131/143/44, and 4 May 1939, P.R.O., F.O. 371/E3298/143/44.

31. Houstoun-Boswall, Baghdad, to Foreign Office, 26 April 1939, P.R.O., F.O. 371/E3286/297/44.

Mosul. Marauding Kurdish tribesmen had resumed their incursions across the Syrian frontier. French authorities captured some of them and found them armed by the Turks and in some cases led by Turkish army officers out of uniform. When the French protested these incidents, Saracoğlu blandly commented that the officers were acting without instructions. Yet when the German army occupied Prague and it seemed that French forces would be tied down in action along the Rhine, the Turkish government audaciously offered to assume France's mandate over Syria. Paris rejected the offer, and London reacted philosophically. The Foreign Office thought these difficulties would continue until Turkey, having no oil, obtained a source in Mosul or elsewhere.[32] The British sympathized with the French but were themselves badgered by another Turkish demand to be permitted to participate in the defense of Egypt.[33] The Turks seem almost to have forgotten the Italians in Albania, although the Italian invasion had been given as the immediate reason for the compact with Britain. When King Zog I of Albania, fleeing from Mussolini's troops, appealed for asylum in Turkey, the Ankara government refused him. Zog reminded İnönü that he was a fellow Muslim, but the king, his queen, Geraldine, and their son had to find quarters in Athens.[34]

Papen was deeply disappointed by the Friendship Declaration but emphasized to Berlin that Germany had not yet irrevocably lost the Turks. He knew that there was no perfect harmony between the Ankara government and Britain and France, although he discovered that Syria and Egypt were specific points of stress only several weeks later.[35] Before he could put the most pessimistic interpretation on the Friendship Declaration, Numan Menemencioğlu came from the foreign ministry to reassure him. Though the declaration was initialed, the Turk pointed out that it would be some time, even months, before the Turkish legislature ratified the instrument. Menemencioğlu hinted that İnönü's ministry might decide not to push it or even decline to bring it before the legislature at all. Mobilization, Papen

32. Cawthorn, War Office, to Baxter, Foreign Office, Secret, 5 July 1939, P.R.O., F.O. 371/E4878/297/44.

33. Lampson, Cairo, to Foreign Office, 15 May 1939; Foreign Office to Lampson, 17 May 1939, P.R.O., F.O. 371/R4041/66/67.

34. Papen to Foreign Ministry, 27 April 1939, A.A. 913/135.

35. Erdmannsdorff to Foreign Ministry, 20 June 1939, A.A. 96/191.

was told, had always been a staggering drain on the Turkish economy. Since the government had nearly reached the bottom of its own resources, the British, if they wanted a viable ally, would have to advance, not merely subsidies, but the entire cost of Turkish preparedness.

According to Numan, there was really no unanimity of Turkish opinion behind the declaration of 12 May. İsmet İnönü was at odds with his generals, Marshal Fevzi Çakmak was shouting declamations of pro-German sentiment in cabinet meetings, and War Minister Ali Fuad Erden had blurted out before the president and the prime minister that the Germans were the only "vital" people in Europe, the only ones whose alliance was worth cultivating. Papen made much of Menemencioğlu's disclosures in his report to Berlin.[36] He probably realized that the Turkish minister would not have dared reveal details of a cabinet meeting without considerable forethought and calculation. İnönü's *amour propre* was known to be well developed; he would cut down any colleague who compromised it by an unauthorized statement or a slip of the tongue. These revelations were deliberately meant to spur the German ambassador to surpass Anglo-French inducements to the Turks. The British were afraid he might be able to do it. They feared the clique of pro-German generals around the Turkish president and regarded Foreign Minister Saracoğlu as the only official reasonably immune to their harrying.[37] Knatchbull-Hugessen persuaded Saracoğlu to revive an old regulation forbidding Turkish military personnel from accepting private entertainments from foreign dignitaries. In this way, Papen was to some extent kept apart from Çakmak and his cronies, though it was still thought necessary to have the German ambassador shadowed by Saracoğlu's secret police.[38]

Shortly after the publication of the Friendship Declaration, Papen was called to Berlin. The British thought his departure meant the end of his mission to Turkey and of his career in government service.[39] Actually, the ambassador was

36. Papen to Foreign Ministry, 11 May 1939, A.A. 96/157.

37. Palairet, Athens, to Foreign Office, 6 June 1939, P.R.O., F.O. 371/R4662/661/67.

38. Knatchbull-Hugessen to Oliphant, 12 June 1939, P.R.O., F.O. 371/R5176/661/67.

39. Knatchbull-Hugessen to Foreign Office, 7 June 1939, P.R.O., F.O. 371/R4690/661/67.

summoned home to brief his superiors on the consequences of the Friendship Declaration. Despite his assurances, the Wilhelmstrasse was verging on a rupture of relations with Turkey. Mob animosity had also begun to hit at Turks resident in the Reich. In Karlsruhe, Mannheim, and Berlin, young Nazis broke up Muslim religious services and damaged Muslim fraternity property. A few Turkish students were beaten up and many more wired for money to buy ship passage home. In a long memorandum to State Secretary Ernst von Weizsäcker, Papen argued that such violence must be curbed and reprisals against Turkey avoided. To do anything else would rupture the lucrative Turco-German export-import trade valued, at the end of 1938, at about two hundred and eighty million marks annually. Reprisals would also jeopardize repayment of the one hundred and fifty million marks credit recently extended to Ankara. In the event of hostilities, the Turks might jump at the chance to wipe out repayment as an exigency of war. The ambassador admitted that it was tempting to consider embargoing imports of Turkish wheat, barley, and tobacco. But if the Reich refused to take these crop imports, it would forfeit shipments of Turkish chrome that went with them, for the Turks had always made chrome deliveries part of a package. Germany drew one-third of her chrome requirement, which was indispensable to the manufacture of high-grade steel, from Turkey. Other deposits sometimes used were in the Union of South Africa, Rhodesia, the Philippines, Yugoslavia, and Greece. But the first three, as Papen and the foreign ministry were aware, were vulnerable to some kind of British regulation or threat; while the last two were accessible to Italian preemption.

Of Italy, Papen questioned whether her alliance was really worthwhile or should be continued much longer. To persuade Turkey to sign an alliance with Germany, the ambassador would have returned to Ankara some of the Dodecanese islands taken by Italy from the Ottoman Empire in 1911. He called Weizsäcker's attention to the island of Castelrosso, within three miles of the Anatolian coast. He argued that it was not indispensable to Italian security and that continuing Italian occupation of it was a standing insult to Turkish sovereignty. Italy claimed that the island was a vantage point from which to bomb the Suez Canal or blockade the

Straits, but Papen reasoned that the war would not be won in the eastern Mediterranean, but rather on Britain's land bridge to India through Transjordan and Iraq. An allied Turkey at the very least could do sentinel duty on the perimeter of this area and perhaps even intervene to combat British-Indian troops. This line of thought echoed that of Fritz Grobba and Col. Hans Rohde, with the important difference that the ambassador warned against any simultaneous arrangements with ibn-Saud or other Arab rulers. In this he was very much a man of the First World War. He remembered that the Arabs had thrown in their lot with the British, rendering them picturesque though somewhat unsteady service, while all German attempts to strike a bargain with the Arabs, such as those made in Tripoli and Persia, had failed.[40]

Papen's brief convinced the German government to accept the Friendship Declaration without any sustained grumbling. It was rumored that Hermann Göring supported his position.[41] Consequently, Turkish agricultural imports into Germany were not embargoed, the German military mission to Ankara was continued, and heavy equipment contracted with German industry was delivered, though not always on schedule. For their part, the Turks did little to popularize the Friendship Declaration in their press and carefully avoided all criticism of German policy. They again announced that they would not fight for Poland and vetoed a British request that they guarantee the frontiers of Rumania. Knatchbull-Hugessen maintained that such a guarantee was implicit in both the Balkan Pact of 1934 and the Friendship Declaration, but Ankara rejoined that it would fight only for its own ground. Partly because of Turkey's attitude, Weizsäcker was able to browbeat the Rumanian foreign minister Grigore Gafencu when he visited the Wilhelmstrasse in June 1939. Gafencu was warned not to take any step to follow Turkey into Britain's camp. In Yugoslavia, no such warnings were necessary. The Yugoslav foreign minister immediately objected to the Friendship Declaration, stated that

40. Papen to Weizsäcker, 20 May 1939, A.A. 96/no number (*DGFP*, 6:544–46); Papen to Foreign Ministry, 6 June 1939, A.A. 96/184.
41. Rendel to Foreign Office, 4 August 1940, P.R.O., F.O. 371/R6885/375/7.

it did not obligate the Balkan Pact membership to support British military policy, and threatened to secede from the pact if London or Ankara attempted to involve the Balkan Peninsula in an Anglo-German quarrel.[42]

These Balkan repercussions raised hopes in Berlin that the Friendship Declaration would never be developed into an Anglo-Turkish military alliance. But the Wilhelmstrasse failed to reckon with Italy or with the ancient animosity between Arabs and Turks. The Arab world had never become reconciled to the Turkish occupation of Alexandretta and in June 1939 the Iraqi ambassador in Ankara tried to interest the Germans in claiming a protectorate over Christian assets in Alexandretta. Papen rebuffed the Iraqi spokesman and kept their encounter secret. He could not, however, keep secret the arms transactions, being negotiated in Berlin by Halid Alhud, between the German government and Saudi Arabia. Ibn-Saud, it will be remembered, had wanted the business transacted in the strictest confidence, principally to avert British wrath.

The Italians, according to their minister in Jidda, Luigi Sillitti, approved any contracts the king and the Germans wanted to write. But subsequently the Italian foreign ministry reconsidered its policy and claimed that Sillitti had exceeded his instructions in his remarks to Fritz Grobba. More likely, the Italians had misled Grobba in the first place in order to compromise German influence in the Middle East. On 20 June 1939, in its Arabic broadcasts originating from Radio Bari in southern Italy, Rome disclosed all of the details of the arms traffic between Germany and Saudi Arabia. Officials in Berlin, Jidda, and Ankara were taken entirely by surprise, none more so than Franz von Papen, who saw suddenly dissipated all the Turco-German goodwill which, thanks in no small part to his own efforts, had survived the Friendship Declaration of 12 May. Nothing the ambassador said could now convince the Turks that his government was not supporting their hereditary Arab enemies. They reopened military discussions with the British and French and also advised Berlin that they would look to the Western

42. Lothar Krecker, *Deutschland und die Türkei im Zweiten Weltkrieg*, pp. 41–48. E. R. Lingeman, *Turkey: Economic and Commercial Conditions in Turkey* (London, 1948), pp. 173ff.

Powers, as well as to Japan, to supply their industrial needs in the future.[43]

It may be argued that another event far better known than the arms traffic between Germany and the Arabs impelled the Turks to negotiate a definitive military alliance with Britain and France. This was the conclusion of the Russo-German Nonaggression Pact of 23 August 1939. The pact with Communist Russia was a flagrant contradiction of all Hitler's anti-Bolshevik pronouncements since the beginning of his political career. But fear of a two-front war and the necessity of isolating Poland prior to attacking her persuaded Hitler to send Ribbentrop to Moscow to sign a treaty with the Russians. Publicly, the treaty bound Germany and the Soviet Union to nonaggression. In secret clauses, it deeded to Stalin spheres of influence in Finland, Estonia, Latvia, eastern Poland, and Bessarabia. The treaty stunned the Turks. It associated Germany with Russia whom, despite occasional periods of rapprochement like the one at the Montreux Conference, the Turks detested far more cordially than they did the Arabs. A panicked Saracoğlu went to Moscow and tried to negotiate a Russo-Turkish nonaggression pact to offset the treaty between the Soviets and the Nazi leadership. But the Soviet foreign minister, Vyacheslav Molotov, confronted him with such unacceptable demands—the Russian was reported to have required the return of Kars and Ardahan to the Soviet Union—that Saracoğlu failed to reach an accord and returned to Ankara empty-handed.[44] İnönü's government, it may be thought, then had no choice but to insure itself against the Russo-German menace by accepting military guarantees from the British and French. However, it will be recalled that the Turks had always made their continuing association with Britain and France contingent on the benevolent attitude of the Soviet Union. In May, the Foreign Office had promised to work for Soviet association

43. Grobba to Foreign Ministry, 20 June 1939, A.A. 4364/no number; Ott to Foreign Ministry, 7 July 1939, A.A. 96/288; Papen to Foreign Ministry, 28 July 1939, A.A. 96/218.

44. Papen to Foreign Ministry, 24 August 1939, A.A. 96/243 (*DGFP*, 7:260–61); Schulenburg to Foreign Ministry, 17 October 1939, A.A. 96/555. See also Koeves, *Satan in Top Hat*, pp. 297–310, for an account, largely uncorroborated, of Papen's role in the Russo-German Nonaggression Pact.

with the Friendship Declaration and had sent a British mission, led by William Strang, to Moscow in June 1939. The Soviet government stalled talks with Strang's delegation because it was negotiating with representatives from Berlin at the same time. In this suit for Stalin's friendship, the Germans won, and the Turks could well have argued that the failure of British diplomacy in Moscow released them from the terms of the Friendship Declaration of 12 May. They did not do so because only in association with Britain and France could they bargain for the satisfaction of their territorial claims against the Arabs.

Hitler himself expected that his pact with the Russians would frighten the Turks into canceling the Friendship Declaration, and he sent Ribbentrop to Moscow partly with this goal in mind.[45] In this the Führer was disappointed, as he was with certain other aspects of Molotov's policy toward the Turkish Republic. Though Hitler requested it, the Soviet foreign minister would neither demand the dismissal of Saracoğlu nor the abrogation of the Friendship Declaration as inimical to Soviet interests.[46] In Ankara, Papen, surely without Ribbentrop's authorization, did all he could to minimize the significance of the Russo-German Nonaggression Pact. He told the Turks that it was mainly an attempt by Hitler to assure uninterrupted delivery of raw materials from eastern Europe. To Knatchbull-Hugessen, Papen had made the rather astonishing statement that he regretted that the British were not able to sign an accord with the Russians before the Germans did. Had the British successfully concluded their negotiations in Moscow, Papen's view was that "the position would be more favorable for discussions between Great Britain and Germany."

> His argument was that when the Soviet Treaty was concluded we should feel ourselves so strong that we could open discussions with Germany without danger of loss of face. Germany would also find the atmosphere more propitious after the conclusion of the Russian negotiations.[47]

45. Krecker, *Deutschland und die Türkei*, p. 54.
46. Schmidt to Moscow Embassy, 22 September 1939, A.A. 96/416.
47. Knatchbull-Hugessen to Halifax, 5 August 1939, P.R.O., F.O. 371/C11144/16/18.

The main points of these discussions with Britain, as Papen sketched them for Ribbentrop, would have been a general peace in Europe based upon the restitution of an independent Czechoslovakia, but without Sudetenland, and the preservation of Poland, after the Polish Corridor had been ceded to Hitler by agreement of the Great Powers. Papen felt his general "peace plan" would have eliminated the necessity for polarizing bilateral pacts like those between Turkey and the Anglo-French and between Germany and the Soviet Union. But Ribbentrop tabled Papen's proposals indefinitely and returned the ambassador a sharp reprimand.[48]

Meanwhile, the Wehrmacht invaded Poland on 1 September 1939, and the European war that Papen and his British and French counterparts had hoped to avoid became reality. The Turkish government used the new situation to drive a hard, almost brutal bargain with Britain and France in exchange for its alliance. London and Paris were interested in immunizing the Balkan Peninsula against the extension of hostilities and also in keeping Italy neutral. (Mussolini did not declare war until spring 1940.) But Saracoğlu and Menemencioğlu at once adopted a masterful and intimidating attitude toward Knatchbull-Hugessen and René Massigli, the French ambassador to Turkey, and presented some hair-raising demands that, if met, would have quickly goaded Italy into the war. Knatchbull-Hugessen and Massigli wanted to word the treaty to define the aggressor as a "European Power" warring in the eastern Mediterranean. Saracoğlu and Menemencioğlu attempted to hold out for the more explicit description of "European power with a Mediterranean seaboard." The Turks were well aware this phrase could refer only to Italy and would almost certainly provoke her, but they did not care because, in the words of the British ambassador, "Turkey cherishes a hope of being able to try conclusions with Italy whom she regards as her natural enemy."[49] Foreign Office Middle Eastern experts, reading Knatchbull-Hugessen's dispatch, entirely concurred in it and did not know how to advise the ambassador in shaping

48. Papen, *Memoirs*, pp. 456–57; Papen to Foreign Ministry, 2 September 1939, A.A. 96/256.

49. Knatchbull-Hugessen to Foreign Office, 1 October 1939, P.R.O., F.O. 371/R8303/2613/67.

his language toward the importunate Turks. They wanted to emphasize the war against Germany in the discussions but admitted that

> if the Turks thought that by signing the treaty they might re-strain the Italians from coming into the war, this might confirm them in their view not to sign the treaty at the present moment, since it may almost be said that their object in signing the treaty is to drag France and ourselves into war with Italy.[50]

So eager were the Turks for a fight against Italy that they proposed to change the projected treaty from a defensive to an offensive engagement. At one point, they offered the use of Turkish troops if London and Paris would declare war on Mussolini first and invade Italian territory, but they were much less responsive when asked for proposals to deal with Germany.[51] Then, and throughout the Second World War, the Turks would counter such proposals with pleas of ma-terial shortages and financial exigency. This Turkish badger-ing about an Italian campaign drove the British to consider desperate measures to avoid antagonizing the Italians. The Foreign Office still believed it was possible to turn Musso-lini, and especially Italian public opinion, in a pro-British direction. It considered having the British government order large amounts of Italian wheat to curry favor with Italian farmers and contract for several ships to be built in Italian yards to supply work to Mussolini's unemployed. The pro-ponents of this scheme knew full well that Britain might be paying for ships that would be used against her in the event Mussolini declared war. However, the positive effect on Italian public opinion was considered so important that some Foreign Office officials would have given Italy the raw materials to build the ships. Foreign Secretary Halifax final-ly rejected the notion of such gratuities to Italy.[52]

Besides the question of war aims, the Turks, British, and French also disagreed over the supreme command and the lines of operation that their respective forces would follow

50. Sargent to Cadogan, 6 September 1939, P.R.O., F.O. 371/R7146/2613/67.
51. Knatchbull-Hugessen to Foreign Office, 1 October 1939, P.R.O., F.O. 371/R8303/2613/67.
52. Loraine to Sargent, 14 April 1940, P.R.O., F.O. 371/R5403/48/22.

in a Mediterranean war. London and Paris assumed that
Turkish forces would be subordinate to one of their own
senior commanders, but Ankara insisted that overall control
of operations be assigned to Gen. Fevzi Çakmak, chief of
the Turkish general staff.[53] İnönü's government also made
it clear that Turkish military cooperation was not to be
understood to prejudice or eliminate any of Ankara's prior
claims to French-controlled Syria or British-administered
Iraq. Instead of jointly resisting Turkey's attitude, the
French parted company from the British to accommodate it.
In July they sent a military mission led by Gen. Charles
Huntziger to Ankara to formulate a plan of Mediterranean
operations with the Turks. Huntziger claimed that he had
British approval for all the matters he raised, but in fact
the British government had no prior notice of his agenda
for discussions and soon thought it went far beyond anything
they had intended. Sensing that the enormity of Turkish demands might make trouble, the Foreign Office even considered signing an alliance treaty with Ankara without a protocol of specific military operations attached.[54] But Huntziger
anticipated its reservations, agreed that the French and
British would defer to Çakmak's ultimate authority, and
remarked that it would probably be necessary to deploy
Turkish troops in Palestine and Egypt.[55] He said nothing
about Syria, perhaps because he wished to deflect Turkish
territorial aspirations from French- to British-held ground.

Huntziger's allusion to Palestine and Egypt somehow
leaked out of Ankara and soon became grist for the rumor
mills of Middle Eastern capitals. Cairo politicians feared
it as a portent of a Turkish occupation of Egypt, a notion
that, despite repeated efforts, the British ambassador, Sir
Miles Lampson, could not lay to rest. Lampson categorically
denied that any consideration had ever been given to introducing the Turks into Egypt, although, probably unknown to him, some officials in the London Foreign and War

53. Knatchbull-Hugessen to Foreign Office, 1 August 1939, P.R.O.,
F.O. 371/E5544/143/44, and 6 August 1939, P.R.O., F.O. 371/E5565/
143/44.
54. Knatchbull-Hugessen to Foreign Office, 21 July 1939, P.R.O., F.O.
371/E5247/143/44; 21 July 1939, P.R.O., F.O. 371/E5248/143/44; 26 July
1939, P.R.O., F.O. 371/E5315/143/44.
55. Newton, Baghdad, to Foreign Office, 9 August 1939, P.R.O., F.O.
371/E5719/474/93.

offices were speculating that Turkish troops might have to be used along the Nile if demands on British manpower were too severe elsewhere. The Huntziger talks equally agitated the Iraqi government in Baghdad, which several times offered the use of its troops to the Anglo-French coalition to forestall a suspected offer of Mosul to the Turks in exchange for Ankara's military support. Declining the offer, the British assured the Iraqis that the status of Mosul would remain unchanged. However, the Baghdad government was still uneasy and almost neurotically alert to the threat of Turkish irredentism.[56] Finally, Turkey's Balkan neighbors wondered whether any territorial concessions had been made at their expense to persuade Ankara to declare war against Germany. British and German documents do not indicate that a rectification of Turkey's European frontier was proposed. Nevertheless, the Turks did successfully insist that Balkan military personnel be excluded from the Ankara staff conferences for fear that, as full allies of the British and French, the Balkan states would be entitled to their guarantee against Turkish expansionism.[57] They also convinced Huntziger to agree that Turkey would recover the Dodecanese islands in the event that the Anglo-French coalition, allied with Ankara, won the war.

But, according to Huntziger's minutes of his conferences, captured by the Germans when they occupied Paris in 1940, the French general never agreed that London and Paris would declare war on Italy first. He was stupefied when the Turks demanded such a declaration, accompanied by the entry of the French navy into the Strait of Otranto, where the Turks wanted it to shell Italian convoys carrying supplies to Mussolini's troops in Albania. This naval action was to be coordinated with a simultaneous Turkish amphibious landing in the Dodecanese, and the islands would immediately come under Ankara's jurisdiction. Huntziger warned the Turks that they underestimated the Italian fleet, dismissed their whole notion of tactics as "primitive," and threatened to walk out of the meeting. Yet the French am-

56. Newton, Baghdad, to Foreign Office, 21 August 1939, P.R.O., F.O. 371/E5909/474/93; 23 November 1939, P.R.O., F.O. 371/R10596/661/67. Knatchbull-Hugessen to Foreign Office, 7 October 1939, P.R.O., F.O. 371/R8565/661/67.

57. Knatchbull-Hugessen to Foreign Office, 21 July 1939, P.R.O., F.O. 371/E5247/143/44.

bassador, René Massigli, deemed it prudent to soothe the Turks at this point and suggested that their schemes would be favorably considered in the future. The British dissented. Adm. Andrew Cunningham, chief of Mediterranean naval operations, labeled the Turkish proposals outrageous and dismissed General Çakmak as professionally incompetent.[58]

The Turks never won over the British and French to their political and military ideas, but in matters of economics and finance they were completely victorious. The Foreign Office gave Knatchbull-Hugessen license to meet any reasonable Turkish demands, though by "reasonable," the Turks meant a 25 million pounds credit of war materials and an additional transfer to them of 15 million pounds in gold bullion. This loan the Turks proposed to pay back in farm commodities, chiefly in a huge tobacco delivery to Britain. Lord Halifax, the foreign secretary, was appalled when he first saw these terms. He declared Britain could not ship out so much gold bullion without endangering payment on arms contracts already placed in the United States and Canada. Furthermore, Turkish tobacco was largely unmarketable in Britain, where smokers preferred American or Rhodesian blends. However, the foreign secretary was convinced to acquiesce by Knatchbull-Hugessen and by Percy Loraine, who minuted the dispatches from Ankara. Albeit reluctantly, Halifax authorized Knatchbull-Hugessen to sign the military alliance with İnönü's government.[59]

The final draft, published on 19 October 1939, provided that Britain and France would render Turkey all aid if she were attacked by a "European Power"—the Turks had to settle for that simple description. In return, Turkey assumed the same obligation to help her allies, but only if the action developed in the Mediterranean theater. The Turks would not fight on a western European front. On the other hand, a secret clause committed the Anglo-French to intervention

58. Woermann to Papen, 18 October 1940, A.A. 1303/Pol. XI 2801. Andrew B. Cunningham, *A Sailor's Odyssey: The Autobiography of Admiral of the Fleet, Viscount Cunningham of Hyndhope*, pp. 214–15, 218, 223.

59. Foreign Office to Knatchbull-Hugessen, 25 August 1939, P.R.O., F.O. 371/R6794/661/67, and 28 August 1939, P.R.O., F.O. 371/R6797/661/67; Knatchbull-Hugessen to Foreign Office, 26 August 1939, P.R.O., F.O. 371/R6795/661/67.

on Turkey's behalf if the aggressor force only reached the frontiers of Bulgaria or Greece, without violating Turkish territory itself. Still another secret article exempted Turkey from any operation against the Soviet Union. The twenty-five million pounds credit and the fifteen million pounds bullion loan were confirmed. A concluding secret proviso made the whole pact inoperative until the British and French delivered the money and materials.[60]

The British and French had scored nothing more than a propaganda victory, as Papen suspected, though Ribbentrop in Berlin believed they had gotten much more. The foreign minister summoned the Turkish ambassador, Hüsrev Gerede, gave him a severe dressing down and threatened that Turkey might suffer the fate of Poland. Saracoğlu and İnönü were reported to have been very irritated by these remarks, but they were equally irritated when the London press lashed out at them for maladroit administration at home and deceitful, double-dealing relations abroad. Obviously, though the British had their treaty, their own newspapers showed that they were dissatisfied with it. For this reason, Papen continued to hope that he would soon write a treaty of his own.[61]

60. Loraine to Foreign Office, 8 September 1939, P.R.O., F.O. 371/R7244/661/67; Foreign Office Minute by Broad, 8 September 1939, P.R.O., F.O. 371/R7256/661/67. Frank Marzari, "Western-Soviet Rivalry in Turkey, 1939," pp. 63–77, 201–20. Sir Ernest Llewellyn Woodward, *British Foreign Policy in the Second World War*, 1:24–27. Krecker, *Deutschland und die Türkei*, pp. 62–63.

61. Ribbentrop to Papen, — October 1939, A.A. 96/no number; Papen to Foreign Ministry, 9 January 1940, A.A. 96/26.

Chapter 3

Mediterranean Triangle:
Turks, Arabs, and Italians

The first seven months of the Second World War were a time of calculated inaction. After his rapid conquest of Poland, Hitler did not concentrate on a western offensive and had the Wehrmacht assume positions largely of defense. A small British expeditionary force landed in France, and the French themselves invaded the German Saarland, only to be quickly driven out. The bitterest fighting occurred in Finland, which the Soviet Union attacked in late November 1939, under the terms of the nonaggression pact with Germany of the previous August. Meanwhile, Hitler talked nebulously of negotiated peace with Britain, confirming to him his gains in eastern Europe, restoring the old German territories in East Africa, and awarding him additional enclaves in central Africa.[1]

Mussolini did not declare war on Britain and France until 10 June 1940. When he signed the Pact of Steel with Hitler, Il Duce warned that Italy, short of equipment and raw materials, would not be ready for war for three years. He demanded that Germany supply him with twenty million tons of coal, iron, fuel, and ammunition. The German High Command replied that these large quantities were unavailable, and therefore Italy remained nonbelligerent when Poland was invaded. Hitler nonetheless asked Rome to place its forces on alert so that Britain and France would be discouraged from intensifying their attacks on the western front. Mussolini failed even in this. Instead, he summoned the British ambassador and assured him that no Italian operations were contemplated against the Western allies. Hitler

---

1. There are accounts of the "phony war" in Winston S. Churchill, *Blood, Sweat, and Tears*; Cyril Falls, *The Second World War* (London, 1948); Grigore Gafencu, *Prelude to the Russian Campaign: From the Moscow Pact to the Opening of Hostilities in Russia*, trans. E. Fletcher-Allen; William L. Langer, *Our Vichy Gamble*. For Hitler and colonial questions, see Klaus Hildebrand, *Von Reich zum Weltreich: Hitler, NSDAP und koloniale Frage, 1919–1945*, pp. 674ff.

was irritated, but his admonitions could not persuade Il Duce to intervene or even to be courteous to the German military attaché, Gen. Enno von Rintelen. For some months, Rintelen was forbidden to make the customary inspections of Italian defenses. When he was finally permitted to tour Italian army emplacements, he found that the most intensive preparations were being made along the frontier of German-controlled Austria, while the border with France was relatively neglected. Rintelen protested but was met with a curtness verging on defiance. The Italian crown prince frankly told him that he would do all in his power to keep Italy neutral; Mussolini sent Italian troops to fight with the Finns against the Russians. He also sold Britain 650,000 rifles, which London immediately turned over to the Turks in the hope of bringing them into the war against the Axis. The Rumanian foreign minister, Gafencu, asked Mussolini if he was not afraid of pushing Hitler too far. Il Duce replied that, throughout history, German armies had never been able to maintain their positions south of the Alps.[2]

If Germany was dissatisfied with the Italians, Britain and France were having no better experience with the Turks. Throughout early 1940, they tried in vain to make Ankara pay its first dividend on the dearly bought October alliance. If the Turks would not begin a general mobilization, Knatchbull-Hugessen and Massigli indicated that they would be content with the dismissal of Fevzi Çakmak, chief of the Turkish general staff, whose influence they regarded as too pro-German. İnönü declined to remove Çakmak. The allies then proposed to compromise by accepting Çakmak as titular supreme commander of Balkan operations if a senior British or French general did the actual strategical planning. The ambassadors proposed Gen. Maxime Weygand for this job, and Ankara permitted the Frenchman to inspect Turkish defenses preparatory to accepting the assignment. In the end, however, he was not approved as Çakmak's assistant, and the enraged Weygand returned to Paris. Çakmak himself never forgave this attempt to foist a foreign commander

2. Enno von Rintelen, *Mussolini als Bundesgenosse: Erinnerungen des deutschen Militärattachés in Rom, 1936–1943*, pp. 68–76; Grigore Gafencu, *Last Days of Europe: A Diplomatic Journey in 1939*, trans. E. Fletcher-Allen, pp. 162–63; Weizsäcker to Mackensen, 17 February 1940, A.A. 217/182. (For list of abbreviations, see p. 221.)

on him and became the implacable opponent of intervention for Britain and France.[3]

He was, however, not reluctant to fight for a goal clearly
in Turkey's interest. In February 1940 the allies again requested and were refused an order for general mobilization.
But though Turkey would not participate in a war with
Germany, the allies learned that she was close to a confrontation with Bulgaria. Saracoğlu asked George Kiosseivanov,
the Bulgarian prime minister, to yield to Turkey some land
west of the Maritza River frontier so that the defenses of
İstanbul could be deepened. In return, Saracoğlu promised
that Turkey would assist Bulgaria to recover the Dobruja
from Rumania after the war. Kiosseivanov refused this deal
and alleged that the Bulgarians would have Hitler's support
if Saracoğlu threatened to send Turkish troops over the
Maritza line. The Turk then backed down, and British and
French diplomats were relieved that a crisis had been
avoided. However, this setback diminished Saracoğlu's prestige, and Knatchbull-Hugessen was afraid of losing the only
Turkish official whose pro-allied sentiments he thought
genuine. Because he seemed to have mismanaged Balkan
affairs and aligned Turkey with the weaker side in the European war, many members of İnönü's government began calling on Saracoğlu to resign in favor of Numan Menemencioğlu. Nonetheless, Saracoğlu narrowly held his post.[4]

When Germany resumed its western offensive and Belgium capitulated after a short resistance on 28 May 1940,
the Turkish foreign minister panicked and publicly declared that his alliance with Britain and France had been
a mistake. He expected Turkey to opt imminently for an
alliance with the Reich and offered to negotiate it if İnönü
would leave him in office and be content to sack only his
colleagues. There seemed little likelihood of Saracoğlu's
political survival. İnönü and his generals openly congratulated Papen on the victory of German arms. But the German

3. Rohde to Foreign Ministry, 2 February 1940, A.A. 217/76, and 8
February 1940, A.A. 217/82. Paul Reynaud, *In the Thick of the Fight,
1930–1945*, pp. 256–57.
4. Papen to Foreign Ministry, 20 February 1940, A.A. 217/106. Knatch-
bull-Hugessen to Foreign Office, 3 February 1940, P.R.O., F.O. 371/
R1868/316/44. Rendel, Sofia, to Foreign Office, 15 August 1940, and
Minute by Clutten, P.R.O., F.O. 371/R/7073/84/7. Lothar Krecker,
Deutschland und die Türkei im Zweiten Weltkrieg, pp. 71–72.

ambassador decided to intervene to hasten Saracoğlu's disgrace and, in so doing, overplayed his hand and inadvertently sustained his adversary in power. Earlier in the year, during the Finnish campaign, Knatchbull-Hugessen and Massigli had secretly debated reprisals against Russia's Black Sea ports with the Turkish foreign minister. They had asked Saracoğlu to open the Straits so that an Anglo-French flotilla could bombard Odessa and draw off Red Army units from the Finnish front. Throughout extended discussions, Saracoğlu appeared favorable to this proposal, but he finally rejected it as inconsistent with strict neutrality.

Details of all these talks were leaked to the German embassy in Ankara, and Papen planted them with neutral newspaper correspondents. When the story broke, the Soviet Union issued the sternest warnings to Ankara, and Saracoğlu denied his remarks to the allied ambassadors in a manner that seemed implausible to British observers. They thought that Papen's aim was to compromise and finally get rid of Saracoğlu. The Foreign Office also believed that the German ambassador was attempting to instigate a Russo-Turkish conflict, which would force Ankara to seek an alliance with Berlin. However, though İnönü was dissatisfied with his foreign minister and perhaps would have been ready to substitute the more pro-German Menemencioğlu for him, he was too much a Turkish patriot to tolerate foreign interference and intrigue. He authorized Saracoğlu to reprimand Papen severely. The German diplomat was reminded that modern Turkey was not the Ottoman Empire where a foreign envoy at his whim had been able to have the sultan's ministers appointed or dismissed. Regardless of how they felt about Saracoğlu, many Turks shared the sentiment İnönü expressed, and public opinion shifted in the foreign minister's favor.[5]

Meanwhile, Italy declared war on Britain and France on 10 June 1940. Officials in London and Paris thought the Italian declaration was a clear *casus belli* that obligated Turkey to intervene.[6] But the Turks astonished the allies and de-

5. Knatchbull-Hugessen to Foreign Office, 8, 9, and 11 July 1940; Campbell, Belgrade, to Foreign Office, 11 July 1940, P.R.O., F.O. 371/R6670/203/44. Papen to Foreign Ministry, 29 May 1940, A.A. 217/385, and 16 July 1940, A.A. 1303/3640.

6. Foreign Office to Knatchbull-Hugessen, 10 June 1940; Knatchbull-Hugessen to Foreign Office, 11 June 1940, P.R.O., F.O. 371/R6510/316/44.

lighted the Germans by maintaining their neutrality. They advanced two arguments to justify their policy. First, they had contracted their alliance with both Britain and France, but the French government, retreating before the Wehrmacht, evacuated Paris on the very day that Il Duce declared war. On 17 June 1940 a new government was formed under Marshal Pétain with the avowed intention of seeking armistice terms from the Germans. The Turks argued that they could not be expected to go to war with Britain as their only ally.[7] They also claimed that their intervention would provoke the Soviet Union, which had never been brought into the Anglo-French-Turkish bloc. A special protocol of the October alliance relieved Turkey of any responsibility liable to involve her in hostilities with Russia. Yet, upon inquiry, the Foreign Office found out that the Kremlin had made no threat of war, nor had it mobilized troops on the Turkish frontier or demanded the cession of certain border towns, as the Turks alleged.[8]

Fear of Russia and despair of France undoubtedly were important determinants of Ankara's continuing neutrality, but there were also acquisitive and aggressive reasons at work. Anticipating Italy's entry into the war, the British Foreign Office had originally defined Turkey's obligations under the October alliance as follows:

> The allies will have the right under the tripartite treaty of October, 1939 to require Turkey immediately to lend them all aid and assistance in its power. It is essential that there should be no hesitation in putting these dispositions into effect. The measures designed to render Turkish assistance effective should be the rupture of diplomatic relations with Italy, general mobilization, the placing of naval and air bases at the disposal of the allies. In addition it would be most desirable that the Turkish government should declare war on Italy and occupy the Dodecanese as contemplated.[9]

7. Knatchbull-Hugessen to Foreign Office, 18 June 1940, P.R.O., F.O. 371/R6510/316/44.

8. Cripps, Moscow, to Foreign Office, 14 June 1940; Newton, Baghdad, to Foreign Office, 17 June 1940, P.R.O., F.O. 371/R6510/316/44. Sir Ernest Llewellyn Woodward, *British Foreign Policy in the Second World War*, 1:245–47. Krecker, *Deutschland und die Türkei*, pp. 87–89.

9. Foreign Office to Knatchbull-Hugessen, 28 May 1940, P.R.O., F.O. 371/R6269/58/22.

This program for presentation to the Turkish government was formulated in a draft dispatch to Knatchbull-Hugessen by Alexander Cadogan, permanent under secretary of the Foreign Office. It was dated and sent to Ankara on 28 May 1940. But three days later Cadogan changed his mind and ordered the ambassador to withdraw the offer of the Dodecanese islands.[10] He thought that he had good reasons for doing so. Since he had drafted his initial instructions to Knatchbull-Hugessen, the French military situation had deteriorated so rapidly that the French minister in London, Roger Cambon, advised the Foreign Office that his government would be unable to help in an assault on the Dodecanese.

Moreover, Turkey's associates in the Balkan Pact, Greece and Yugoslavia, showed no enthusiasm for the enterprise. The Greeks reported that their finances were so bad that they could hardly afford to defend themselves against a possible Italian invasion, much less try to anticipate it by attacking Italian authority in the Dodecanese islands. Yugoslavia was in favor of bribing Italy out of the war. Belgrade indicated that it would help Athens resist an Italian attack on continental Greece but that it would not fight to maintain Greek jurisdiction on Crete and Corfu, should Mussolini choose to land his forces on those islands. Finally, Bulgaria, never a member of the Balkan Pact and always apprehensive of its policies, was likely to mobilize and declare war against whichever of its neighbors rearmed. The Bulgarians would fight for the Dobruja, not against Italy. In fact, the extension of war to the Balkan Peninsula was expected to persuade Bulgaria to conclude an alliance with Germany.[11] Thus, only Britain and Turkey would be left to assault the Dodecanese, with Britain supplying much of the manpower and paying most of the bill.

The Turks did not sympathize with any of these motives of British policy and were furious at being denied the islands. The Foreign Office rather maladroitly tried to point out to

10. Nichols, for Cadogan, to Knatchbull-Hugessen, 31 May 1940, P.R.O., F.O. 371/R6269/58/22.

11. Campbell, Paris, to Foreign Office, 31 May 1940; Rendel, Sofia, to Foreign Office, 2 June 1940; Palairet, Athens, to Foreign Office, 3 June 1940, P.R.O., F.O. 371/R6269/58/22.

Dr. Aras, now the Turkish ambassador in London, that Egypt, a fellow Muslim state, had immediately severed relations with Italy upon her declaration of war and placed all Egyptian military and naval facilities at the disposal of Britain. Aras was asked if Turkey, though reneging on a declaration of war against the Axis, would at least allow British ships to operate in Turkish territorial waters to attack Italian commerce. He retorted that Turkey was no British colony like Egypt, reiterated the demand for the Dodecanese, and evinced a new interest in Albania, the tiny Balkan kingdom that had been a Turkish possession before the First World War. The Turks wanted the British to concentrate their attack on Italy in Albania rather than in North Africa, where an Italian army could be expected to move out of Libya into Egypt and toward the Suez Canal.[12]

Papen believed the Turks would never have dared to violate their alliance commitments to Britain and France unless they were preparing to cover themselves with a declaration for Germany and Italy. He claimed that President İnönü had told him that such a decision was under consideration in the Turkish cabinet. The German ambassador was ready to pay dearly for it. The Turks wanted to buy long-range guns, electrical equipment, and aircraft motors from German industry with their credits. The High Command in Berlin, mindful of the growing dimensions of the European war, preferred to reserve such equipment for use in the Reich or to allocate it to Italy. But Papen intervened energetically to convince a skeptical Ribbentrop and a hesitant High Command to consign 21 million Turkish pounds worth of this critical weaponry to Ankara on credit. Ottavio de Peppo, the Italian ambassador to Turkey, protested Berlin's readiness to accommodate the İnönü government and wondered aloud whether the Turks had replaced the Italians as Hitler's favorite allies.[13]

Another people who wondered the same thing were the Arabs. All their overtures for German support were doomed because of the Reich's preference for the elusive Turkish alliance. This was now especially true in light of Turkey's

---

12. Halifax to Knatchbull-Hugessen, 11 June 1940; Foreign Office to Knatchbull-Hugessen, 14 June 1940, P.R.O., F.O. 371/R6510/316/44.
13. Papen to Foreign Ministry, 13 June 1940, A.A. 217/429.

neutrality despite Italy's declaration of belligerence. The Italians, however, were not so considerate of Turkish reactions because they possessed territories, Libya and the Dodecanese, to which Turkey had once had title. In conjunction with its North African military operations and to win the goodwill of the Arab peoples, the Italian government on 7 July 1940 solemnly declared through Luigi Gabrielli, its minister to Iraq, that it favored the creation of a large and independent Arab state free of any kind of European imperialistic influence. This declaration was contrary to every previous Italian response to the Arab independence movement, and it bewildered the Germans and caused them to make inquiries with Foreign Minister Count Ciano. Ciano at first claimed that Gabrielli in Iraq had exceeded his instructions but later admitted that he had authorized his representative to give some vague verbal assurances to Iraqi dignitaries.[14] Ciano was not normally so careless, and it may be that in encouraging Arab hopes and inciting Turkish jealousy, the Italian foreign minister intended to drive a wedge between Ankara and Berlin. Whatever his motives, the Arab nationalists naturally assumed that German and Italian policy toward them ran parallel, and they began to approach the Reich's representatives soon after the Italian declaration in Iraq.

In Turkey at least three Arab petitioners contacted Franz von Papen in the summer of 1940. The ambassador found their presence inconvenient and embarrassing and kept his responses cool and moderately obstructive. All three interviews were arranged to take place at Therapia, the German summer embassy near İstanbul, by Zoltan de Mariassy, the Hungarian minister to Turkey, who was known to have close contacts with Count Ciano. Papen himself was little more than cordial to his Arab guests and did nothing to make them comfortable. The first he met was an unnamed Egyptian. Claiming to speak for King Farouk, this Egyptian wanted the Germans to take immediate control of Italian forces in Libya under Marshal Rodolfo Graziani. Grazi-

14. Grobba to Papen, 27 September 1940, A.A. 1303/no number. This summarizes the history of Gabrielli's declaration, which occurred a few months earlier. Łukasz Hirszowicz, *The Third Reich and the Arab East,* p. 80.

ani's forces then heavily outnumbered the British army in Egypt under Archibald Wavell, but the Italian had done little to press toward the Egyptian frontier since hostilities were declared on 10 June. Farouk supposedly wanted a German general to supplant Graziani, bring some drive into the campaign, and expel the British, especially their ambassador Sir Miles Lampson, of whose bullying Farouk was always complaining. In return for this operation, the Egyptian king promised to Hitler control of the Suez Canal and to Mussolini a communications corridor between Libya and Abyssinia, to be carved out of the Egyptian Sudan.[15]

Papen sent his dispatch of this interview, without supportive comment, to Berlin, where nothing was done about it. The Wilhelmstrasse's decision may have been wrong. At this time, Anglo-Egyptian defenders on the Libyan frontier were badly undermanned and demoralized. Many of the officers and men were serving punishment detail at half the pay rate customary in Cairo and Alexandria. They would probably have quickly cracked under an Italo-German attack. But, on the other hand, King Farouk was petulant and unstable. He detested Sir Miles Lampson and his staff, but was English in education and taste. He might withdraw his support from the Germans as unpredictably as he now offered it. And, while many Egyptian politicians had pro-Axis proclivities, one of the most important political parties at Cairo, the Saadists under Ahmed Maher, urged the government to cooperate loyally with Britain and seek leadership of the Arab world with British backing. The Saadists and all other prominent Egyptians recognized the Turks as their chief rivals for this leadership. Farouk and his family were the declared enemies of İnönü's government, and any German encouragement to the monarch would have quickly aroused the resentment of Ankara. German policymakers had to weigh all these factors. While they deferred any commitments to the Egyptian king, the Churchill ministry was given time to ship out reinforcements to General Wavell's hard pressed command. In September 1940, after weeks of mulish inaction, Graziani finally took the offensive against Egypt and scored some initial successes. Then, in December, Wavell hit back hard, stemmed the Italian advance, and

15. Papen to Foreign Ministry, 4 July 1940, A.A. 1303/501.

took massive numbers of prisoners while sustaining relatively few casualties in his own forces.[16]

Soon after dealing with the Egyptian emissary, Papen held talks with Naji Shawkat, the Iraqi minister of justice. Shawkat was well known to the British for his recurrent inquiries about Turkish designs against his country. He complained to the German ambassador that the Turks had withheld his travel visa for some months. Now that he had finally reached Therapia, he asked Papen and the German government to declare their support for the complete independence of Iraq from British control. In return, he promised that Baghdad would resume diplomatic relations with Berlin, which had been broken when the war began, and furnish military assistance to Axis forces in the event they invaded the Middle East. Papen inquired if the whole Iraqi army would come over to the German side, but Shawkat answered that he had only skirmishes and guerrilla operations against British emplacements in mind. Papen belittled this kind of intervention and sent home the Iraqi official without encouragement.[17] Despite the rebuff, another agent arrived from Baghdad within a month. He was Osman Kemal Haddad, private secretary of the grand mufti of Jerusalem, Haj Muhammad Amin al-Husseini.

The mufti was the most tireless Arab collaborator with the Axis, though all his schemes proved abortive. Haj Muhammad had been the supreme judge of the Palestinian religious courts since 1922 and chairman since 1936 of the Arab Higher Committee, an association to promote internal revolts and conduct relations with foreign powers. Sir Herbert Samuel, a British Jew serving as high commissioner for Palestine in 1922, appointed him to the courts for his breadth of learning and apparent open-mindedness. Once in office, however, the mufti revealed himself an uncompromising opponent of the British mandate and of Jewish immigration to Palestine. He had many supporters, not only in Palestine

16. On conditions in the Egyptian army, see Henry Maitland Wilson, *Eight Years Overseas, 1939–1947*, p. 26. For an estimate of Farouk's character, see Oliver Lyttelton, Viscount Chandos, *The Memoirs of Lord Chandos*, pp. 232–41. The Egyptian political scene is described in Jean Lugol, *L'Égypte et la Deuxième Guerre Mondiale*, pp. 120–22.

17. Papen to Foreign Ministry, 6 July 1940, A.A. 1303/no number; Kroll to Foreign Ministry, 31 July 1940, A.A. 1303/3864. Hirszowicz, *Third Reich*, pp. 78–79.

but also in Iraq, Saudi Arabia, Egypt, and Transjordan. Halid Alhud and Naji Shawkat, both involved in negotiations with the Axis, were among them, as was Rashid Ali al-Gailani, leader of the anti-British Iraqi revolt of 1941. Those who did not support him, the mufti ignored or, it was rumored, had assassinated. Throughout his prewar career, the British administration in Palestine was curiously reluctant to press charges against the mufti. In 1938, in the wake of a particularly bloody fight between Jerusalem Arabs and Jews that Haj Muhammad was believed to have incited, General Wavell, then commanding officer of the Palestinian army, tracked him down to the Temple quarter, where he had sought sanctuary, and almost arrested him. But the mufti escaped, fled to Syria, where the French authorities provided him with comfortable lodgings and transportation to Iraq, and finally set up his headquarters in Baghdad. Both the British and French governments justified their leniency to the mufti by claiming that any harsher policy would have alienated Muslim opinion and made the recruitment of Muslims into their colonial forces more difficult.[18]

The proposals that the mufti sent to Papen in August 1940, by the hand of Osman Kemal Haddad, were thorough in content and lavish in implication. A cunning master of intrigue had obviously honed them. Germany and Italy were asked to sign an eight-point declaration promising independence to every Arab state. Both were to promise the abolition of the Anglo-French mandates and to pledge never to use the mandate device themselves. In return, Iraq would reopen diplomatic relations with Berlin—they had never been broken with Rome—instigate anti-British revolts throughout the Middle East, and transfer to the Axis valuable concessions in its oil fields. Foreign investments other than those of Britain and France would be declared inviolable and all interest and dividends would be paid unimpaired. Complete freedom of worship would be assured to resident foreigners. Osman Kemal Haddad gave the impression that the mufti could bring regular Iraqi army units into action against the

18. Elie Kedourie, "Wavell and Iraq, April-May 1941," pp. 373–86. Joseph B. Schechtman, *The Mufti and the Fuehrer: The Rise and Fall of Haj Amin el-Husseini*, pp. 70–76, 93–97. Schechtman's is an interesting but biased account. A more balanced summary of the mufti's early career is found in Yehoshua Porath, *The Emergence of the Palestinian-Arab National Movement, 1918–1929*, pp. 76–77, 189–94.

British, not just the irregular companies suggested earlier by Naji Shawkat. Haddad also spoke of purging all pro-British ministers from Middle Eastern governments. He mentioned particularly Nuri as-Said, the senior pro-British politician at Baghdad and several times prime minister or foreign minister of Iraq in the interwar period. According to Haddad, Nuri as-Said and the whole British connection were despised by the Iraqi people and would be tolerated only as long as Iraq had to fear the Turks, with their well-known and long-standing claims against Mosul and adjacent Syria.[19]

About the middle of August Osman Kemal Haddad left İstanbul for Berlin, though only after a lengthy argument with Turkish customs and immigration officials who tried to prevent his departure. Papen does not seem to have intervened to ease his difficulties with the Turkish authorities. Arrived in the German capital, Haddad repeated his proposals in several conferences with State Secretary Ernst von Weizsäcker and Fritz Grobba, the German minister to Iraq before the rupture of relations and now an adviser on Middle Eastern affairs in the foreign ministry. Unknown to the mufti's envoy, Papen sent an elaborate policy paper to Weizsäcker that made the Arab's visit to Germany a failure. The ambassador argued that, with Italian troops ensconced in Libya and the Dodecanese islands, Germany must achieve closer relations with Turkey unless she intended to resign the whole Mediterranean to Mussolini. Turkey, he continued, remained the Reich's only land approach to the Middle East, and if the Wilhelmstrasse dallied now with Iraqi emissaries and the cause of Arab nationalism, the Turks were liable to be irreparably alienated and riveted in their Anglo-French alliance, while Italy would be propitiated without any real prospect of her becoming a more resolute ally in the near future.[20]

Papen's opinion confirmed Weizsäcker's own doubts about the Arabs. The state secretary took several weeks to decide about the declaration for Arab independence; during this tedious delay, Osman Kemal Haddad revealed the least attractive side of his personality. To his original proposals

19. Papen to Foreign Ministry, 6 August 1940, A.A. 63/602 (*DGFP*, 10:415–16); Weizsäcker to Mackensen, 9 September 1940, A.A. 63/Pol. VII 2730g. Hirszowicz, *Third Reich*, pp. 82–84.

20. Papen to Weizsäcker, 3 October 1940, A.A. 1303/4828.

he added a demand that Germany pay the mufti a monthly subsidy of twenty thousand pounds sterling. When Ciano heard about it, he commented that it tallied with his own experience of Haj Muhammad. For years he had paid the mufti millions of lira to carry out anti-British activity but in return had gotten only the destruction of a few oil refineries of no strategical importance and quickly repaired in any case. The Italian foreign minister said he still favored Arab independence but preferred someone other than the mufti to lead the fight for it. The Germans also heard that Haj Muhammad had been unable to keep Haddad's trip to Berlin a secret from the Anglophile politicians in Baghdad. One of them, most probably Nuri as-Said, had alerted the British and the Turks who, predictably, began to complain about this surreptitious traffic between the mufti and the Wilhelmstrasse.

Therefore Weizsäcker returned the declaration for Arab independence to Osman Kemal Haddad unsigned. Instead, the state secretary proposed a compromise. Germany and Italy offered to broadcast a message to the Middle East that would affirm that the Axis viewed "Arab strivings for independence with warm friendship." The governments in Berlin and Rome furthermore "cherished the wish" that the Arabs would take their "natural and historical place" among the peoples of the world. This message was actually transmitted in Arabic from stations in Berlin and Bari on 23 October 1940, but it was not simultaneously released to the European press. Only the relatively few Arabs prosperous enough to own a wireless ever knew about this Axis proclamation at all, and Osman Kemal Haddad and the mufti denounced it as totally inadequate and unacceptable. The Arab emissary and the state secretary had a furious row, but Weizsäcker would not change his mind and curtly retorted that where Arab independence already existed, Germany would support it. Where it did not exist, the Arabs must fight for it.[21]

Weizsäcker's rebuff to the Arabs could not have been more timely. On 28 October 1940, Italian forces invaded Greece

---

21. Grobba to Ribbentrop, 27 August 1940, A.A. 63/Pol. VII 2614 (*DGFP*, 10:556–59); Mackensen to Weizsäcker, 10 September 1940, A.A. 63/2730g, and 14 September 1940, A.A. 63/1677. Papen to Foreign Ministry, 14 September 1940, A.A. 63/743; Weizsäcker to Papen, 18 October 1940, A.A. 63/534. Hirszowicz, *Third Reich*, pp. 90–92.

from Albania. This was a contingency clearly covered by Ankara's military alliance with Britain and France. But, as in the previous June, the Turks broke their pledge and remained neutral. Had Weizsäcker made an agreement with the Arabs, the İnönü government might have intervened against the Italians. Neither the British nor the Germans were prepared for Mussolini's Greek adventure. Hitler, who at that time wanted peace in the Balkans, had long suspected that Il Duce might try to expand his foothold from Albania, but he could obtain no precise information about the direction the Italians would take. Mussolini ordered his generals to avoid consultation with German military personnel; when Enno von Rintelen, the German military attaché, queried Pietro Badoglio, chief of the Italian general staff, about a Greek campaign, Badoglio flatly denied that it was in the offing. The Italian general, however, privately opposed the Greek invasion and warned Mussolini that it could never succeed without substantial German assistance.

On the other hand, Count Ciano predicted a quick victory, with Italian vanguards having to move no farther east than the town of Arta in Epirus in order to pressure the Greek government to surrender. The Italian foreign minister relied on certain Greek politicians, whom he had liberally bribed, to call for an early capitulation. These turncoats did not appear, the doughty Greeks fought back furiously, and in a short time they cleared the Italians out of their country and chased them back into Albania. The Fascist retreat became a rout, and it was soon evident, as one Turkish diplomat put it, that Italy had become "a nail in Germany's coffin." Yet officials in Ankara made no effort, by activating the alliance with Britain, to drive that nail home.[22]

The British denounced Turkey's policy as inexcusable. The Foreign Office had believed, probably unrealistically, that the mere threat of Turkish intervention in response to Italian aggression would have dissuaded Mussolini from his course.[23] Now that he had mounted his attack on Greece, the British expected the Turks to help Greece with all avail-

22. Rintelen, *Mussolini*, pp. 106–8; Pietro Badoglio, *Italy in the Second World War: Memories and Documents*, trans. Muriel Currey, pp. 27–28; Stohrer to Foreign Ministry, 8 November 1940, A.A. 217/3798.

23. Rendel, Sofia, to Foreign Office, 8 October 1940, P.R.O., F.O. 371/R7861/4/7.

able means. Turkish diplomats pled that those means were inadequate for combat. The Turks emphasized their lack of a strong air force and of adequate antiaircraft defenses, a point that modern Turkish historians cite in vindication of their country's policy in 1940.[24] İnönü's government, however, made a distinction between Axis aggression against Yugoslavia and against Bulgaria as part of the Greek campaign. If the Germans were to invade Yugoslavia to support another Italian drive against Greece, the Turks indicated that they would do nothing, even though Ankara and Belgrade had been allied in the Balkan Pact since 1934. But, if the Germans penetrated Bulgaria, Turkey's immediate neighbor, the İnönü government declared itself perfectly able and ready to fight.[25] At the same time, the Turks raised their old demands for territorial compensation in the Dodecanese islands, Bulgarian Thrace, and Albania.[26] They even evinced a new interest in controlling the Greek port of Salonika, which, since they controlled the Straits, would have given the Turks the predominant position in the Aegean Sea. Ambassador Knatchbull-Hugessen's advice was "to press the Salonika argument very hard" in order to bring Turkey into the war against Italy, but Under Secretary Alexander Cadogan thought Salonika too high a price to pay.[27]

Until the end of the year, the Turks continued unsuccessfully to seek territorial increments. What disturbed them particularly was that while the British refused to bargain with them, it was rumored that the Foreign Office had made a deal with Stalin to improve Anglo-Soviet relations. In the summer

24. For instance, Türkkaya Ataöv, *Turkish Foreign Policy, 1939–1945*, pp. 81–89. Ferenc Váli, the Hungarian historian, in his survey of Turkish foreign policy, remarks that, at the time they made their alliance with Britain and France, Turkish leaders expected Hitler to lose interest in the Balkans. Váli implies that at that point the Turkish officials were not concerned about violating the stipulations of the alliance because they did not expect them to become operative. Váli's argument is difficult to accept because Hitler's troops were already in Czechoslovakia, on the periphery of the Balkans, in 1939, and the Turks had no grounds for assuming that they would not move farther. Ferenc A. Váli, *Bridge Across the Bosporus: The Foreign Policy of Turkey*, p. 30.

25. Knatchbull-Hugessen to Foreign Office, Important, 4 December 1940, P.R.O., F.O. 371/R8697/316/44.

26. Foreign Office to Knatchbull-Hugessen, 30 October 1940, P.R.O., F.O. 371/R8130/316/44.

27. Knatchbull-Hugessen to Foreign Office, 28 November 1940, P.R.O., F.O. 371/R8697/316/44.

of 1940 the Churchill ministry instructed Sir Stafford Cripps, the British ambassador in Moscow, to discuss all outstanding problems, including control of the Straits. Stalin demanded unrestricted passage from the Black Sea for Soviet ships, regardless of Turkey's regulatory authority. That authority had been conferred by the Montreux Convention, signed by both Britain and the Soviet Union. Nevertheless, the Soviet dictator implied that the convention would have to be either modified or ignored. Cripps did not agree to Stalin's plans but did not unequivocally reject them, either. Instead Knatchbull-Hugessen was ordered to begin a verbal offensive, to persuade the Turks that concessions to Russia would result in a gain for all of anti-Fascist Europe. His arguments left the Turks unimpressed and uneasy. In July Saracoğlu traveled to Moscow to offer Stalin some rectification of the Russo-Turkish frontier in exchange for abandoning any revision of the Montreux Convention. The foreign minister argued that a sovereign and independent Turkey was the Soviet Union's soundest rampart against Italian imperialism in the Mediterranean.

However, the Soviet leadership was not worried about Mussolini and, with Britain struggling desperately against Hitler, could afford to stick to its demands. Saracoğlu returned to Ankara without an accord and the Kremlin recalled Alexei Terentiev, its ambassador to Turkey, and replaced him with Serge Vinogradov, formerly Terentiev's chargé d'affaires. The British were puzzled by the change but ascribed it, to soothe the Turks, to Terentiev's poor health. The İnönü government, however, suspected that there was something more behind Vinogradov's appointment, which it found wholly unsuitable. The former chargé was very young for his new job and spoke only Russian. He seemed scarcely qualified except, the Turks feared, for a brief tenure preparatory to a complete rupture of relations.[28]

With the Russians threatening at the Straits and the British unaccommodating in the Balkans, Turkey's failure to honor her alliance and declare war against the Axis becomes

28. Knatchbull-Hugessen to Foreign Office, 7 July 1940; Cripps to Foreign Office, 8 July 1940; Knatchbull-Hugessen to Foreign Office, 11 July 1940, P.R.O., F.O. 371/R6670/203/44. Foreign Office to Knatchbull-Hugessen, 5 December 1940, P.R.O., F.O. 371/R8697/316/44. Kroll to Foreign Ministry, 31 July 1940, A.A. 217/584; Papen to Foreign Ministry, 12 September 1940, A.A. 1303/4535.

more understandable, though not morally or legally justifi-
able. These two factors also suggest why the Turks drew
nearer to Germany, whose Arab policy was so encouraging,
in the wake of Mussolini's debacle in Greece. Hitler managed to stem the Italian rout in the Balkans by allocating
German reserves to Il Duce's army. But he realized that he
could never more than temporarily resuscitate his ally and
therefore, in late October 1940, sought additional sources
of help. At the conferences of Montoire and Hendaye, the
Führer opened negotiations with Vichy France and Falan-
gist Spain, but Marshal Pétain declined to put his military
forces at Hitler's disposal, and General Franco was ostensibly
willing to do so only in return for large German donations
of oil, machinery, and wheat. The Spanish leader also presented colonial claims against the French empire that Hitler
found unacceptable.

Papen was surprised to learn that the Turks were kept
well abreast of developments at Montoire and Hendaye by
an excellent secret service system and asked to be invited to
such palavers held in the future. A bit earlier, through their
ambassador in London, they had suggested that Turkey and
the United States be invited to negotiate a general European
peace entailing, among other things, a reorganization of the
Balkan Peninsula. Joseph Kennedy, the American ambassador to Britain, was described as mildly favorable to the
Turkish scheme, but the British government discouraged
it immediately.[29] Papen, on the other hand, was quite ready
to treat the İnönü government as a great power and believed
it could supplement or even supplant Germany's faltering
Italian ally. In November 1940, the Ankara war ministry
finally undertook something like the full mobilization that
Knatchbull-Hugessen had been pleading for without success
since the Nazi blitzkrieg of Poland. Blackouts were imposed
in İstanbul and Ankara, soldiers were substituted for civilian
municipal police, and some of the principal government offices were relocated in the countryside. Gen. Asım Gündüz,
deputy chief of the Turkish general staff, told Papen that
these measures portended a Turkish declaration for the
Axis. From their various missions, the British too heard that

29. Papen to Foreign Ministry, 26 November 1940, A.A. 217/963.
Halifax to Knatchbull-Hugessen, 23 October 1940, P.R.O., F.O. 371/
R8008/316/44.

his generals were trying to browbeat İnönü into allying with the Reich.[30]

On 23 November 1940, Papen called on Numan Menemencioğlu to learn more about the reasons behind the Turkish state of alert. Menemencioğlu attributed it to the Italo-Greek conflict and the likelihood of German intervention. The German ambassador rejoined that, whatever happened, Turkey's frontiers could be guaranteed if the İnönü government declared its acceptance of the Axis new order. The Turkish minister then adjourned the conference, but two days later he invited Papen to his office again. He ridiculed Mussolini's reverses in Greece and urged Germany to use Il Duce's embarrassment to become the dominant partner in the Axis. All decisions, the Turk said somewhat cryptically, should be made in the interests of the Reich alone. He then queried Papen about what Hitler would do if the Italians were driven out of Albania by the Greek army. The ambassador dismissed this as a remote possibility, but in a third interview on 29 November, this time with President İnönü, the Turks returned to the subject of Albania. It was rather unusual for İnönü to concern himself with foreign policy publicly; when Knatchbull-Hugessen or Massigli pressed him to do so, he usually pleaded a constitutional limitation of his power. But with Papen he was direct and candid. He insisted that Italy evacuate Albania and asked point-blank whether Hitler would land German troops in that country. Without hesitation, Papen declared that the Führer would not, because the tiny Balkan kingdom had no strategical significance and was largely irrelevant to the successful outcome of the war. This assurance encouraged İnönü, and he requested that the German ambassador formulate his ideas for a nonaggression pact, together with a program for the reorganization of the Balkan Peninsula in the event that Hitler won the war. He enjoined the strictest secrecy on Papen; otherwise, he would deny that this conversation had taken place. This admonition to secrecy and the inquiry about Balkan reorganization beyond the requirements of mere Turkish security suggest that it was by no

30. Kroll to Foreign Ministry, 31 October 1940, A.A. 217/868. Yencken, Madrid, to Foreign Office, 15 November 1940, P.R.O., F.O. 371/R8608/5/67; Knatchbull-Hugessen to Foreign Office, 29 November 1940, P.R.O., F.O. 371/R8712/316/44.

means impossible that the Turkish leadership was seeking to acquire the economic and cultural primacy in Albania exercised by Mussolini until his recent series of defeats.[31]

Papen immediately prepared a draft treaty, wiring it to the Wilhelmstrasse for approval. He recommended that negotiations with the Turks be strictly bilateral and not subject to Italian approval. He divided his treaty into four articles. In the first, Turkey would declare herself "sympathetic" to the Axis new order and ready to take "an active part" in regulating the Balkan Peninsula and the Middle East. The second article obligated the Turks to abstain from any British operation against German forces, while the third pledged the Axis to respect Turkey's territorial integrity and not to attack her. The last article affirmed that Turkish representatives would be invited to all conferences on Balkan reorganization. Saracoğlu perused these articles before their dispatch to Berlin, amending the territorial guarantee to cover not only Turkey, but also an undefined "Turkish zone of interest."[32]

Ribbentrop perfunctorily censured Papen for failing to respect Italy's privileges as an ally, but his real concern was for the Soviet Union's reaction to the proposed pact with Turkey. The German foreign minister had recently conferred with Molotov in Berlin, where the stony Russian had demanded that Bulgaria, as well as the area from the Caucasus to the Persian Gulf, be reserved to Stalin's sphere of influence. In addition, the Soviet Union was again demanding air and naval bases on the Straits. In the end, Germany was to rebuff Molotov on all these matters; in the meantime, Ribbentrop, as he told Papen, did not want to bind his hands in regard to Turkey. However, because Molotov became less tractable during the next few weeks, Ribbentrop allowed the negotiations with Ankara to amble on. He cautioned Papen to put as little as possible in writing, but he did not object to the amorphous but potentially explosive proposal for a Turkish "zone of interest."

To conciliate the Turks, Ribbentrop even sent his brother-

31. Papen to Foreign Ministry, 25 November 1940, A.A. 217/958 (*DGFP*, 11:702–3); 29 November 1940, A.A. 217/971 (*DGFP*, 11:741–43); 2 December 1940, A.A. 217/977 (*DGFP*, 11:764–65).

32. Ibid. and Ribbentrop to Papen, 3 December 1940, A.A. 217/653 (*DGFP*, 11:777). Krecker, *Deutschland und die Türkei*, pp. 127–28.

in-law, Albert Jencke, to confer with Saracoğlu and Mene-mencioğlu. Papen simply described these discussions as "generous and encouraging," but it seems quite likely that they ranged over territorial shifts and bequests.[33] The British suspected that such meetings were taking place but thought the crux of the discussions concerned Syria and Iraq, not the Balkan Peninsula. Philip Nichols, counselor of the Foreign Office, wrote in a memorandum for Alexander Cadogan that "Syria seems to be the key to the whole [Turkish] position." But C. W. Baxter, his colleague and fellow Middle Eastern expert, advised the under secretary that Turkey had no imperialistic aspirations and that any allegations to the contrary were fabricated by her old enemies, ibn-Saud, king of Saudi Arabia, and the French government, which still smarted under the prewar loss of Alexandretta. Cadogan adopted Baxter's view and did nothing to obstruct an agreement between Ankara and Berlin.[34]

33. Ribbentrop to Papen, 21 December 1940, A.A. 217/715 (*DGFP*, 11:927); Papen to Ribbentrop, 15 February 1941, A.A. 217/140.
34. Memoranda by Nichols and Baxter to Cadogan, 6 November 1940, P.R.O., F.O. 371/R8242/316/44.

Chapter 4

The Alienation of the Arabs

A comparison of German and British official documents
shows that often each government was very well informed
about the most secret diplomacy of the other. But about the
Foreign Office's rejection of Turkish territorial demands,
the Wilhelmstrasse was completely deceived. Relying on a
Vichy French informant, Papen wired Berlin in January
1941 that the British had already conceded the French mandate of Syria to the İnönü government and were about to
follow it with an offer of the Italian-held Dodecanese islands.[1]
The German ambassador did not know that British diplomats could not then have made such a deal even had they
wished to. While the Foreign Office might have accepted the
loss of a French possession in the Levant, it could not have
been as easily reconciled to the surrender of a piece of the
British Empire in the Mediterranean. For, by the beginning
of 1941, the issue was not only the cession of Syria and the
Dodecanese islands, but of the British crown colony of Cyprus as well.

The island of Cyprus, with a population about eighty
percent Greek and twenty percent Turkish, was an Ottoman possession until 4 June 1878, when the sultan signed a
military convention transferring it to Britain. Under the
terms of this convention, the British were to develop the
island as a naval base to help defend Turkey against possible
Russian aggression in the eastern Mediterranean. Legally,
the sultan remained sovereign of Cyprus, but in practice the
British administered it as a crown colony from the beginning.
In 1914, when the Ottoman Empire allied with Germany, the
British retaliated by annexing Cyprus in a proclamation of
5 November. The Greek and Turkish inhabitants were not
consulted about any of these developments, but no serious
protests against them were raised until December 1940.

At that time, when the Greek army was smashing the

1. Papen to Foreign Ministry, 7 January 1941, A.A. 1303/A.62. (For
list of abbreviations, see p. 221.)

66

Italian invaders near the Albanian frontier, a wave of phil-hellenic enthusiasm swept Cyprus, and the Cypriot Greeks began to demand the union of the island with Greece. This provoked the local Turks to call, in somewhat more muted volume, for the incorporation of Cyprus by the Ankara government. Events in Cyprus seem at first to have been spontaneous and not inspired by the Greek government in Athens. *Hestia*, an Athenian newspaper, declared that Britain should relinquish the island to encourage her valiant but beleaguered ally, but even the Foreign Office could find no evidence that this pronouncement emanated from the Greek king and his prime minister, Gen. Joannes Metaxas. The real authors of the Cypriots' enthusiasm, the Foreign Office believed, were the Greek Orthodox clergy of the island, who enjoined their parishioners to sacrifice their wealth and even their lives in the Greek struggle against Fascist aggression. The clergy set an example by donating money and ecclesiastical gems and plate to the cause. The laity signed over their personal jewelry and bank accounts. About twelve hundred Cypriot men went to the mainland and enlisted in the Greek army, and two hundred women from the island volunteered for the Greek Red Cross.[2]

The British government was embarrassed by this movement for Cypriot independence but divided over how to cope with it. Sir Michael Palairet, the British ambassador to Greece, recommended the cession of the island to encourage unity within the allied war effort. Edward Warner and Pierson Dixon, counselors on Middle Eastern affairs at the Foreign Office, also favored making Cyprus a gift to the Greek government. Both men argued that the local population, who an unsympathetic colonial office did nothing to conciliate, would always be disgruntled under British rule, while the cost of fully developing the island's naval facilities had been regarded as prohibitive before the war. Warner and Dixon thought that Cyprus should be transferred to Greece in exchange for the permanent lease to the Mediterranean fleet of Suda Bay in Crete. But Counselor Philip Nichols, who had earlier encouraged concessions to Turkey in Syria and the Dodecanese, now opposed any revision of the status

2. Historical Review by Dixon to Foreign Office, 31 January 1941; translation of *Hestia* article of 17 December 1940, P.R.O., F.O. 371/ R397/198/19.

of Cyprus in favor of Greece. Nichols wrote that if Britain won the war, the Greek government would be perfectly happy to lease Suda Bay without any territorial inducements, while the Turks, who had so far reneged on their alliance with Britain, might be irretrievably alienated from it by any attempt to change the regime on Cyprus. He warned:

> The Turks could, if they wished, argue that the island ought to revert to Turkey since the original basis of its cession by Turkey to Great Britain has long lapsed, i.e. an engagement to defend Turkey against Russia. In any case it is obviously desirable to avoid provoking such an awkward controversy, which might well be the effect of a decision to give the island to the Greeks.[3]

Deputy Under Secretary Orme Sargent adopted Nichols's argument and ordered Ambassador Palairet in Athens to restrain his enthusiasm for Greek irredentism. Palairet was also to persuade the Greek government to discourage Cypriot enlistments in its armed forces. Athens was to be advised that there already existed a Cypriot unit in the British army, which potential recruits to the Greek ranks might instead be invited to join. The Metaxas government promised to turn back Cypriot volunteers and to recommend service in British imperial forces to them. Despite this understanding, enrollment in the British Cypriot unit remained embarrassingly small, Cypriots continued to leave the island for the fighting on the mainland, and the local clergy did not desist from their philhellenic call to arms. British authorities on the island were finally reduced to canceling all travel visas and jailing those Cypriots who persisted in trying to smuggle themselves off the island.[4] They recognized that these measures would never solve the problem, which was to recur throughout the war, but they dared not risk anything more conclusive. As one Foreign Office minute put

3. Palairet, Athens, to Foreign Office, 19 December 1940; Minutes by Warner and Dixon, 21 and 31 January 1941; Minute by Nichols, 13 March 1941, P.R.O., F.O. 371/R397/198/19.

4. Palairet, Athens, to Foreign Office, 14 February 1941, P.R.O., F.O. 371/R1193/198/19; Foreign Office to Palairet, 15 February 1941, P.R.O., F.O. 371/R1270/198/19; Acheson, Colonial Office, to Foreign Office, 24 February 1941, P.R.O., F.O. 371/R1508/198/19. Palairet, Athens, to Foreign Office, 28 February 1941, P.R.O., F.O. 371/R1863/198/19. There is additional material on politics in Cyprus in Palairet, Athens, to Foreign Office, 4 January 1941, P.R.O., F.O. 371/R198/198/19.

it, "the chief difficulty in handing over Cyprus to Greece is that this would meet with the same problem, only in a more acute form, which complicates the question of the Dodecanese—namely the claims of Turkey."[5] In both areas, the London government recognized, rival Greek and Turkish claims were irreconcilable; it was impossible to solve one problem without making the other a point of contention.

Here was a dilemma upon which German diplomacy might have capitalized. The Turks left no doubt that for a price they were willing to disavow their alliance with Britain, especially since the collapse of Italy as a belligerent seemed irreversible. Because of Badoglio's defeats in Albania, Mussolini dismissed him as chief of staff and replaced him with Gen. Ugo Cavallero, who was ordered to take personal charge of operations in the Balkans. But Il Duce realized that he could not end the succession of Greek victories without German intervention, which Hitler pledged him, and he rather reluctantly accepted, at a conference at the Berghof in Bavaria on 19 January 1941. However, the German High Command, in formulating its plan of attack, decided against committing its troops to Albania because of the jagged terrain, which made transportational problems almost insuperable, and because of the area's heavy rains and snows.

Aside from these purely military considerations, the decision was diplomatically congenial to the Turks. Numan Menemencioğlu advised Hans Kroll, Papen's assistant, that Germany should not fight in Albania under any circumstances, because even if the lost ground were recovered by the Wehrmacht, the reputation of Italy was indelibly sullied, and Mussolini could never again be taken seriously as a combatant. In Berlin, the Turkish ambassador sent his chargé d'affaires, Alkend, to the foreign ministry to say much the same thing. Alkend told Minister Fritz Grobba that Turkey was Germany's only cheap and reliable overland route to the British-dominated Middle East. Air transport to Iraq and Transjordan would be expensive, and German shipping through the Mediterranean would be at the mercy of the Royal Navy. Turkey, Alkend continued, was ready to reconsider her collaboration with Britain, which had been undertaken only as a precaution against Italy, now no longer

5. Minute by Bowker, 22 January 1941, P.R.O., F.O. 371/R397/198/19.

a military threat. But Germany must first settle the Arab Question to Ankara's satisfaction.[6]

At this time, Germany's relations with the Arabs complicated her diplomacy toward Turkey fully as much as Britain's obligations to Greece in Cyprus undermined the Anglo-Turkish military alliance of 1939. A few months before, it will be recalled, the Wilhelmstrasse, intent on maintaining good relations with Turkey, had refused to subscribe a comprehensive declaration in favor of Arab independence. However, the Arabs were not easily daunted and again appealed their case early in 1941. Their spokesmen, as before, were the king of Egypt and the grand mufti of Jerusalem. For the second time, in February 1941, Farouk urged the German High Command to mount an attack on the Suez Canal, offering to instigate a revolt of the fellahin against the British defenders when the German invasion began. In return, the Egyptian monarch required that Germany recognize Egypt as the leading Islamic state in the Axis new order and himself as caliph of all the Muslim faithful. The king was anxious that Germany act quickly to protect him, as he put it, against the "rising Muslim consciousness and solidarity" of Turkey.[7]

This last phrase, rather surprising when applied to the secular republic founded by Atatürk, requires a short historical explanation. In 1924, Atatürk abolished the caliphate despite the protests of traditionalist Turks, most of the Muslim world, and the kingdom of Egypt in particular. Some scholars argue that his decision was not intended to be permanent and that even Atatürk never relinquished the hope of dominating Muslim Arabs through this office.[8] However, the caliphate was never revived, though meanwhile Sultan Hussein Kamil, then ruler of Egypt, made plans to reconstitute the office in Cairo. Hussein Kamil argued that the caliphate did not depend on direct descent from the Prophet Mohammed, that the office could be elective, and that he had the necessary votes from the faculty of al-Azhar, the most

---

6. Enno von Rintelen, *Mussolini als Bundesgenosse: Erinnerungen des deutschen Militärattachés in Rom, 1936–1943*, pp. 116–17, 124–25. Grobba to Papen, 11 December 1940, A.A. 1303/298; Kroll to Foreign Ministry, 6 February 1941, A.A. 1303/no number.

7. Kordt to Foreign Ministry, 19 February 1941, A.A. 237/164.

8. Dankwart A. Rustow, "Politics and Islam in Turkey, 1920–1955," pp. 69–107.

distinguished Muslim university in the world. He attempted to persuade Sir Edmund Allenby, the British high commissioner for Egypt, to support his project, but Allenby had no wish to meddle in a religious controversy between Egypt and Turkey.

Hussein Kamil was never acclaimed as caliph, nor was his successor, King Fuad I, though he too had the powerful support of al-Azhar and of its rector, Sheik Mustafa al-Maraghi. Fuad bequeathed his ambitions to his son Farouk, who succeeded him in 1936. The young monarch wanted not only the caliphate like his predecessors, but also a coronation ceremony in which Sheik Mustafa al-Maraghi would gird him with the sword of Mehemet Ali, the Albanian founder of the Egyptian royal house. The sheik was very willing to preside at such a ceremony, though it was unprecedented in modern Egyptian tradition, but the British government vetoed the proceedings.[9] Farouk restrained his anger, though not always successfully, but the sheik, a vociferous preacher, publicly fulminated against the British presence in Egypt and demanded its speedy end. When war broke out, Mustafa al-Maraghi, defying the British ambassador, Miles Lampson, compared British democracy unfavorably with the systems of Hitler and Mussolini. The ambassador tried to make Farouk restrain his noisy henchman, but the king, as on so many occasions, was evasive and dilatory.[10]

Farouk's ambition to become caliph was more than a vain dynastic whim. The caliphate, whatever it had meant to Hussein Kamil and Fuad I, had become a question of pressing political importance by the beginning of 1941. The king wanted the office not only to satisfy his vanity but also to enhance and secure his throne against his many critics. He was used to sparring with the British embassy. Somewhat more serious was the opposition of the Wafd party, founded by Zaghlul Pasha at the end of the First World War and directed during Farouk's reign by the lawyer Nahas Pasha. The Wafd membership, drawn mostly from the middle-class intelligentsia, favored the monarchy but wanted to limit it by instituting a constitutional ministry responsible to the

9. Elie Kedourie, *The Chatham House Version and Other Middle Eastern Studies*, pp. 182–99.

10. For a description of al-Maraghi's activities, see Lampson to Foreign Office, 25 September 1941, P.R.O., F.O. 371/J3046/18/16.

legislature, not to the king.[11] Farouk could usually bargain with the Wafdists, many of whom were self-seeking bourgeoisie, but he was not at all sure how to deal with a relatively new force in Egyptian politics, the Ikhwan al Muslimin, or Muslim Brotherhood. The Muslim Brotherhood was founded about 1930 by Hassan al-Banna, an ex-schoolteacher from Ismailia. According to an excellent historical summary prepared by British security forces for Ambassador Lampson, Hassan al-Banna was quiet and unobtrusive and appeared almost cowardly. When the occasion demanded, however, this apparently shy and simple man could prove a fiery and moving speaker. The British appraisal states:

> Those who have met him form an impression of cunning and ambition behind his simplicity. The Ikhwan seek to re-establish the government and institutions of Egypt on pure Koranic principles, to restore the Shari law in place of the present code which is strongly influenced by the Code Napoleon, and to exclude all the elements of Western culture, which they regard as intrusive and deleterious. The Ikhwan seem to draw their numbers largely from the more educated of the lower-middle class, to whom their genuine, if fanatical and impractical, ideals as well as their more solid achievements in social and educational work make an appeal.[12]

Because of this program, the Muslim Brotherhood held no appeal for King Farouk. He disliked its equalitarian goals and feared its tight and disciplined organization. He knew, as did the British, that the Muslim Brotherhood had made a careful study of the Nazi and Fascist organizations and modeled a part of their own system upon them. The *Gwala* or "Rovers," picked members of the Muslim Brotherhood who were subjected to special discipline and training, accepted comparison with Hitler's *Sturmabteilungen*. If King Farouk was lucky, he could perhaps turn these units to his own service. But, lax and cosmopolitan Muslim that he was, he also had to fear that they might turn him out of power. Early in 1941, Hassan al-Banna attacked in writing Farouk's conservative prime minister, Hussein Sirri Pasha, for his departure from Koranic principles. Farouk immediately banished the intemperate al-Banna to Qena, a small town three

11. Kedourie, *Chatham House Version*, p. 217.
12. Lampson to Eden, 24 December 1942, and Appendix A, P.R.O., F.O. 371/J245/158/16.

hundred miles south of Cairo.[13] Yet the monarch knew that he could not use this kind of expedient, however effective it might be temporarily, again without arousing popular wrath. On the other hand, the assumption of the caliphate could be expected to overawe al-Banna, who seemed to be claiming a kind of religious leadership for himself.

Shortly after exiling Hassan al-Banna, Farouk again brought up the matter of the caliphate with the British embassy. To his standing demand that the office be reconstituted in Cairo, the king added two new proposals. First, he asked that Britain subsidize Egyptian cotton growers, whose export trade had been disrupted by the war; second, that Britain approve the cession to the Egyptian Sudan of the district of Abyssinia containing Lake Tana, one of the sources of the Nile. Ambassador Lampson opposed all three proposals. Representatives of all the Muslim states, he held, should discuss the future of the caliphate. Only after the war, he continued, could Britain consider the revision of the frontier between the Sudan and Abyssinia. As to the cotton subsidy, Lampson described it as unthinkable because Englishmen were already being taxed "up to and beyond the hilt." Foreign Secretary Anthony Eden, who took over the office from Halifax in December 1940, traveled to Cairo in March 1941 and completely backed up his ambassador in an interview with the Egyptian king. Eden also complained about the inordinate number of Italians staffing the Egyptian royal palaces, whom the foreign secretary thought were Axis espionage agents.[14]

Eden's attitude decided Farouk to approach the Germans more intensively. The king sent his relative, the ex-khedive Abbas Hilmi II, to the Wilhelmstrasse in April. Speaking excellent German, which he had learned as a student at the elite Viennese academy of the Theresianum, the ex-khedive had several conferences with Ribbentrop's deputies. He promised that Farouk would assist a German attack by staging a revolt against the British, asked the acquisition of Lake

13. Ibid.; James Heyworth-Dunne, *Religious and Political Trends in Modern Egypt*, pp. 15–23.

14. Lampson to Eden, 18 March 1941, P.R.O., F.O. 371/J1004/18/16; 27 March 1941, P.R.O., F.O. 371/J1141/18/16. These documents are accounts of Eden's talks with King Farouk and resumés of Lampson's earlier negotiations. On Farouk's Italian servants, see Gordon Macready, *In the Wake of the Great*, p. 113.

Tana in return, and offered a large part of Farouk's personal fortune for German secret service activities. One such activity, Abbas Hilmi suggested, ought to be the assassination of the Turkish president, İsmet İnönü, to whom the Egyptian ascribed aggressive designs against the Arab world.[15]

The Wilhelmstrasse took several weeks to assess the credibility of Abbas Hilmi. Some foreign ministry experts suspected that he was working, not to make Farouk caliph, but to restore himself as ruler of Egypt.[16] The ex-khedive's case was also complicated by the ministry's nearly simultaneous negotiations with Osman Kemal Haddad, who was again in Berlin as the envoy of the grand mufti. The Germans did not want to receive Haddad and tried to stop him at the Swiss frontier. But the Arab persisted in completing his mission and forced on Ribbentrop still another draft treaty in favor of Arab independence. Like the earlier version, it contained an affirmation of indivisible Arab independence, repudiation by the Axis of the mandate device, property and religious guarantees to non-Muslims, and a communications corridor for the Italian army between Libya and Abyssinia. Additionally, and almost perfunctorily, it mentioned and supported Farouk's claims to Lake Tana. The most significant change in the new draft declaration was, however, the mufti's suggestion that future negotiations with the Arabs be conducted in the Japanese embassy in Baghdad, Iraq. This idea disturbed the Germans. Hitherto, the Wilhelmstrasse and the various German legations in Switzerland had proved convenient points of contact. But Switzerland and Germany were too far away from the mufti's direct influence, and the involvement of the Japanese might afford him a means to bring diplomatic pressure on the Reich government. On behalf of the mufti, Osman Kemal Haddad asked for a large consignment of German arms to insurrectionary elements in Baghdad. He proposed that these arms be shipped by way of the Soviet Union and Iran, so that the route through Turkey could be avoided and the Germans

15. Woermann to Ribbentrop, 15 April 1941, A.A. 237/307.
16. Woermann to Weizsäcker, 27 September 1941, A.A. 237/904. Abbas Hilmi II was deposed by the British in December 1914 because of his pro-German sympathies. After that, he lived in exile, mostly in Switzerland.

not be compromised with the İnönü government. The Japanese embassy in Iraq supported this transaction, even in the event of objections from Ankara.[17] But with Ribbentrop, who seemed to be teetering on the edge of an alliance with the Turks, Osman Kemal Haddad made no headway.

The Nazi foreign minister marshaled a whole battery of expert opinions against the mufti's agent. Ribbentrop observed that since the beginning of 1941, Germany's relations with the Soviet Union had been deteriorating so rapidly that Stalin might confiscate any German weapons passing through his territory to Iraq. Moreover, not all Iraqi politicians were pro-Axis. Men like the Anglophile Nuri as-Said, for instance, could be expected to divulge this arms traffic to the British and the Turks. Count Ciano concurred that the Arabs were untrustworthy. He predicted that the mufti, given some German aid, would try to extort more and more. Otto Abetz, the German ambassador to France who Ribbentrop consulted, expressed fear of the Arabs' postwar commercial ambitions. He warned that the Arabs would demand independence for black Africa as soon as they had achieved their own. The Arab, according to Abetz, was the black's natural mentor and the brains of a future Afro-Arab bloc that would in time elbow the British and French out of Africa and prevent the Germans from regaining a colonial foothold on the continent. For the Army High Command, Field Marshal Wilhelm Keitel simply declared that the Wehrmacht had no guns to spare for the Arabs. Ernst Woermann, under secretary of the foreign ministry, also recommended noninvolvement, but he made a distinction between the mufti and his movement. Woermann believed it safe to ignore the mufti's associates, but not the mufti himself. The man's control and charisma were too great to be disregarded by any of the belligerents in the Middle East. Woermann had learned that the Japanese were sufficiently impressed with Haj Muhammad to promise him equipment for a whole Iraqi division. It might be unwise to allow Japan to steal too great a march on Germany in the Middle East. Therefore, though no German arms were given to the mufti,

17. Papen to Foreign Ministry, 28 January 1941, A.A. 63/78; Grobba to Weizsäcker, 7 March 1941, A.A. 63/ Pol. VII 123. Łukasz Hirszowicz, *The Third Reich and the Arab East*, pp. 120–21.

the German government, on Woermann's recommendation, made him a personal gift of one hundred thousand Reichsmarks in gold.[18]

The only dissenting opinion was given by Fritz Grobba, former German minister to Iraq and Saudi Arabia and the foreign ministry's veteran consultant on Arab affairs. Much more than Woermann, Grobba was concerned about the growth of Japanese political and commercial influence in the Middle East. To that threat, it will be recalled, he had been alert during his prewar service in Jidda. Since that time, his distrust of Japan had not abated and had even degenerated into a personal dislike of Hiroshi Oshima, the Japanese ambassador in Berlin. Grobba felt that Oshima was far too free with hospitality and encouragement to Arab emissaries in the German capital. Therefore, he argued that the Reich should make countervailing offers to the Arabs to prevent them from becoming clients of Tokyo. Unlike his colleagues, doubts about the Arabs' trustworthiness did not trouble Grobba. His primary concern was with the Arab states' strategical position, which the Germans might use to destroy British communications between India and the Mediterranean.

He expected Turkey to object to German arms for the Arabs but thought that an offer of control over all Syria at the end of the war would stop any sustained Turkish protest. On his own initiative, Grobba tried to arrange for an alternative to the roundabout and risky route through the Soviet Union and Iran for arms consignments to the Arabs. He conferred with Abdul Medjid, economics minister of Afghanistan, who happened to be in Berlin, and induced him, in return for a handsome bribe, to connive in a scheme to make delivery to Iraq through Turkey. Matériel actually intended for Baghdad would, under this plan, have been labeled with Afghan addresses—Abdul Medjid would have vouched for

18. Woermann to Ritter, 4 February 1941, A.A. 63/54 (*DGFP*, 12:18–19); Woermann to Weizsäcker, 21 February 1941, A.A. 63/137 (*DGFP*, 12:121), and 26 February 1941, A.A. 63/160 (*DGFP*, 12:168–69); Memorandum by Ripken on "Weapons Allocations to Iraq," 6 March 1941, A.A. 63/no number. On Iraqi politics, see Majid Khadduri, "General Nuri's Flirtations with the Axis Powers," pp. 330–34. For more on Ambassador Abetz's views, see Otto Abetz, *Das offene Problem: Ein Rückblick auf zwei Jahrzehnte deutscher Frankreichpolitik*, pp. 185ff. Hirszowicz, *Third Reich*, pp. 122–23.

their authenticity—and Turkey, since Afghanistan was neutral, would have been unable to raise any legal objections to passage of these goods across her territory. At some point in Iran, the weaponry would have been rerouted to points in Iraq.[19]

Ribbentrop vetoed Grobba's plan and Hiroshi Oshima took offense at it. Within a short time, Grobba was eased out of his job at the foreign ministry. Osman Kemal Haddad was also sent back to the mufti without a signed declaration for Arab independence or any arms contract. Instead, State Secretary Weizsäcker furnished Haddad with a letter he himself had drafted, commending the cause of Arab independence but omitting any promise of real help for it. Ribbentrop also assured the mufti's secretary that German secret service operations in the Middle East would be stepped up. These operations, described in a memorandum by Adm. Wilhelm Canaris, chief of the Abwehr, were to be the collection of military intelligence, sabotage of British military installations, and collaboration with the Arabs in guerrilla warfare. To Weizsäcker's letter was added the previously mentioned gift of one hundred thousand gold marks.[20] However, Osman Kemal Haddad's second mission, like his first, was a failure, and gradually Arab leaders throughout the Middle East realized this. King ibn-Saud of Saudi Arabia, through Fuad Hamza, his ambassador to France, had already warned Otto Abetz that Arab leaders were getting tired of the preference and favors that Germany gave the Turks in return for comparatively little. The Saudi Arabian monarch threatened to remove his "restraining hand" from the Arab nationalists and abet insurrections against the Vichy French colonial administration in North Africa and the Levant.[21]

Despite admonitions like this, however, Germany refused to alter her pro-Turkish course. About the same time that Osman Kemal Haddad was given his second rebuff, the Wilhelmstrasse decided against King Farouk's offer to attempt to change the Turkish leadership by violence. Papen's staff in Ankara had been questioning Muhittin Birgen, a disgruntled

19. Woermann to Weizsäcker, 9 April 1941, A.A. 63/288.

20. Ribbentrop to Haj Muhammad Amin al-Husseini, 8 April 1941, A.A. 1303/2101; Canaris to Weizsäcker, 25 March 1941, A.A. 63/OKW Amt. 526. Hirszowicz, *Third Reich*, p. 129.

21. Abetz to Foreign Ministry, 8 March 1941, A.A. 63/785.

deputy in the Turkish National Assembly. Birgen told the Germans that İsmet İnönü had his deficiencies and detractors. The president was very unpopular in some political quarters. But none of the men mentioned as successors to İnönü—the generals Fevzi Çakmak, Rauf Bey, and Kâzım Karabekir—possessed his national prestige or political sticking power. Birgen thought civil chaos would follow İnönü's removal from office, by assassination or otherwise, and that this upheaval could not be advantageous to Germany in any way. Therefore, the Wilhelmstrasse discouraged the machinations of King Farouk and the ex-khedive Abbas Hilmi.[22]

German arms had been denied them, but Arab leaders knew of one other supply source that they could try to tap. After an armistice with Germany in June 1940 had removed Vichy France from the war, a large stockpile of French war matériel had been impounded in Syria. These armaments were under the jurisdiction of the Italo-German armistice commission, which was negotiating their final disposition, as well as many other questions, with Vichy French delegates at Wiesbaden. In the meantime, however, the Arabs were able to pick up small arms from French soldiers garrisoned in Syria. For instance, the troopers illegally sold them rifles for three pounds apiece.[23] At the end of April 1941, Fuad Hamza proposed that the entire cache be sold to his king. Ribbentrop did not want to risk a quarrel with King ibn-Saud, which would probably have followed a clear refusal. Instead, the German foreign minister put the question up to the Vichy French government.[24]

At that time, Pétain's foreign minister was Adm. François Darlan, also vice-president of the Vichy Council of State and minister of the interior, of information, and of defense. Historians still cannot agree in their interpretations of Darlan's diplomatic methods and goals, but all concur, as did the admiral's contemporaries, that no man in the Vichy government held a greater concentration of power. His enemies quipped that the admiral had rarely been to sea. This was untrue; it was true that no naval officer in France

22. Kroll to Foreign Ministry, 8 May 1941, A.A. 1303/1412.

23. Woermann to Weizsäcker, 24 January 1941, A.A. 62/5.

24. Rahn to Foreign Ministry, 11 May 1941, A.A. 62/no number. See also Georges Catroux, *Dans la Bataille de Méditerranée: Égypte, Levant, Afrique du Nord, 1940–1944*, pp. 104–21. Werner Otto von Hentig, *Mein Leben: Eine Dienstreise*, pp. 337–40.

had greater experience in civil administration and diplomatic negotiations. In the interwar period, Darlan had represented France at several international naval conferences and there conceived a deep envy and resentment of the British empire and fleet. Britain, he felt, had stunted France's colonial and maritime expansion. This envy developed into a boiling hatred of the British when they found it necessary to shell the French fleet at Mers-el-Kébir, Algeria, on 4 July 1940, to prevent it from falling into Hitler's hands. Darlan wanted to expel the British from all Africa so that the continent could be reserved as the basis of an amicable colonial settlement between France and Spain. He hoped, too, that Nazi Germany could be persuaded to treat France as a full equal in the Axis new order; at any rate, he was sure that France would become "a second-class Dominion, a continental Ireland," if Britain won the war.[25]

When the Germans, embarrassed into action by Saudi Arabia, approached Darlan about an arms sale to the Arabs, the admiral insisted that nationalist disturbances not be allowed to spread to Syria, Tunisia, Algeria, and Morocco. Otherwise, he was not unencouraging, and he liked Rudolf Rahn, one of Abetz's protégés, whom the Wilhelmstrasse appointed to be its delegate to the Syrian negotiations.[26] Darlan was ready to make three major concessions: the Germans could use French arms stockpiles in Syria; French port facilities at Bizerte, Tunisia; and the harbor at Dakar in French West Africa. These points, often called the Protocols of Paris, were conceived as part of a general settlement to benefit not only the Arabs, but also the Afrika Korps under General Rommel, sent to help Mussolini's troops in North Africa in early 1941. In return, Darlan asked that Germany reduce her occupation charges, ease restrictions on traffic between Vichy and occupied France, and release between seventy thousand and eighty thousand French prisoners of war. It would not have been difficult or dangerous for Germany to grant all Darlan's conditions immediately. Many of the prisoners had served in the First World War and were

25. I have followed the most recent treatment of Darlan, from which the foregoing remarks are drawn, Robert O. Paxton, *Vichy France: Old Guard and New Order, 1940–1944*, pp. 109–15.

26. Abetz to Foreign Ministry, 9 May 1941, A.A. 62/1423. Rudolf Rahn, *Ruheloses Leben: Aufzeichnungen und Erinnerungen*, pp. 154ff.

more fit for convalescence than for combat. Yet Ribbentrop, with Hitler's approval, was slow and sparing in satisfying Darlan's terms. One scholar suggests that Hitler was interested only in looting the French and confiscating their property, not in compounding terms with their Vichy leaders.[27] But the German government also had to keep in mind the effect of concessions to the Arabs on relations with Turkey.[28] Berlin's motives were ruthless, but it was a calculated ruthlessness. Because the Germans moved with deliberate slowness in negotiating with the French, the Arabs received only a fraction of the arms available in Syria. Exasperated, they surprised the British, Germans, and Turks by breaking into revolt in Iraq.

27. Paxton, *Vichy France*, pp. 112, 117–18. See also Ritter to Abetz, 5 May 1941, A.A. 358/no number; Abetz to Foreign Ministry, 6 May 1941, A.A. 358/1387.

28. Ambassador Knatchbull-Hugessen learned from "a good source" that Germany was prosecuting her efforts for an alliance with Turkey throughout the period of the latest exchanges with the Arabs. See Knatchbull-Hugessen to Foreign Office, 18 February 1941, P.R.O., F.O. 371/R1506/236/44.

Chapter 5

Turkey and the Iraqi Revolt, 1941

The failure of ibn-Saud, Farouk, and the mufti to enlist German support revived fears throughout the Arab world that the Reich and the İnönü government were about to conclude a military alliance entailing a partition of the Near and Middle East. Other events in early 1941 suggested the same possibility to British observers. On 17 February 1941, Turkey and Bulgaria signed a nonaggression pact. Knatchbull-Hugessen protested to Turkish officials that, at the very least, this agreement was untimely, because it relieved Bulgaria of any anxiety about her southern frontier and permitted her to slip more easily into the Axis orbit without fear of Turkish reprisals. He was soon proved justified in his apprehension. On 1 March 1941, Bulgaria adhered to the Tripartite Pact, making her a partner of Germany, Italy, and Japan.

The British ambassador also suspected that Turkey was trying to stabilize relations with Bulgaria so that her army could seize Salonika while Greek forces were engaged in fighting the Italians. When questioned, Foreign Minister Saracoğlu brushed aside all these British apprehensions and characterized the understanding with Sofia as a perfectly logical development within the framework of the Balkan Pact. It had always been a goal of Ankara's diplomacy to include Bulgaria in the Balkan security system, and the most recent accord, Saracoğlu said, was merely a step in that direction. But the British government was not reassured.[1] Nor did Turkey's policy toward Greece allay London's dissatisfaction. On 6 April 1941, the Wehrmacht invaded Greece and before the end of the month had subjugated the mainland and the Greek islands of Thasos, Lemnos, and Samothrace. In April the British had transferred fifty-seven thousand men from Wavell's North African command to help stiffen

1. Knatchbull-Hugessen to Saracoğlu, 15 February 1941, P.R.O., F.O. 371/R3940/91/7, and 18 February 1941, P.R.O., F.O. 371/R3941/91/7; Knatchbull-Hugessen to Eden, 22 February 1941, P.R.O., F.O. 371/ R4370/91/7. (For list of abbreviations, see p. 221.)

the Greek resistance, but this gesture proved to be as futile as it was magnanimous. Gen. Sir Henry Maitland Wilson, Wavell's subordinate, was able to evacuate most of the British forces to Crete. The Turks, however, though treaty-bound to assist in the struggle for Greece, remained neutral, pleading lack of matériel. Yet, for other operations, Ankara considered its preparations completely adequate. Saracoğlu suggested to the Germans that Turkey garrison the Greek islands of Chios, Samos, and Mytilene for the duration of the war, but the Wilhelmstrasse responded that the Army High Command had already detailed German units for the job.[2] The Turkish government was undoubtedly irritated but did not make an issue of the future of the Greek islands. It hoped to acquire an even greater prize, Iraq and the oil fields of Mosul.

The Iraqis had no intention of succumbing to Turkish annexation and staged a revolt in Baghdad at the end of April 1941. The aim of the Iraqi rebels was to have their country declared a nonbelligerent zone. Their movement was anti-British in that they wished to prevent the collaboration of Iraqis with the British Indian army. It was also anti-Turkish, since the Baghdad insurgents wanted to immunize their frontiers against Turkish imperialism. But the outbreak was not clearly pro-German, as it is so often depicted. Neither German nor British archival documents conclusively demonstrate that Germany instigated the Iraqi revolt, though the Germans did try to take advantage of it once it had begun. These attempts, as it turned out, proved inept and unsuccessful. Writing of the Iraqi revolt in his history of the Second World War, Winston Churchill said that if Hitler had acted with more determination at Baghdad he could have captured "a great prize at little price." The British prime minister thought that the German air force was superior to Britain's and sufficiently large to begin the conquest not only of Iraq, but of Syria and Iran as well. He believed that Hitler did not react more aggressively in the Middle East

2. Kroll to Papen, 29 April 1941, A.A. 1303/1314; Ritter to Papen, 29 April 1941, A.A. 1303/372. For an account of British intervention in Greece and Crete by one who participated, see Alan Moorehead, *African Trilogy*, pp. 137–44. For British appeals to Turkey, see Sir Ernest Llewellyn Woodward, *British Foreign Policy in the Second World War*, 1:546–48.

because the Luftwaffe was engaged in the bombardment of Crete. But Churchill himself hints that his explanation does not go far enough, and he leaves the relative inactivity of Hitler something of a mystery.[3] However, British correspondence recently opened to scholars, as well as German records available for inspection since the war, show that Hitler had good reason to move cautiously in Iraq. The Führer and his foreign ministry recognized that the course of events in Baghdad was more pan-Arab and anti-Turkish than it was pro-Nazi. Accordingly, Berlin had every right to doubt the commitment of the Iraqi leaders to the Axis cause.

The head of the April revolt was Rashid Ali al-Gailani, prime minister of Iraq. The Foreign Office set him down as a neo-Nazi, chiefly because he was not a British sycophant, not because it had incontestable evidence that al-Gailani accepted the principles of Fascism. Al-Gailani was a well educated lawyer from an old Baghdad family. One of his ancestors, Abdul Kader Gailani, had preached Islam in India in the tenth century and founded an important Sunnite sect to which seventy thousand Indians, four thousand Afghans and four thousand Egyptians belonged at the time of the Second World War. Rashid Ali first became prominent when Nuri as-Said, the pro-British Baghdad politician, obtained a job for him as private secretary to the young and high-riding King Ghazi I of Iraq. That position ended when Ghazi accidentally smashed his sports car into a telephone pole and died instantly. But al-Gailani remained in Nuri's good graces, claimed to share his pro-British proclivities, and affirmed that he would strive to maintain cordial relations with Britain whenever he held public office.[4] However, neither he nor most other Iraqi leaders understood good relations to mean the active participation of their country in Britain's war effort. The keynote of Iraqi policy was well expressed by Jamil Madfai, then prime minister, in an address to the Chamber of Deputies in Baghdad on 21 December 1940. Madfai declared:

3. Winston S. Churchill, *The Second World War*, vol. 3, *The Grand Alliance*, pp. 266ff.

4. Allan A. Michie, *Retreat to Victory*, pp. 80–84; Maurice D. Peterson, *Both Sides of the Curtain: An Autobiography*, p. 151; Fritz Grobba, *Männer und Mächte im Orient*, p. 177; Majid Khadduri, *Independent Iraq, 1932–1958: A Study in Iraqi Politics*, p. 161; Papen to Foreign Ministry, 15 May 1941, A.A. 350/556.

> As an independent state, Iraq should in all her proceedings seek
> her national interest and the realization of her national aspira-
> tions and avoid being carried away on a course inconsistent with
> these interests and aspirations.[5]

He made these remarks in response to a rumor that Britain
was demanding to be allowed to recruit Iraqis into her armed
forces. The British were definitely demanding that Iraq
sever relations with Italy, as she had severed them with Germany at the beginning of the war. Because he could not
convince his colleagues that he would remain adamant
against British pressure, Madfai had to dissolve his cabinet
in January 1941. The British hoped that Emir Abdul Illah,
regent for the boy king Feisal II, would be able to recall
Madfai to power. The Foreign Office even authorized Sir
Basil Newton, British ambassador at Baghdad, to pay out
bribes to do so. But Britain was not the only power subsi-
dizing Iraqi politicians. The Japanese, who did a great deal
of trading in the Persian Gulf, also bribed officials. There is
no evidence, however, that the Germans tried to influence
the succession to Prime Minister Jamil Madfai. Their embassy in Baghdad was closed, and their nearest representative
was Erwin Ettel, German ambassador at Teheran, Iran. It
is not clear whether or not he had Japanese help, but Rashid
Ali al-Gailani succeeded Madfai in the prime ministry.[6]

Like his predecessor, al-Gailani was an advocate of neutrality, but he was a much stronger proponent of Arab solidarity against Britain than Madfai. He privately assured the
Egyptian envoy in Baghdad that his government would do
everything possible to help the Egyptians achieve a British
withdrawal from their country, and he wanted an independent Palestinian state established immediately, instead of in
ten years as outlined in the British White Paper issued in
1939.[7] However, al-Gailani did not stay in power long
enough to work toward either of these goals. Nuri as-Said,
his foreign minister, refused to deviate from British policy

5. Copy of speech enclosed in Newton to Eden, 27 January 1941, No.
589, P.R.O., F.O. 371/E137/1/93.
6. On British "financial assistance" to friendly Iraqi governments,
see Cadogan to Newton, 31 January 1941, No. 85; on Japanese involvement, see Newton to Foreign Office, 7 January 1941, No. 20, both in
P.R.O., F.O. 371/E137/1/93.
7. Lampson to Foreign Office, 17 January 1941, P.R.O., F.O. 371/
E223/1/93.

in either the Egyptian or Palestinian questions. Furthermore, Nuri pressed for the rupture of relations with Italy, again dissolving the Iraqi cabinet on 13 January 1941. London now saw the first definite sign of a pending revolt. The British expected that the regent would appoint Nuri as-Said to lead the new government, but the Iraqi army forced Abdul Illah's hand. The regent was obliged to name Gen. Taha el-Hashimi, a declared enemy of British influence, to the prime ministry. Even so, Sir Basil Newton thought Taha was a more acceptable choice than were some of his army colleagues. There were nationalists more radical than General Taha in the ranks, particularly four scheming and ambitious officers who called themselves collectively the "Golden Square." All were colonels and long had been anathema to the British embassy, which tried to have them dropped from the payroll. Their names were Salah ed-Din es-Sabbagh, Fahmi Said, Mahmud Salman, and Kamil Shabib.[8]

The Golden Square was a mildly fascist organization, but it took its ideology from neither Berlin nor Rome but from a local intellectual, Dr. Sami Shawkat, Iraqi minister of education and another protégé of Nuri as-Said. Sami Shawkat preached a doctrine of national revival based on a return to the simplicity of the early Arabs. He persuaded the government to equip its high school students with military uniforms and train them in rifle practice. His followers, among them the four colonels, were fiercely anti-imperialistic and denounced the Anglo-Iraqi Treaty of Mutual Defense of 1930. Legally, the British mandate ended and Iraq became an independent state in 1932. But as long as the mutual defense treaty was in force, the presence of the former mandatory continued to loom large. The treaty gave Britain two air bases, at Habbaniya, west of Baghdad, and at Shu'aiba, near Basra; the use of all Iraqi communications in time of war or threat of war; and precedence for the British envoy over representatives of all other foreign powers.[9] It should be noted that the treaty did not allow for the establishment of bases outside the Baghdad and Basra areas nor for the admission of additional military personnel to man them. The

8. Newton to Foreign Office, 3 and 4 February 1941, Nos. 97 and 102, P.R.O., F.O. 371/E353/1/93. Woodward, *British Foreign Policy*, 1:571–73.

9. Khadduri, *Independent Iraq*, p. 166.

Golden Square, Sami Shawkat, and all their followers wanted this treaty annulled.

Many army officers did not think that Gen. Taha el-Hashimi would prove capable of this task; indeed, the Golden Square never regarded General Taha as anything more than a caretaker for the return of Rashid Ali to power. Al-Gailani recovered the prime ministry on 3 April 1941.[10] London had already recalled Sir Basil Newton, its ambassador, because that amiable gentleman had been unable to secure the formation of a durable and friendly Iraqi government for Britain. As Newton's replacement, the Foreign Office appointed Sir Kinahan Cornwallis, a tough, courageous, but somewhat willful colonial official with twenty years experience in the Middle East. Cornwallis was resolved to bring the quarrel with the Iraqi nationalists to a head. It is worth noting, however, that the personnel of the RAF base at Habbaniya petitioned the Air Ministry in London, and through it the Foreign Office, to be lenient and helpful with al-Gailani. The Habbaniya military felt that Rashid Ali was sincere when he said that he wanted to avoid a quarrel with Britain at all cost. The men of the air base were afraid that al-Gailani had already lost so much ground with his extremist supporters by seeking rapprochement with Britain "that he may be expunged by his own people before we can exploit a change of heart to our advantage." The RAF unit predicted that then "the alternative to Rashid's administration would be a full military dictatorship under [Col.] Salah ed-Din es-Sabbagh, which even if short lived would increase Axis efforts here."[11]

Nevertheless, Ambassador Cornwallis ignored these forebodings and advised London to withhold recognition of Rashid Ali's government in order to bring down his cabinet.[12] Besides the Iraqi prime minister, the British envoy especially disliked two of its members, the lawyer Junus Sabaui, who had translated *Mein Kampf* into Arabic, and Naji Shawkat, the minister of justice, who had approached Franz von Papen in July 1940 for protection against Turkish

10. Cornwallis to Foreign Office, 3 April 1941, No. 262, P.R.O., F.O. 371/E1253/1/93.

11. Air Ministry to Foreign Office, 24 April 1941, P.R.O., F.O. 371/E1667/1/93.

12. Cornwallis to Foreign Office, 3 April 1941, No. 268, P.R.O., F.O. 371/E1253/1/93. Woodward, *British Foreign Policy*, 1:574–75.

imperialism.[13] Churchill entirely approved Cornwallis's course. In his history of the war, the British prime minister commented that he did not care what happened "up-country at Baghdad."[14] Apparently he was too busy supervising British forces involved in the defense of Greece to probe deeply into those kaleidoscopic shifts of Iraqi politics that brought in al-Gailani and turned out the more congenial Nuri as-Said. In effect, Churchill gave Kinahan Cornwallis a free hand.

Having recommended nonrecognition to Britain, Cornwallis called on the governments of Egypt, Saudi Arabia, Turkey, and the United States to adopt the same policy toward the al-Gailani regime.[15] As might have been expected, al-Gailani's fellow Arabs in Cairo and Jidda did not entirely acquiesce. The Egyptian and Saudi Arabian governments withheld de jure recognition from Baghdad, but continued to deal with Rashid Ali on a de facto basis.[16] More surprising was the reaction of the United States. The State Department in Washington agreed to have no official relations with al-Gailani but insisted on maintaining informal liaison with the Iraqi prime minister. The State Department believed that its representatives in Baghdad should be as helpful as possible so that al-Gailani and his army backers would not be goaded into violence and open hostilities. The British government, however, was very angry at American policy and Lord Halifax, then British envoy in Washington, was instructed to urge the Americans to "use a rather bigger stick with Iraq." But Halifax was unsuccessful. Indeed, some elements in the State Department believed that Rashid Ali's cause was just and that, but for his efforts for strict neutrality, Turkey would have seized Iraq as a prize of war and gone on to attempt to regain the whole Ottoman Empire.[17]

13. Ettel to Foreign Ministry, 14 April 1941, A.A. 358/223; Grobba to Woermann, 15 April 1941, A.A. 358/no number. Łukasz Hirszowicz, *The Third Reich and the Arab East*, p. 139.

14. Winston S. Churchill, *The Second World War*, vol. 3, *The Grand Alliance*, p. 255.

15. Cornwallis to Foreign Office, 3 April 1941, No. 264, P.R.O., F.O. 371/E1254/1/93.

16. Cornwallis to Foreign Office, 9 April 1941, P.R.O., F.O. 371/E1448/1/93.

17. Halifax to Foreign Office, 8 April 1941, P.R.O., F.O. 371/E1341/1/193. See also Assistant Secretary Berle to Murray, Chief of Near Eastern Affairs, 11 October 1940, *FRUS, 1940*, vol. 3, p. 961.

The Soviet Union, which the Foreign Office did not solicit, granted Rashid Ali full recognition, causing the British to think briefly that the Iraqi regime was not a German, but rather a Soviet Russian, front.[18]

Meanwhile, Ambassador Cornwallis went his imperious way. He decided to confront Rashid Ali with a list of inadmissible demands. The first was that British forces be allowed unrestricted passage from the Persian Gulf to Transjordan and Palestine, the second, that Iraq yield permanent British bases in addition to Habbaniya and Basra. Third, al-Gailani was asked to sever relations with Italy. Finally, the prime minister was ordered to carry out a sweeping purge of the Iraqi officer corps. In addition to these specific demands, Nuri as-Said suspected that the British embassy was inciting a secessionist movement among certain tribes of northern Iraq.[19] Cornwallis well knew that only the first of his demands was compatible with the Anglo-Iraqi treaty of 1930, and even he admitted that al-Gailani fulfilled the requirements of that treaty as far as the communications of the British Indian army were concerned. The Iraqi prime minister sent special instructions to all provincial and municipal authorities ordering them to render all service and hospitality to British troops in transit through the country. Against the protests of the Golden Square, he also appointed an officer known to be friendly to Britain, Gen. Ibrahim al-Rawi, to supervise the disembarkation of British troops, already on the way from India, at the port of Basra.[20]

But al-Gailani stuck to a strict interpretation of the treaty of 1930 and would not discuss the creation of additional British bases; nor would he allow the units from India to linger in his country. He was willing to allow future troop reinforcements to pass through but wanted each contingent to have departed Iraq before another was landed at Basra. Many British foreign service officials thought that al-Gailani's

18. Foreign Office Minute by Seymour, 12 May 1941, P.R.O., F.O. 371/R5380/112/44.

19. Churchill, *The Grand Alliance*, pp. 253–67; Lord Birdwood, *Nuri as-Said: A Study in Arab Leadership*, p. 182.

20. Cornwallis to Foreign Office, 17 April 1941, P.R.O., F.O. 371/E1546/1/93. Cornwallis to Foreign Office, 17 April 1941, P.R.O., F.O. 371/E1545/1/93. Woodward, *British Foreign Policy*, 1:576.

position was legally correct,[21] but Kinahan Cornwallis over-
rode critics and overlooked technicalities. In a manner remi-
niscent of the high noon of British imperialism in the
nineteenth century, the ambassador explained his motives:

> From the political point of view as I see it from here rapid . . .
> communication is very important. Basra is naturally of supreme
> importance to us strategically, but on the other hand in Iraqi
> eyes it is comparatively speaking of minor political importance,
> and though the arrival of troops should have an immediate and
> wholesome effect throughout the whole of Iraq, it will soon
> wear off if none of them are seen further north. If we are to
> establish our position more firmly and safeguard our strategic and
> other interests throughout Iraq, we must show the flag here
> [Baghdad]. Baghdad is the hub of Iraq.[22]

In other words, the British ambassador was attempting to
reduce Iraq to the mandate status it had held before 1932.
He wanted the country fully fortified as a necessity of war.
But such developments would have exposed Iraq to German reprisals and, as the Arabs feared, to Turkish reprisals
if Ankara chose to ally with Berlin for the sake of annexing
Iraq as a prize of war. Rashid Ali's government expected
Turkey and Germany to make a treaty carving up Iraq, but,
with an urgency born of desperation, made one last attempt
to neutralize the intrigues of the Turks and to wean the Germans away from supporting them.

Rashid Ali, through his brother Kamil, who was Iraqi minister to Ankara, asked Turkey to serve as mediator between
himself and Britain. Knatchbull-Hugessen urged Saracoğlu
to accept the assignment, and the Turkish foreign minister
agreed, although it is likely that he did so most reluctantly.
As mediator, Turkey would be bound to abjure a self-
interested policy and to renounce any advantage from the outcome of the Anglo-Iraqi dispute. In April 1942, a year after
the crisis, Knatchbull-Hugessen, in a private letter to Sir
Orme Sargent, deputy under secretary of state, revealed that
the Turks would have much preferred to participate in the

21. Bullard, Teheran, to Foreign Office, 10 April 1941, P.R.O., F.O.
371/E1465/1/93.
22. Cornwallis to Foreign Office, 18 April 1941, P.R.O., F.O. 371/
E1577/1/93.

violent repression of Rashid Ali's regime and then to have remained on patrol in Iraq, as either Britain's or Germany's ally, to keep the situation there quiet.[23] But al-Gailani had temporarily outmaneuvered them.

About 21 April 1941, al-Gailani appealed to Germany, but only after he had unsuccessfully attempted to compromise with the British ambassador. The Iraqi prime minister would still not permit the landing of British Indian army units at Basra until all earlier arrivals had left the country. Nor would he agree to the establishment of more British bases in Iraq. But he offered to permit an increase of three thousand British personnel in the encampments at Basra and Habbaniya.[24] Cornwallis rejected this proposal, the regent Emir Abdul Illah fled Baghdad for the refuge of a British warship in Basra port, and Iraqi army units began to concentrate around Habbaniya, cutting its communications with the outside. The Germans, contacted by Iraqi diplomats in the Reich embassies at Ankara and Teheran, watched these developments with keen interest but were not eager to accelerate them. Apparently, Rashid Ali wanted diplomatic recognition and nothing more from Berlin. In his opinion, the extension of such recognition would be enough to preclude German attempts to partition Iraq or to abet Turkish schemes to occupy the country. Hans Kroll, Papen's second-in-command, asked Kamil al-Gailani if his brother wanted German troop support, but the Iraqi diplomat replied that the dispatch of the Wehrmacht would be premature. He also asked Kroll to urge Berlin to minimize any radio criticism of the British authorities, who might be provoked into having the Iraqi leadership assassinated.

The German foreign ministry, consistent with its pro-Turkish policy, would not be maneuvered into granting even recognition to al-Gailani. Instead, State Secretary Weizsäcker decided that the Reich would only broadcast congratulations to Sherif Sharaf, head of the cadet branch of the Hashemite ruling house, whom the Golden Square had imposed as the new regent of Iraq. Ironically, this congratu-

23. Knatchbull-Hugessen to Foreign Office, 17 April 1941, P.R.O., F.O. 371/E1544/1/93; Knatchbull-Hugessen to Sargent, 22 April 1942, P.R.O., F.O. 371/R3192/24/44.

24. Cornwallis to Foreign Office, 18 April 1941, P.R.O., F.O. 371/E1565/1/93; 28 April 1941, P.R.O., F.O. 371/E1782/1/93. Knatchbull-Hugessen to Foreign Office, 3 May 1941, P.R.O., F.O. 371/E1912/1/93.

latory broadcast, transmitted in German and Arabic, drew much of its material from T. E. Lawrence's *Seven Pillars of Wisdom*, wherein the British adventurer commended Sherif Sharaf, who was Lawrence's comrade in the First World War, for his modesty, patriotism, and unselfishness. The Italian embassy in Baghdad criticized this German broadcast as insufficient and almost insulting and offered to put its code facilities at the Wilhelmstrasse's disposal for the delivery of more formal greetings to Sherif Sharaf. However, the foreign ministry would not use the Italian code, objecting that it had been the source of distortions and leaks in the past.[25]

Al-Gailani's government commanded a well-trained army of four infantry divisions, with a modern air force of about sixty planes. At the Habbaniya base, the British had only training planes and one bomber. Equipment that could have been brought from India would not have much improved the British force. Lord Linlithgow, the viceroy of India, thought his aircraft were inferior to the Iraqi and even to the Iranian air forces. The Indian army also had no antitank or antiaircraft equipment and was, in Linlithgow's judgment, unfit for a major offensive.[26] Still, Sir Claude Auchinleck, the commanding field general in India, did not share this pessimistic estimate, and the German Army High Command did not believe that the Iraqis could reduce the British at Habbaniya without outside aid. On 26 April 1941, the High Command put the question of aiding the Iraqi coup on the agenda of one of Hitler's staff conferences. Its inclusion was a last-minute move because Field Marshal Keitel, chief of the High Command, was out of town and unavailable for comment. Keitel's deputy in the Iraqi discussion was a Colonel Brinckmann, who recommended that Germany not become militarily involved at Baghdad. Brinckmann observed that the decision was being made much too late and believed that the British had already landed about fourteen thousand

25. Kroll to Foreign Ministry, 21 April 1941, A.A. 358/414; Ribbentrop to Papen, 21 April 1941, A.A. 358/274; Ettel to Foreign Ministry, 24 April 1941, A.A. 358/299. The Wilhelmstrasse's observations about Italian security leaks may have been initiated by the Army High Command. General Kesselring complained about the Italians in this regard when so many of his supply ships to Rommel were sunk by the British. See Albert Kesselring, *Kesselring: A Soldier's Record*, pp. 129–30, 137.

26. Compton Mackenzie, *Eastern Epic*, pp. 79–84; Michie, *Retreat to Victory*, p. 86.

men at Basra, with German intelligence reporting another twenty thousand auxiliaries on the way from India. In the military view, these odds were insuperable. However, State Secretary Weizsäcker, who had long opposed support to the Arabs and who later declared in his memoirs that Germany did not instigate the quarrel between al-Gailani and Britain, now revealed some reasons that had caused him to reconsider his hitherto negative attitude. The Wilhelmstrasse had picked up reports that Japan and the Soviet Union were interested in intervening in Iraq. Though Weizsäcker did not recommend that large amounts of aid be given to al-Gailani, he did feel that token help must be extended to prevent either Japan or the Soviet Union from jeopardizing Germany's future influence in the Middle East. To head off Japanese and Russian competition, Hitler thereupon decided to send a small team of Luftwaffe experts to Baghdad to analyze the situation in depth.[27]

This decision for even minimal intervention in Iraq was never popular with the German armed services. Göring assigned only three fighters to make the initial reconnaissance flight to Baghdad. Maj. Axel von Blomberg, the son of Hitler's former Reichswehr minister, led this small squadron. While the planes were flying into Baghdad, in full view of Rashid Ali and an Iraqi welcoming committee, Blomberg was shot in the head and died instantly. Apparently an Iraqi marksman mistook his plane for an enemy aircraft and fired at it from the ground. But Fritz Grobba, who the foreign ministry had sent to Iraq via Syria as its representative attached to the German military forces and who witnessed the scene, claimed that Blomberg was hit from above by a British pursuit plane. Whatever the facts regarding Axel von Blomberg's death, Iraqi embarrassment was very great and German resentment very deep. The other members of the German detachment became very uneasy, moody, and demoralized. They made no secret of their dislike for the Iraqi assignment and seized the first excuse to abandon it. The Germans quickly found that Blomberg's death was an omen of still worse things to come.

Despite his profuse apologies, al-Gailani was not a coop-

27. Woermann to Weizsäcker, 26 April 1941, A.A. 358/350. Ernst von Weizsäcker, *Memoirs*, trans. John Andrews, p. 247. Hirszowicz, *Third Reich*, pp. 146–50.

erative ally, though it must be remembered that he had preferred German recognition over German relief forces. He
had promised plenty of fuel, but when the Luftwaffe team
landed, it found only a week's supply, five hundred thousand
liters, available in the Baghdad area. The Germans then
flew a chemist into Mosul to process inferior grades of oil,
and urgent requests for high-test fuels were addressed to
the Soviet Union and Iran. Both governments refused to
comply for fear of diplomatic complications with the British.
The Berlin High Command was also derelict. It had decided
that many antiaircraft guns, of which the Iraqi forces had
few, would be flown to Baghdad, but only two were dis-
patched. The Germans assumed that the Vichy French in
Syria would make up any deficiencies, but, as has been pointed
out, the German and Vichy French governments had not
settled the details of this exchange. The Italians were of
no help at all. Ciano requested that Gailani declare Saudi
Arabia, Yemen, and French North Africa, where the Italians
had long-standing ambitions, immune from the revolutionary repercussions of the Iraqi movement. But the prime
minister would make no commitment, and Ciano remained
virtually aloof from the Baghdad putsch.[28]

Meanwhile, in Ankara, Papen worked to consummate an
alliance with the Turks. Saracoğlu again seemed to be bid-
ding for an understanding when, on 17 May 1941, he discussed recent Wehrmacht victories in Greece with the German ambassador. The Turkish minister speculated that, with
Greece in tow, Germany's next logical move should be an
attack on the Suez Canal. Saracoğlu claimed that if such
an attack were successful, it would serve even Britain's best
interests, because the Churchill government would be forced
to make a sensible peace and could then combine its forces
with Germany's against world Communism. At any rate,
Saracoğlu did not believe that Rommel could take the
canal from the west. The only sound approach was from the
north, through Syria, Palestine, and the Sinai Peninsula,
with supplies coming regularly through Turkish Anatolia.
If Germany demanded the right of transit across Anatolia

28. Grobba, *Männer und Mächte*, p. 237. Grobba to Foreign Ministry,
12 May 1941, A.A. 350/9; 19 May 1941, A.A. 350/54; 20 May 1941, A.A.
350/64. Woermann to Ribbentrop, 2 May 1941, A.A. 358/363; Woermann to Rome Embassy, 7 May 1941, A.A. 358/no number.

or delivered any ultimata to Ankara, Saracoğlu warned that she would be refused and opposed with all the force of Turkish arms. But if Berlin could offer him some "face-saving device," with which he could silence the partisans of the alliance with Britain in the Turkish legislature, then the foreign minister was ready to repudiate the Anglo-Turkish treaty and open to Germany the overland passage to Egypt.

He was prepared to justify his policy by arguing that the alliance, which France had also signed, had become invalid when the Vichy government made an armistice in 1940 and withdrew from the war. In return, however, Saracoğlu demanded that Germany furnish the Turkish army with the most modern weaponry and recognize Iraq as part of the Turkish sphere of influence. Papen responded that arms would be forthcoming when Turkey had publicly concluded the military alliance with Germany. In the case of Iraq, however, the German ambassador declared that Saracoğlu could regard the bargain as already sealed. Papen affirmed that the Reich had no interest in Iraq and favored a return to the *status quo ante* there, that is, to Turkish jurisdiction as it had existed until the imposition of the British mandate after the First World War.[29]

There is little reason to doubt that the Turks were sincere about this alliance proposal. They were already threatening military reprisals against the Iraqi revolutionary regime, alleging that it had disrupted Turkish trade through the Persian Gulf.[30] Moreover, a few days before he talked with Saracoğlu, Papen was told by President İnönü that he personally endorsed the resumption of the "old, friendly relationship" with Germany and a treaty that would make the Wehrmacht's communications with Baghdad absolutely assured. All the Turkish president wanted in return was a territorial award, a long-term nonaggression pact, and Germany's pledge never to ally with enemies of the Turkish Republic. When Papen alluded to the difficulties that the German military mission was already having in Iraq, İnönü discounted them and said in heavily accented English,

29. Papen to Foreign Ministry, 17 May 1941, A.A. 1303/no number.
30. Knatchbull-Hugessen to Foreign Office, 26 April 1941, P.R.O., F.O. 371//E1753/1/93; Cornwallis to Foreign Office, 30 April 1941, P.R.O., F.O. 371/E1848/1/93.

"Where there's a will, there's a way." This episode, together with Saracoğlu's more pointed observations, dispelled whatever doubts even the circumspect Ribbentrop had. The German foreign minister wondered only whether İnönü, having countenanced a treaty with Germany, could survive a possible pro-Allied attempt to unseat him.

Papen doubted that the Turkish legislature could muster sufficient opposition to the president to oust him. He therefore asked for and received authorization to formulate a draft treaty with Ankara. As the ambassador sketched it, this projected Turco-German alliance offered the İnönü government a cordon of land west of Edirne; two or three Aegean islands off the coast of Anatolia; and lastly, "the advancement of Turkish interests in the southern and eastern neighboring zones," that is, Syria and Iraq. The Wilhelmstrasse intimated that still more land would be ceded in the Edirne sector once the objections of King Boris III of Bulgaria had been overcome, or the monarch himself removed. Papen specifically recommended the elastic phraseology about "neighboring zones" so that the Turks could take the fullest advantage of any advances made by the German military mission in Iraq. The draft treaty was cabled to Berlin on 23 May 1941, but Saracoğlu saw it before it was sent and, indeed, collaborated on the text. Yet no sooner did it reach the German capital than the Turks began to equivocate about their responsibilities under it and by the end of the month, executing a complete diplomatic volteface, they returned to their policy of nominal association with Britain and strict neutrality toward all the belligerents.[31]

Neither Ribbentrop nor Papen ever understood why the Turks reversed themselves. The ambassador lamely volunteered that İnönü was afraid of British "reproaches." The foreign minister complained that the first consignment of matériel for Turkey was already aboard a ship nearing the port of Haidar Pasha, opposite İstanbul. He also charged Papen to remind Saracoğlu that he was not an old-time pasha

31. Papen to Ribbentrop, 14 May 1941, A.A. 217/552; Ribbentrop to Papen, 16 May 1941, A.A. 217/388 (*DGFP*, 12:828); Ribbentrop to Papen, 17 May 1941, A.A. 217/442; Papen to Ribbentrop, 16 May 1941, A.A. 217/565; Papen to Ribbentrop, 23 May 1941, A.A. 217/598 (*DGFP*, 12:866–67); Papen to Ribbentrop, 27 May 1941, A.A. 217/629 (*DGFP*, 12:886–89). Hirszowicz, *Third Reich*, pp. 183–84. Lothar Krecker, *Deutschland und die Türkei im Zweiten Weltkrieg*, pp. 156–58, 161.

and that modern Turkey did not control the resources of the Ottoman Empire. The Reich, Ribbentrop railed, with only a fraction of its army, could wipe out Turkey within a week.[32] Yet the German government never attempted to use military force to make Turkey sign a new treaty, any more than the British attempted to coerce the Turks into honoring a treaty that was already signed. The reason that the relatively weak republic was able to hold both great powers at bay was well expressed at this time by Gen. Asım Gündüz, deputy chief of the Turkish general staff. His remarks were intended to reassure Britain, but could serve just as well to awe Germany. Gündüz told Knatchbull-Hugessen:

> Turkey at the present moment [is] in the position of a fortress. Direct attack on fortresses or direct passage through fortresses is always difficult, and for this reason the Germans would not wish to attack Turkey, and are in fact already suffering considerable disadvantages in having to go around Turkey.

In Gündüz's opinion, the republic was a reservoir of manpower for whichever of the combatants it decided to support. The Turks, the general claimed, "could muster close on fifty divisions," whereas neither Germany nor Britain, with their worldwide commitments, could deploy nearly so large a force in the eastern Mediterranean. Gündüz may have exaggerated the number of his divisions—the British thought he did[33]—but both London and Berlin still wanted to bring them into the war.

However, the Germans could no longer expect to offer, nor the Turks to receive, Iraq as the price of their collaboration. Even while Papen and Saracoğlu deliberated such a settlement in Ankara, the Japanese government unexpectedly intervened to prevent it. On 18 May 1941, Grobba wired Berlin that Tokyo's envoy to Iran was proposing to put the Iraqi government under official Japanese protection. The Japanese ambassador in Teheran was also criticizing German assistance to Rashid Ali as dilatory and inadequate. He demanded that Japan be consulted about all German Middle

---

32. Ritter to Papen, 26 May 1941, A.A. 217/434; Ribbentrop to Papen, 3 June 1941, A.A. 217/501 (*DGFP*, 12:954–56).

33. All Gündüz's remarks are in Knatchbull-Hugessen to Foreign Office, with minutes, 22 May 1941, P.R.O., F.O. 371/R5495/236/44.

Eastern policy in the future and announced that, in the meantime, the Japanese general staff was preparing a plan of defense for Iraq.[34] Japan based her rights in the Middle East on the Tripartite Pact signed with Germany and Italy on 27 September 1940. This pact pledged the signatories to mutual support in their spheres of influence, but these spheres were not precisely defined. Japan was, of course, to exercise hegemony over Asia in the Axis new order, but Tokyo now made it clear that it considered Asia to extend far enough west to include the Middle East.

This bold Japanese assumption startled the Germans and caught them unprepared, even though Tokyo had hinted earlier that it was prepared to contest the jurisdiction of the eastern Mediterranean. On 23 February 1941, Ribbentrop and the Japanese ambassador, Oshima, had quarreled about German and Turkish collusion over the postwar settlement of the Middle East. The Japanese diplomat denounced Berlin and Ankara as frankly imperialistic and warned Ribbentrop that Japan was reserving her rights in Asia and Africa. The German foreign minister terminated this conversation as quickly as he could, assuring Oshima that "there would be no problem." But the Japanese were not satisfied and, within a few days, began negotiations to supply the Iraqi army with weaponry. They did not conceal the arms traffic from Germany, their military attaché, Lieutenant Colonel Murasawa, keeping the High Command in Berlin fully informed. Japan also probably subsidized al-Gailani and other Iraqi politicians from the beginning of 1941.[35] Germany had been able to tolerate all this earlier Japanese activity because her own attitude toward the Arab world wavered between ambivalence and hostility. But when, during the Baghdad rebellion, Prince Fumimaro Konoye, the Japanese foreign minister, presumed to dictate strategy to the Germans, the Wilhelmstrasse felt that it had to call a halt. Konoye insisted that German warships speed to Basra and blow up the British vessels unloading at the port, so that Japan's profitable prewar export trade with the peoples of the Persian Gulf could be restored. At the same time, he urged the German

34. Grobba to Foreign Ministry, 18 May 1941, A.A. 350/49.
35. Ribbentrop to Papen, 2 March 1941, A.A. 1721/56; Schlobies to Ankara Embassy, 8 March 1941, A.A. 1721/Pol. VII 1000g.

government to commandeer Lufthansa commercial airplanes to fly to Afghanistan, where the Japanese had stockpiled materials for the relief of the Iraqi insurgents.[36]

Germany vetoed all Konoye's demands. The prince was advised that it would be pointless to extend his protection to Rashid Ali unless Japan was ready to declare war on Britain. Japan's export business, the Germans added, was unessential to either the outcome of the war or the Iraqi revolt.[37] Konoye did not press his arguments, and the Wilhelmstrasse professed to overlook them. But neither the Germans nor the Turks could now forget Japanese aspirations in Iraq, and certainly Berlin had no wish to offend the Japanese and test the Tripartite Pact before it was tempered. Here, then, was still another reason why the Germans avoided deeper involvement at Baghdad. The same considerations held for the Turks. Through Kamil al-Gailani, the Iraqi ambassador in Ankara, they knew that Rashid Ali was closely associated with the Japanese and that the communiqués from Tokyo threatened the arrival of a new competitor for Iraq.[38] The Japanese might be willing to share Iraq's resources with the Turks, or they might move to take them out of Ankara's reach entirely. Neither the Germans nor the Turks knew what Japan's future course would be, but both wanted to avoid making of it a trial of strength. For this reason, Berlin and Ankara did not prosecute their aims in Iraq to the fullest, did not, as Churchill put it, capture the great prize at little price. Turkey backed off from an alliance with Germany, abruptly but, as it proved, permanently.

Meanwhile, events in Baghdad, apart from considerations of higher policy, discouraged the Germans. After Blomberg's death, Berlin sent Gen. Helmuth Felmy to command the Luftwaffe squadron. Al-Gailani was apparently unimpressed by the new leader's higher rank and seemed in every way uncooperative. The Germans were short of high-test fuel. Soon they found themselves short of money. Al-Gailani ordered his compatriots to sell nothing to the German military mission unless they paid in Iraqi dinars or gold. The prime minister refused to validate the Reichsmark as legal

---

36. Grobba to Foreign Ministry, 18 May 1941, A.A. 350/49.

37. Ettel, Baghdad, to Foreign Ministry, 31 May 1941, A.A. 350/434.

38. Knatchbull-Hugessen to Foreign Office, 21 April 1941, P.R.O., F.O. 371/E1619/1/93, and 24 April 1941, P.R.O., F.O. 371/E1692/1/93.

tender. The military then tried to convert some German property, impounded at the start of the war, into ready cash. But Rashid Ali, maddeningly legalistic, argued that the regent Abdul Illah had promulgated the original decree of confiscation, and only he could cancel it. The regent was in exile at Amman, Transjordan. The Germans also tried but failed to persuade al-Gailani to institute anti-Semitic laws modeled on their own. The Jews of Baghdad, heedless of Rashid Ali's identification with the Axis, supported their prime minister wholeheartedly, donating money and small arms to his forces.[39]

The British and most other pro-Allied foreigners were penned up during May in the Habbaniya air-force base or in the British embassy in Baghdad. The Luftwaffe bombarded Habbaniya but did little damage to Baghdad. Their hits at the base were minimally effective because, the German pilots complained, they had been given a defective map of Habbaniya by an Italian engineer who had worked on the base before the war. Consequently, the British throughout the area were fairly comfortable during Rashid Ali's rebellion. Freya Stark, the distinguished British orientalist, who was an eyewitness of the Baghdad disturbances, says that the besieged continued to sleep on the roof of the British embassy. Evidently they had more to fear from the heat of the summer nights than from Göring's aviators. Stark admired the leadership of Ambassador Cornwallis but thought the British were partly responsible for the trouble with Rashid Ali because of their aloofness and arrogance toward Iraqi citizens. As the mandatory power, they had not done enough to provide vocational training and jobs for Iraqi youths.[40] There was a

39. All the information in this paragraph is drawn from Grobba to Foreign Ministry, 27 May 1941, A.A. 350/120, 131. Seiler to Foreign Ministry, 24 July 1941, A.A. 4722/no number. Grobba, *Männer und Mächte*, p. 163.

40. See the following eyewitness accounts. Freya Stark, *The Arab Island: The Middle East, 1939–1943*, pp. 158–59. Freya Stark, *Dust in the Lion's Paw: Autobiography, 1939–1946*, pp. 78–82, 104. Somerset De Chair, *The Golden Carpet*, pp. 118, 123, 127. De Chair was an intelligence officer with the relief column. Cornwallis privately tended to agreed with Stark. He admitted there were many unemployed Iraqi youths, of no particular political persuasion, who supported Rashid Ali. Britain did not, or could not, do anything to teach them skills after the suppression of the revolt. Instead they were all interned by the police on Cornwallis's orders. Cornwallis to Foreign Office, 26 July 1941, P.R.O., F.O. 371/ E4194/1/93.

great deal of juvenile delinquency, lawlessness, and looting under Rashid Ali's rule, so much that the governments of Egypt and Transjordan thought the political revolt in Baghdad was turning into a social revolution with equalitarian overtones. Accordingly, the monarchical regimes in Cairo and Amman considered revising their sympathetic attitude toward al-Gailani.[41]

The British took brilliant advantage of Germany's stalemated diplomacy to recover control of Iraq. Two relief armies were sent to Baghdad, a fast-moving column from Palestine and a larger force from India. The Palestinian column was subject to the command of General Wavell, who opposed its dispatch. Wavell, whose forces had already been reduced when some of them were assigned to the defense of Greece, feared that this new depletion would ruin the salients he planned to throw out against Rommel in the Libyan desert. He predicted that intervention in Iraq would arouse all the Arab peoples in a holy war. Col. John Glubb, the flamboyant drillmaster of the Transjordanian army, tended to agree with Wavell. He declared it pointless as well as arduous work to reimpose the Hashemite King Feisal II and his regent, Abdul Illah, on Iraq. The dynasty, according to Glubb, was popular only with the Bedouins; a republican regime might better suit the city dwellers. Nevertheless, Churchill overruled Wavell and Glubb, the relief army was ordered to depart Jerusalem, and it survived a series of minor disasters while crossing the burning Transjordanian desert. The Transjordanian contingent of the relief force refused to cross the Iraqi frontier, and the Arab drivers, hastily recruited to operate a melange of run-down vehicles, made little attempt to keep them in service, often willfully pushing their cars into ditches. After the relief force crossed the Iraqi frontier, things went better. A British advance unit captured an Iraqi communications installation and warned the Baghdad insurgents that they were approaching the city with heavy tank support. The British actually lacked significant armor, but the Iraqis panicked and abandoned their forward positions. The Germans objected halfheartedly and then prepared to decamp themselves. On 29 May 1941, the

41. Colonial Office to Foreign Office, 17 April 1941, P.R.O., F.O. 371/ E1570/1/93.

Luftwaffe left Baghdad. Two days later, Fritz Grobba, who accused the German airmen of cowardice, made his own escape. Al-Gailani, his ministers, and the grand mufti, who exhorted the airmen to make a stand against the British, all escaped into Iran. The British entered Baghdad on 1 June, never having bothered to declare war on Iraq.[42]

It was due to Papen that the Reich managed to salvage anything at all from the Iraqi rebellion. He turned the military debacle into a propaganda victory. At the height of the fighting in Baghdad, İnönü had demanded a nonaggression pact from Berlin as part of his price for opening the Turkish route to German forces going to the Middle East. With the British having recaptured the Iraqi capital, there seemed no point in continuing discussions for a pact, but Papen continued to favor it. To the German ambassador, the most important advantage of such a pact would be its psychological effect on the British. It would show London and the world, he believed, that the last remaining ally of the British empire, expecting its defeat, had deserted to the enemy. Ribbentrop was not in a mood to grant anything to the mercurially exasperating Turks, but since it cost him nothing, he authorized the signature of a treaty of friendship and nonaggression between Berlin and Ankara on 18 June 1941.[43]

Its effect on the Foreign Office and Britain's friends was as depressing as Papen had anticipated. In addition to protesting the pact at Ankara, the British government marshaled American pressure against Turkey. The Americans were told that, while the pact itself was innocuous, it would continue to create the worst possible impression everywhere. The State Department then instructed John V. MacMurray, the United States' ambassador at Ankara, to warn Saracoğlu that his recent arrangement with Germany was having a "negative" effect on American public opinion. However, the Turkish foreign minister retorted that, in that case, Washington must

42. Ian S. Playfair, *The Mediterranean and Middle East*, 2:177–87, 192, 196. Alec S. Kirkbride, *A Crackle of Thorns: Experiences in the Middle East*, p. 132. Michie, *Retreat to Victory*, p. 84. De Chair, *The Golden Carpet*, pp. 70–71, 106, 108–18. Khadduri, *Independent Iraq*, p. 224. Grobba to Foreign Ministry, 31 May 1941, A.A. 350/166.

43. Papen to Ribbentrop, 18 June 1941, A.A. 217/751. Krecker, *Deutschland und die Türkei*, pp. 171–72. Türkkaya Ataöv, *Turkish Foreign Policy, 1939–1945*, p. 94.

manage its public opinion as best it could.[44] In the Balkans, the pact's effects were particularly corrosive. Laird Archer, head of the United States Near Eastern Foundation for Public Health, who was doing relief work in Athens when the pact was published, declared that it undermined the spirit of partisans who continued to fight the Wehrmacht after the Greek capital was captured. Archer and other Americans tried to convince the Athenians that Turkey was only buying time with the pact until she could declare for the Allies at a more opportune point. But the Greeks dismissed this argument as wishful thinking and feared that Turkey would annex portions of the Greek frontier with German concurrence.[45]

In his memoirs, Knatchbull-Hugessen glossed over the pact, calling it a stalling device, but privately he excoriated Turkish diplomacy for plumbing a new moral depth. With İnönü, Saracoğlu, and the senior army officers all turning cool and reserved toward him, his post was becoming distinctly uncomfortable. Yet the British ambassador suspected that Papen was not altogether secure in his job, either. He speculated that his German adversary meant the nonaggression pact not only as a propaganda bludgeoning but also as a beckoning to London to make a negotiated peace. The British ambassador conjectured that Papen espoused the pact to stymie his Nazi critics at home and to hold his job long enough to serve as broker in an Anglo-German accord to be arranged in Turkey. This scheme, according to British embassy informants, had the support of Göring and of Saracoğlu, whom Papen had invited to moderate a general peace conference. Saracoğlu was reported to be eager to turn an Anglo-German coalition against Communist Russia, Turkey's most hated foe, and, if he could manage it, to acquire enough prestige to take the presidency from İsmet İnönü.[46] Knatchbull-Hugessen may have exaggerated Saracoğlu's

44. Memorandum of the British Embassy, Washington, 15 June 1941, *FRUS, 1941*, vol. 3, pp. 854–55; MacMurray to Hull, 18 June 1941, *FRUS, 1941*, vol. 3, pp. 859–61. Woodward, *British Foreign Policy*, 1:582–83.
45. Laird Archer, *Balkan Journal*, p. 232.
46. Knatchbull-Hugessen to Foreign Office, 25 June 1941, P.R.O., F.O. 371/N3197/78/38; Foreign Office to Knatchbull-Hugessen, 30 June 1941, P.R.O., F.O. 371/R6532/236/44. Hughe Knatchbull-Hugessen, *Diplomat in Peace and War*, pp. 161–67.

presidential ambitions, but he was right about his anti-Communism. When Hitler attacked the Soviet Union on 22 June 1941, the whole Turkish leadership was jubilant. Later, Papen was to make still clearer and more persistent bids for a negotiated peace, though Churchill's parliamentary addresses eloquently excluded anything less than unconditional surrender.

The nonaggression pact of 18 June 1941 demoralized not only the Allies but also the Arabs, an effect that the Germans might not have intended. The accord with Ankara was the culmination of all their disappointments with Nazi Germany and after it mass Arab help like the Iraqi rebellion was never again available to the Reich, whatever pro-Axis intrigues individual Arabs might engage in. The absence of widespread pro-German feeling in the Middle East after the middle of 1941 was one reason for the High Command's decision against renewing operations in Iraq. Some of the survivors of the Luftwaffe expedition to Baghdad admitted that they had evacuated prematurely and recommended another attempt to make the city the base of German Middle Eastern campaigning. John MacMurray, American ambassador to Turkey, fully expected the Germans to reappear in Iraq, and Gen. Alfred Jodl, chief of the general staff in Berlin, briefly considered planning an attack on Turkey to batter a passage through Anatolia to Mosul and Baghdad. But Jodl feared the rigors of campaigning in the Taurus and Amanus mountains, fully as rugged as the terrain the Italians had known in Albania, and he pronounced the Wehrmacht unfit for this kind of operation, at least for the remainder of 1941.[47]

The only person to contest this decision seriously was the grand mufti. Like Rashid Ali al-Gailani, he was now a fugitive in Iran. He asked the Germans to rescue him by plane at either Tabriz or Teheran, but the Wilhelmstrasse, anxious to avoid further wrangling, curtly informed him, through its envoy Erwin Ettel, that no aircraft was available. When Haj Muhammad offered to risk the overland route to Europe through Turkey, Woermann in Berlin notified him that he would not be permitted to travel farther than the Bulgarian

47. MacMurray to Hull, 7 July 1941, *FRUS, 1941*, vol. 3, pp. 878–81. Papen to Foreign Ministry, 2 June 1941, A.A. 217/658; O.K.W. Memorandum to Ribbentrop, 24 August 1941, A.A. 51/no number.

frontier. However, the Italian embassy, without German approval, smuggled the mufti out of the Iranian capital on one of its own planes, and Haj Muhammad arrived in Rome at the end of October. Mussolini accorded him a jovial reception, promised support for Arab "liberation," and embarrassed the Wilhelmstrasse into receiving the Arab leader despite its fully expressed reluctance. The mufti still carried his declaration for Arab independence, which he insisted on discussing with Hitler, along with more insurrections in the Arab world, when he and the Führer met on 28 November 1941.

The import of the declaration and the memory of the Iraqi imbroglio irritated Hitler to the point that he did not make even a pretense of courtesy. Though he knew coffee drinking customarily accompanied all polite discussion in the Middle East, Hitler neglected to have even one cup served and substituted barley water instead. He never shook the mufti's hand, refused to endorse the cause of Arab independence, and left his guest confused and mortified.[48] Back in Iraq, the mufti's former revolutionary confederates were even less fortunate. The British put most of them in concentration camps and had a few shot for treason. Even when revolutionaries had succeeded in escaping to Turkey, Knatchbull-Hugessen noted that the Turkish police readily extradited them to the Iraqi authorities and that Papen's embassy never intervened to impede these extradition proceedings. Some of the revolutionaries who survived the proscriptions returned to politics after the war, and it is not surprising that they maintained their anti-Turkish stance. In July 1958, such men were instrumental in overthrowing the government of Nuri as-Said; this coup was caused partly by Nuri's negotiation of a regional security pact with Turkey. Nuri and King Feisal II were murdered and the ministries in Baghdad taken over by a military clique led by Brigade Commander Abdul Karim Qasim. Qasim's first cabinet contained few experienced ministers, but one was the former informa-

48. Weizsäcker to Ettel, — June 1941, A.A. 63/no number; Ettel to Foreign Ministry, 13 June 1941, A.A. 63/475; Kroll to Foreign Ministry, 14 October 1941, A.A. 63/1279; Bismarck to Foreign Ministry, 1 November 1941, A.A. 63/2770. Hirszowicz, *Third Reich*, pp. 218–21. Joseph B. Schechtman, *The Mufti and the Fuehrer: The Rise and Fall of Haj Amin el-Husseini*, p. 123.

tion officer for Rashid Ali, Siddig Shanshal, appointed minister of news and guidance in 1958.[49]

In Egypt, the collapse of al-Gailani's putsch had a sobering effect on King Farouk and probably spared the British serious trouble at the hands of the more extreme Arab nationalists. Just after the flight of Rashid Ali, British intelligence in Cairo discovered the existence of a widespread plot to assassinate the civil and military leaders of the British administration. But the Egyptian conspirators were waiting for the success of al-Gailani and looking to Germany to help him. When the Reich did not intervene in strength, the plotters deferred action and were detected by British agents. All were put under arrest.[50] King Farouk was not implicated in the affair, but he was profuse with congratulations to Ambassador Lampson. He asked the British envoy what he could do to further the Allied cause, and informants in his household described him as quite sincere and as having undergone a complete change of heart toward the Axis. This estimate proved overly sanguine, but Farouk for the time being made a number of gestures to strengthen the British position. He dismissed some of his objectionable Italian domestics, threatened Sheik al-Maraghi and other agitators with police restraint, and, most important to the British envoy, allowed him to name a new chief of the security section of the Egyptian department of the interior. The security section had hitherto been lax toward suspected Axis agents, but now Lampson put it in charge of Babli Bey, former superintendent of the police school, whom the ambassador described as efficient, honest, and pro-British.

The embassy expected to be less troubled by Egyptian connivance with Berlin and Rome in the future. Lampson was also gratified that Farouk dropped his demand for Lake Tana and part of Abyssinia.[51] However, in Ankara, the Turks, deprived of Iraq, were still intent on annexation. In a pri-

49. Knatchbull-Hugessen to Foreign Office, 11 November 1941, P.R.O., F.O. 371/R10088/15/44. Waldemar J. Gallman, *Iraq Under General Nuri*, pp. 37–39, 203–4, 215.

50. Lampson to Foreign Office, 2 June 1941, P.R.O., F.O. 371/J1737/18/16.

51. Lampson to Foreign Office, 10 June 1941, P.R.O., F.O. 371/J1822/18/16, 23 September 1941, P.R.O., F.O. 371/J3040/18/16, and 27 September 1941, P.R.O., F.O. 371/J3079/18/16. See also Lampson to Foreign Office, 17 February 1942, P.R.O., F.O. 371/J813/38/16.

vate letter to Oliver Lyttelton, British minister of state for the Middle East, Knatchbull-Hugessen charged that while the Turks professed to eschew expansion, they actually coveted a great deal more territory, especially if they could justify it as vital to their security. He expected them to try to gain control of Samos, Mytilene, and the other Greek islands as their minimum gains from the war, and to plot with Germany for still larger loot as long as the Reich was scoring great victories on land. In his opinion, the İnönü government was completely indifferent to British triumphs at sea and in the air.[52] At the time Knatchbull-Hugessen wrote these views, the Wehrmacht had just begun what seemed to be another string of victories. It had invaded the Soviet Union, and Turkish ambition turned from the Persian Gulf to the Caucasus Mountains.

52. Knatchbull-Hugessen to Lyttelton, Cairo, 13 July 1941, P.R.O., F.O. 371/R7421/236/44.

Chapter 6

Turkey and the Russian Campaign: Cyprus and the Caucasus

Pan-Turanian Intrigues

The Iraqi revolt was the watershed of Turco-German relations in World War II. As indicated, some German general staff experts still continued to plan for an attack on the Suez Canal, using Iraq as a heavily fortified flank against a counterattack by the British Indian army. And Turkey took out insurance against the day when Berlin might order such an operation by signing a nonaggression pact with the Reich government. But Ankara officials now knew that they could not again inveigle the Wehrmacht into attempting the conquest of northern Syria and the Tigris-Euphrates Valley. Nor could they blithely dare to provoke Ribbentrop, who had threatened to wipe out Turkey within a week, for a second time. It is probable that in delivering Ribbentrop's harangue, Papen blunted its cutting edge and drained off some of his chief's virtiol. But the Turks were still chastened and even frightened. They were put on notice that henceforward they would have to conduct their affairs with Germany more modestly and deferentially. They were compelled, in fact, to change their aims from annexing contiguous territories to trying to establish spheres of influence and jurisdictional zones in areas well beyond the frontiers of the old Ottoman Empire. Germany's initially rapid penetration of the Soviet Union made this new policy more than promising for Ankara.

The Turkish government was delighted with the German invasion, and Saracoğlu even claimed that his adroit diplomacy had brought it about. By offering Hitler the nonaggression pact of 18 June 1941, the Turk reasoned, he had secured the Germans' southern flank and lured them into an attack on Russia. This, he opined, was good for both London and Ankara, because it removed some of the German pressure from the British and deflected it entirely from the Turks. Saracoğlu was so pleased with his cunning success, as he considered it, that he suggested that Churchill might commend him for it in a speech to the Commons. The Foreign Office was appalled at the Turkish minister's audacity and dismissed his interpretation of the Russo-German conflict as "absurd." It denied that the British government was in any way in Turkey's debt and refused to see the nonaggression pact as anything more than still another betrayal of the Anglo-Turkish alliance. London ordered Knatchbull-Hugessen to remind Saracoğlu that Hitler often signed pacts with those he intended to assail. He had pledged peace to Russia in 1939 even as he pledged it to Turkey in 1941, yet he had broken his word to the Soviets and might even now be meditating violence against the Turks. If he and his colleagues would understand true cunning, the British warned Saracoğlu, they must read *Mein Kampf*.[1]

When he realized that the British regarded his claim as tasteless and unfounded, Saracoğlu gradually retracted and then denied his boast that he had contrived the Russo-German war.[2] But, at the instance of Papen, he attempted to deprive the Soviet Union of all outside help. The German ambassador suggested, and Saracoğlu vigorously recommended, that Britain and the United States abstain from the quarrel between Germany and the Soviet Union. If the British desisted from extending assistance to the Soviet dictator, Papen implied, then Hitler was willing to allow London a free hand in western Europe, while reserving to himself only hegemony in the East. The Foreign Office, of course, met this bargain with a complete rejection; Papen took this in his stride and was later to hazard a similar rejection. But the Turkish government seemed genuinely puzzled by Britain's unresponsiveness and badly shaken when Winston Churchill, despite his lifelong aversion to Communism, accorded the benefits of a full alliance to Joseph Stalin.[3] Knatchbull-Hugessen did not dissent in any way from the prime minister's decision, but he warned:

1. Knatchbull-Hugessen to Foreign Office, 22 June 1941, P.R.O., F.O. 371/R6401/1934/44; Knatchbull-Hugessen to Foreign Office, 23 June 1941, and Cadogan to Knatchbull-Hugessen, 28 June 1941, P.R.O., F.O. 371/R6399/1934/44. Sir Ernest Llewellyn Woodward, *British Foreign Policy in the Second World War*, 2:20–21. (For list of abbreviations, see p. 221.)

2. Knatchbull-Hugessen to Foreign Office, 28 June 1941, P.R.O., F.O. 371/R6868/236/44.

3. Knatchbull-Hugessen to Foreign Office, 22 June 1941, P.R.O., F.O. 371/R6867/236/44; 30 June 1941, P.R.O., F.O. 371/R6965/236/44.

Once Russia had become our ally, difficulties were inevitable. Monsieur Saracoglu's resentment at his treatment in Moscow in 1939 has never disappeared. In addition to this and to the traditional Turkish fear of Russia, there were more immediate causes of distrust. A serious one was the supposed suggestion made by Monsieur Molotov during his visit to Berlin in November, 1940, that the Straits should be handed over to Russia. Beyond these, there was a chronic complaint that the Soviet government had remained studiedly unresponsive to all advances made to them from Ankara.[4]

The British ambassador went on to say that he thought the rumors about Molotov's demands for the Bosporus and the Straits were largely illusory. But by the middle of 1941, he admitted that the Turks had other valid grievances against the Soviet regime. Ankara uncovered proof, which the British embassy regarded as conclusive, that Moscow was stirring up an independence movement among the Kurdish tribes of eastern Turkey. Turkish police had apprehended Russian agents all along the Black Sea shore and, in several cases, were all but certain that the Soviet navy was sinking Turkish merchant ships at night. On 25 August 1941, a combined Anglo-Soviet force began the occupation of Iran, quickly deposing the shah for pro-German sympathies and exiling him to the British island of Mauritius. The British and Russians likewise expelled the German ambassador, Erwin Ettel, and several Axis espionage agents. The British and Soviet governments defended the occupation of Iran as a necessity of war and solemnly affirmed to Turkey that it was not intended to be permanent. Nonetheless, Knatchbull-Hugessen could see that the İnönü government was not placated and that all these episodes confirmed the Turks in their pro-German proclivities, which the failure in Iraq had temporarily dampened.

Hitler's Russian campaign was hardly six weeks old when it became evident that the Turkish irredentists were for the time being looking away from their former Arab provinces and toward the Turkish peoples of the Soviet Union. Those were reported to have long preferred the mild dictatorship

4. This quotation and the following observations of the British ambassador are all from his year-end summary of Turkish diplomacy to Anthony Eden. See Knatchbull-Hugessen to Eden, 5 February 1942, P.R.O., F.O. 371/R1471/24/44. Experts at the Foreign Office labeled this "a really first-class dispatch."

of Atatürk's successors to the brutalities of Joseph Stalin. At the beginning of August 1941, Ankara's ambassador to Berlin, Hüsrev Gerede, called on Weizsäcker and advised him that the Wehrmacht could make excellent propaganda use of the Russian-Turkish peoples among whom it was now moving. Ambassador Gerede said it was his personal opinion that a "Turanian" state should be organized by the Axis new order in the shank of land between the Black and Caspian seas. Gerede claimed that everyone in Baku spoke Turkish and yearned for independence from Soviet domination. Weizsäcker answered that he could not yet tell how army policy in conquered Russia would evolve, but in his private notes of this conversation the state secretary recalled that Papen reported being sounded on the fate of the Russian "Turanians" by several prominent Turks in Ankara. After he had discussed Gerede's overtures with Ribbentrop, Weizsäcker instructed Papen to investigate the business more deeply.[5]

Meanwhile, the Army High Command was so intrigued by the Turkish ambassador's remarks that it invited him and Ribbentrop to General Headquarters in late August. However, in the presence of the generals, Gerede retracted virtually all his previous declarations. This meeting was held on the very day that the Anglo-Soviet invasion of Iran began, and the Allies' summary treatment of that country possibly made the Turkish envoy more circumspect.[6] For whatever reason, he now said the Pan-Turanian idea was dead in Turkey, and his government had no territorial aspirations beyond its present frontiers. Ribbentrop interrupted to inquire whether this policy would change if the Soviet Union were to collapse entirely, but Gerede replied that he lacked the authority to make any predictions. In Ankara, Papen also noted a change when he interviewed İnönü and Saracoğlu. He wanted to have their ideas about the reorganiza-

5. Weizsäcker to Ribbentrop, 5 August 1941, A.A. 217/494 (*DGFP*, 13:284); Weizsäcker to Papen, 21 August 1941, A.A. 217/no number. The U. S. State Department had already noticed, and complained, that Turkey often used her ambassadors, apparently without official authorization, to probe highly sensitive questions. Memorandum by Berle, 9 October 1940, *FRUS, 1940*, vol. 3, pp. 957–61. Lothar Krecker, *Deutschland und die Türkei im Zweiten Weltkrieg*, pp. 210–11.

6. King Farouk was very shaken by the deposition of the Iranian shah and afraid of losing his own throne. See Lampson to Foreign Office, 5 October 1941, P.R.O., F.O. 371/J3162/158/16.

tion of Crimean Russia and the disposition of Soviet war and merchant vessels lying in Crimean ports. To these queries, both Turks answered that no discussion was appropriate until the German armies actually reached Batum and beyond.[7]

Despite Gerede's assertions, Pan-Turanianism was not dead, either in republican Turkey or in Soviet Russia, where it was regarded as a potentially dangerous centrifugal force. In 1938, Fitzroy Maclean, later Churchill's personal representative to the Yugoslav partisan Tito, traveled through Baku, Batum, and Erivan, reputed to be centers of Pan-Turanian activity. Maclean found these cities among the most impressive in the Soviet Union. The civic architecture was handsome and the streets well repaired; the food shops were full, and, unlike the rest of Russia, there were no queues in front of them. The Englishman thought the regime was trying to appease the secessionist tendencies of the local inhabitants with especially favorable treatment, but he concluded that those tendencies remained incorrigible, nonetheless.[8] Whether İnönü and his foreign ministers actively encouraged them must, until the Turkish archives are opened, remain a moot question. But the Ankara leadership was not absolutely opposed to Pan-Turanianism. İnönü seems to have abetted it with a kind of benign tolerance. A hotbed of militant Pan-Turanianism was the Turkish Historical Society of Ankara, with which the president often met. He once joked that some of the members would not be satisfied until the Turkish frontier was pushed back to the walls of Vienna, but he did not rebuke them.

He also personally advanced the official careers of some outspoken Pan-Turanians. Papen cited the case of Memduh Şevket, Turkish ambassador to Afghanistan, as an example of this kind of presidential patronage. Şevket was known to have talked often about his country regaining much of the Soviet Union, and consequently Afghan officials were afraid that his appointment would compromise relations with Moscow. But İsmet İnönü insisted on it, and the government in Kabul, however apprehensively, received Memduh Şevket as the Turkish envoy. The German

---

7. Ribbentrop to Papen, 25 August 1941, A.A. 217/888 (*DGFP*, 13: 373–75); Papen to Foreign Ministry, 30 August 1941, A.A. 217/1124.
8. Fitzroy Maclean, *Eastern Approaches*, pp. 174–75.

ambassador also reported that as soon as the Wehrmacht crossed the Soviet frontier, the Turkish government hurriedly began to consult with some of Abdul-Hamid's former ministers who had espoused Pan-Turanianism under the sultanate. For two decades the Kemalist revolution had condemned these men to political obscurity, but with the German drive eastward opening up new possibilities of expansion, their advice seemed timely.[9] These old Ottoman functionaries, like İnönü himself, could well remember the days when Turkish troops briefly occupied parts of Russian Armenia and Azerbaijan during the early period of Lenin's revolution.

British officials also had evidence of Turkey's Pan-Turanian ambition. About a year after Gerede's encounters with the Wilhelmstrasse and the German general staff, Ahmet Umar, Turkish consul in Damascus, paid a call at the city's British consulate. Umar, well liked and thought to be pro-Allied, was considered an official spokesman of his government, even though he denied it, since he had just returned to Syria from Ankara. Alleging that his initiative was purely personal, Umar asked R. A. Beaumont of the British consulate whether London would agree to some expansion of Turkish territory at the expense of Soviet Russia. In return, Umar believed Ankara would renounce any intrigues against Bulgaria and Iraq if the Allied coalition guaranteed gains in Azerbaijan and the Caucasus. The Turkish consul admitted that his government would have preferred to see its jurisdiction revived in parts of the Arab world, but it had recently suffered so many disappointments in that area that it was not prepared to risk fresh humiliations. Ankara was ready to accept the formation of some sort of Arab confederation under British "influence" and a "puppet ruler," probably King Abdullah of Transjordan. But Turkey had to be compensated in Soviet territories, and even then, Ahmet Umar argued, Syria should be subject to a special regime. France was too unpopular to be restored there, and the British army, which had invaded the country and beaten the Vichy forces under Gen. Henri Dentz in June 1941, could not remain indefinitely. The best solution, the Turkish diplomat suggested,

9. Papen to Foreign Ministry, 5 August 1941, A.A. 691/3018. Edward Weisband, *Turkish Foreign Policy, 1943–1945: Small State Diplomacy and Great Power Politics*, p. 70.

was to award Ankara the trusteeship of Syria. The Foreign Office, however, took no action, even though it considered the interview to be officially inspired and the Turkish proposals sinister.

Commenting on the overtures of the Turkish consul, Harold Caccia, former chargé d'affaires at Athens and a Middle Eastern consultant in 1942, compared the question of the Caucasus and Azerbaijan with the acquisition of Alexandretta in 1938. "The Turks," he wrote, "hope to be able to get away with something of this kind again." His fellow Middle Eastern expert, George Lisle Clutton, agreed. He warned Foreign Secretary Eden to guard against Pan-Turanianism. It was latent, not moribund, and the Turkish government was doing nothing to discourage it. If the Soviet Union collapsed, Clutton speculated, the Turks would readily accept Transcaucasia from Germany unless the British were able to threaten reprisals. They might also demand a border rectification with Iran if they suspected the British response would be feeble or acquiescent. And under no circumstances would Clutton rely on the Turks to abjure their threats to Arab independence.[10]

Thus British as well as German sources strongly suggest that Pan-Turanianism was not simply a mass enthusiasm popularly engendered, but an official program of the Turkish government, continuously though surreptitiously cultivated. Ankara preferred to use subordinate diplomats or non-official spokesmen in order to obscure the origins of the Pan-Turanian movement, but there was little doubt that those origins were in the highest echelons of the Turkish leadership. In August 1941, Papen reported that the Turks were about to send an impressive emissary—albeit an irregular one—to Berlin to discuss Pan-Turanian aspirations. The emissary was Nuri Paşa, brother of the celebrated Enver Paşa, Ottoman minister of war who was most responsible for allying the sultan's empire with the Wilhelmian Reich in 1914. Enver was long since dead, but his brother Nuri, who had tried to raise the Libyan tribes in a holy war in the Kaiser's cause, had survived the First World War to become a moderately prosperous factory owner in republican Turkey.

10. Beaumont to Foreign Office, 13 August 1942; Minute by Clutton, 6 September 1942, and Minute by Caccia, 11 September 1942, P.R.O., F.O. 371/R5618/2713/44.

Ostensibly, Nuri was visiting Germany to place industrial orders at the annual Leipzig Trade Fair. Actually, his mission was to propound his theories of the Pan-Turanian reorganization of the Middle East before the highest dignitaries of the German government.

At the first report of his coming, the Wilhelmstrasse, which always made audiences difficult for the various Arab agents to obtain, arranged its schedule to accommodate him. Papen was ordered home on "sick leave" so that he could analyze and advise on Nuri's remarks. The ambassador immediately assured the foreign ministry that Nuri was no free-lance firebrand, but the accredited spokesman of the İnönü government, though Ankara chose to keep his credentials somewhat sub-rosa. Papen found out that Saracoğlu had briefed Nuri immediately before the latter left Turkey. Ambassador Gerede had also been instructed to pay Nuri's expenses in Berlin. As Papen quite rightly observed, had either Saracoğlu or Gerede objected to Pan-Turanianism, they would have revoked Nuri's passport.[11]

Nuri was thus certain of support from home and of a cordial welcome, even of a kind of indebtedness, from the Germans. As the brother of an important First World War ally, he thought the Reich owed him a debt of gratitude. Accordingly, Nuri was imperious to Under Secretary Woermann at their first meeting in Berlin. The Turk, who had probably been coached by Saracoğlu, was sharp and self-assured. Nuri first criticized imperial Germany's maladroit handling of Turkish public opinion twenty-five years earlier. The Germans, he claimed, were still wont to take exclusive credit for the victory of Gallipoli in 1915, even though the jagged hills of that peninsula were covered with the graves of the Turkish defenders. Since that time, the pasha continued, Germany had forgotten her old Turkish comrades and tended to conciliate the Arabs. The Arabs Nuri described as a weak, incompetent, and treacherous lot, who had sold out the sultan in the First World War and might do the same to Nazi Germany. Nuri predicted that any Arab political federation would first squander and ruin

11. Weizsäcker to Ribbentrop, 22 August 1941, A.A. 217/no number; Ribbentrop to Papen, 22 August 1941, A.A. 217/885; Weizsäcker to Woermann, 10 September 1941, A.A. 691/590 (*DGFP*, 13:473–74).

the achievements of Western technology in the Middle Eastern area, and then, because of the Arabs' inherent incapacity for administration, disintegrate. To guard against such calamaties, Germany should be prepared, at the very least, to assign to Ankara after the war the sections of the Baghdad Railway that ran through Syria to Turkey. As Nuri reminded Woermann, such an eventual transfer of ownership to the Turks had been part of the original understanding with Sultan Abdul-Hamid, in any case. It might as well have been Saracoğlu making these remarks, though the Turkish foreign minister preferred to keep his association with Nuri Paşa under cover and to deny it when he was pressed.[12]

A week later, Nuri and Woermann conferred again, and the Turk revealed the main part of his mission. First, he delimited for the German minister what areas of Asia he considered "Pan-Turanian." These were the Crimea, Transcaucasia, Azerbaijan, the land between the Ural Mountains and the Volga River, and the Daghestan and Tatar Autonomous Soviet republics. In addition to these provinces, Nuri also claimed Turanian enclaves in Syria, Iraq, and northern Iran. Finally, he would have had the Turanian state embrace "East Turkestan," that is, the Chinese province of Sinkiang. Quite obviously, his schemes were a blend of old and new, with some points drawn from Ottoman times and others conceived under the republic. To these claims, Woermann replied that Germany had neither cultural nor economic ambitions in any of the areas mentioned, nor did her conquering armies contemplate a long-term tenure in these parts of Russia. He therefore offered Nuri Paşa a general assurance of support, though he pointedly commented that all these Pan-Turanian proposals ran counter to Atatürk's precept that Turkey was a purely national state. Nuri asserted that Atatürk's foreign policy had been only temporary, necessitated by the weakness of the infant Turkish Republic and fear of Soviet Russia. But the Wehrmacht now stood on Soviet soil and was gaining more ground every day. According to Nuri, Turanian expansion was very popular with the Turkish people and with the Turkish army, and if the government in Ankara did not advance the cause or proved nega-

12. Woermann to Weizsäcker, 17 September 1941, A.A. 691/869.

tivistic and timid, the Turkish army could be expected to sweep it away.[13]

Woermann's memorandum of his conversation with Nuri Paşa shows that he was favorably impressed by the Turk and ready to support the return of Turkish control to the Turanian regions, with a few reservations. The under secretary privately questioned whether it would ever be to Germany's advantage to capture the oil fields of Kirkuk, Mosul, Batum, and Baku and then transfer them to İnönü's government. But on all other points, Woermann thought the Reich could safely satisfy the Turanian party. Nuri's contention that the army favored an irredentist policy he accepted on the basis of evidence furnished him by Papen. Shortly after Nuri's Berlin sojourn, Hüseyin Hüsnü Emir Erkilet, one of the Turkish generals living in semiretirement but maintaining contacts with many Russian Turks, petitioned Woermann through the German ambassador. Erkilet revealed that Ankara was making it a practice to smuggle Turkish intellectual and political leaders out of the Soviet Union. The retired general requested German visas for these refugees so that they could travel to Berlin and offer their services to Hitler. As anxious to come to the German capital, Erkilet mentioned especially Ayas Ishaki, whom he described as the leading writer of the Volga-Ural Turks and Abdurrahman bin seyh Zeynullah, grand mufti of all Russian Muslims. These men would be expert at turning out propaganda broadsides for Hitler and, as foreign ministry records indicate, there was a Tatar printing press in Berlin ready to be put into service. Woermann approved subsidies to Turanian intellectuals, though there is no record of their receiving them. In any case, General Erkilet, who was invited to Germany as a guest of the government, did go to Berlin.[14]

In the meantime, the Wilhelmstrasse, at Ribbentrop's express direction, set up a special agency to deal with the Turanian problem under Otto Werner von Hentig, a Middle Eastern expert and a notorious espionage agent in that area during the First World War. Hentig in turn called for a

13. Woermann to Weizsäcker, 26 September 1941, A.A. 691/897. (*DGFP*, 13:571–75). Krecker, *Deutschland und die Türkei*, pp. 212–15.

14. Woermann to Ribbentrop, 26 September 1941, A.A. 217/897; Erkilet to Woermann, 11 October 1941, A.A. 694/no number; Killinger to Foreign Ministry, 4 November 1941, A.A. 217/3580.

positive and forward-moving policy. He wanted to begin with frequent indoctrination broadcasts to Muslim war prisoners in German camps. German planes would be detailed to drop propaganda leaflets over Turanian Russia. In time, specially indoctrinated and equipped Muslim prisoners of war would be released by the Germans to be smuggled over the Soviet frontier for espionage and subversion. For all Muslim war prisoners, Hentig wanted to increase the food ration, and he would have selected internees of obvious talent to staff an elite Muslim officer corps to govern the independent Turanian states that a Nazi victory over the Soviet Union could be expected to create. Papen agreed with Hentig's ideas and warmly endorsed Nuri Paşa, whose vigor and enthusiasm he commended, for chief camp lecturer and propaganda coordinator.

The ambassador cautioned only that prudence and circumspection be used when dealing with Foreign Minister Saracoğlu. Saracoğlu had told Papen that he always handled all the Pan-Turanians with studied restraint. He did not really object to their goals, but he was afraid that if Stalin ever learned of any traffic between the Pan-Turanians and Ankara's officialdom, he might retaliate by liquidating all the Turanians in the Soviet Union. As he confided to the German envoy, Saracoğlu did not want that on his conscience. Nor, he admitted, could he expect to retain control of the Turkish foreign ministry if Moscow took umbrage at his policy. Papen believed Saracoğlu's qualms were genuine and, at any rate, thought it vital to maintain the Turkish minister in power to bring his country into the war on the Axis side and to arbitrate a peace between the Reich and Britain.[15]

The general European situation again seemed to favor a Turkish declaration for the Axis. While the Turks were probing the Wilhelmstrasse about its future policy in Soviet Russia, they were also objecting in London to British policy in the eastern Mediterranean. One of their long-standing concerns in that region was the postwar disposition of the island of Cyprus. The Turks were willing to tolerate British

15. Woermann to Ribbentrop, 6 November 1941, A.A. 691/no number; Hentig to Woermann, 6 November 1941, A.A. 63/959 Anlage 4; Woermann to Weizsäcker, 28 October 1941, A.A. 691/920 (*DGFP*, 13:707); Papen to Woermann, 31 October 1941, A.A. 691/no number.

control of Cyprus, although perhaps not indefinitely. For the sake of the Turkish minority, however, they would never acquiesce in the transfer of the island to Greece. As will be remembered, Greek patriots on Cyprus, inflamed by Greece's heroic resistance to Italian aggression, were calling for just such a union. But Britain, anxious to postpone a quarrel between her Greek and Turkish allies, managed to bring the Cypriot zealots under restraint in early 1941. Yet all parties to this dispute—Turks, Greeks, and Englishmen—knew that this was only a stopgap solution. In March 1941, Anthony Eden, visiting Cyprus to confer with Saracoğlu, was accorded a rather cool reception by the local people, but these same stolid crowds turned Saracoğlu's every appearance into a noisy triumph. The Cypriot Turks, the foreign secretary did not doubt, were a minority but assuredly a compromisingly vociferous one. The Greek government, not yet vanquished by the German army, quickly reacted to these pro-Turkish demonstrations. In Athens, the prime minister, Alexander Koryzis, asked Eden point-blank to promise to cede Cyprus to Greece after the war. Eden informed him that that was not the moment to discuss such a question. Koryzis committed suicide in the wake of his country's defeat, but his successors were not to be put off about Cyprus, and on 29 September 1941, the Greek ambassador left at the Foreign Office, without comment, an *aide-mémoire* demanding Cyprus, the Dodecanese islands, and southern Albania for his country as part of the peace settlement. The Foreign Office disregarded the entire *aide-mémoire*.[16]

It was Koryzis's successor as prime minister, Emmanuel Tsouderos, who determined to revive the Cyprus question and maneuver the British government into a solution favorable to Greece. On 15 November 1941, at a luncheon in London for the Greek community-in-exile, Tsouderos made a speech reviewing the course of the war in the Balkans. He excoriated not only the Italian and German invaders but also their allies the Bulgarians, whom Tsouderos accused of theft and the most sadistic varieties of murder. Greece, he said, was going through "one of the most dreadful periods of her history." But he did not doubt her ultimate victory

16. *Mémoire* by Dixon to Eden, 25 November 1941, P.R.O., F.O. 371/R10112/198/19. Anthony Eden, *The Reckoning: The Memoirs of Anthony Eden, Earl of Avon*, pp. 260–61, 286–87.

over Fascism and barbarism, which she would oppose with the same heroic qualities that had expelled the Turks from the Greek homeland one hundred and fifty years before. This remark, Tsouderos later protested, was not intended to offend Ankara, although the Turks immediately interpreted it as a calculated insult. Still worse, however, was the conclusion of the prime minister's speech, wherein Tsouderos indulged in some very poetic and compromising language. Though Greece was ravaged and bleeding now, he envisaged her tattered and exhausted but still striding toward a prosperous postwar future:

> Dressed in white and with the nimbus of martyrdom round her head, she is not alone; she is followed by her beloved united daughters. One easily knows them from their costumes. Look! there is the woman of Peloponese, the woman of the Dodecanese, the woman of Yanina, the woman of Crete, the woman of Cyprus, the woman of North Epirus, . . . adorned with laurels they follow their mother, going forwards towards victory that will unite them again in peace.

The BBC, apparently without Foreign Office clearance, summarized Tsouderos's remarks as visualizing "a Greece pale but glorious, building up her ruined cities and villages, united and great, and having at her side Northern Epirus, the Dodecanese and Cyprus." When the Cypriot press repeated the British broadcast, it simply said that Tsouderos called for a great Greece, including northern Epirus, the Dodecanese, Macedonia, and Cyprus.[17] The Turks on Cyprus and the İnönü government in Ankara bristled with resentment and fully believed that Britain endorsed the Tsouderos address, particularly because members of the Foreign Office attended the luncheon. As the Turkish Cypriot newspaper *Soz* editorialized on 19 November 1941, "these words have produced great sorrow and anxiety in Turkish circles, and the British government's denial in this respect is awaited with great impatience."[18] Anthony

17. The original text of the Tsouderos speech, together with the BBC and Cypriot variations upon it, are found in The Greek Prime Minister to the Secretary of State, 26 November 1941, P.R.O., F.O. 371/ R10112/198/19.

18. Moyne to Eden, 24 November 1941, P.R.O., F.O. 371/R10171/ 198/19.

Eden was quick to try to allay Turkish anger. On the afternoon of 25 November 1941, he summoned Emmanuel Tsouderos to his offices, roundly criticized his speech as unstatesmanly, and sternly warned him never to refer to the Cyprus issue publicly again. The Greek leader profusely apologized for any inadvertent misunderstanding he had created, but Eden was convinced that his language, however veiled and allegorical, was carefully calculated. The Foreign Office issued a denial that negotiations to cede Cyprus to Athens after the war were under way, but the Greeks were not deterred from future intrigues, nor were the Turks disabused of their suspicion that an Anglo-Greek plot to deprive them of supremacy in the eastern Mediterranean was being secretly hatched. The colonial secretary, Lord Moyne, feared that at the worst Greek partisan groups might stage a revolution against the British authorities on Cyprus. At the very least, he feared, "the Germans are bound to make capital out of Mr. Tsouderos's unfortunate indiscretion about Cyprus and our irritable dementi."[19]

Lord Moyne proved quite right about the German reaction, at least as far as Franz von Papen was concerned. As early as August 1941, Numan Menemencioğlu told Knatchbull-Hugessen that reliable neutral sources were reporting that Hitler himself had designated the Reich's ambassador to make proposals for a separate Anglo-German peace.[20] In October, when Papen was in Berlin to advise on the reception of Nuri Paşa, British intelligence discovered that he had met with a group of anti-Nazi leaders to propound the bases of an understanding with London. Besides Papen, the conspirators were said to include the banker, Hjalmar Schacht; the chief of the general staff, Franz Halder; and the marshals Bock, Falkenhausen, and Blaskowitz. Several high dignitaries of the Roman Catholic church were also thought to be behind the peace move, but the British report does not reveal their names. Hitler was described as using this Berlin circle as his puppets to negotiate peace with Britain; Hitler supposedly

19. Foreign Office Minute, 5 December 1941, P.R.O., F.O. 371/R10334/117/22. Foreign Office Minute, 5 December 1941, P.R.O., F.O. 371/R10335/534/90. For additional British views of Tsouderos's policy, see Foreign Office Minute, 5 December 1941, P.R.O., F.O. 371/R10332/198/19.

20. Knatchbull-Hugessen to Foreign Office, 17 August 1941, P.R.O., F.O. 371/C9236/18/18.

desired peace but knew Britain would never accept it at his hands.[21] As soon as Papen returned to Ankara, he gave an interview to a Spanish journalist named Masoliver, who worked for a Barcelona newspaper, *Vanguardia*, to publicize his ideas. He began by telling the Spaniard that the German army was finding the struggle with Russia tougher than expected but was still confident of final victory. Nevertheless, it was in the interests of all humanity to end this exhausting quarrel, and Germany was ready to bargain. If Britain remained adamant against discussion, the Turks, who wanted peace, would force the discussion by entering the war against her. Whatever Britain's decision, German policy favored a strong, heavily armed Turkey, capable of exercising supreme influence in Iraq, Syria, and Iran. Unless Britain fought on doggedly, Germany had no intention of forcing the British out of Egypt, but she must be willing to share primacy in the Mediterranean with Turkey and Spain in the future.[22]

Almost immediately the Wilhelmstrasse denied that Papen had ever given an interview to any Spanish journalist, though Masoliver produced notes of his conversation that the German envoy had read and signed. But the German foreign ministry did not repudiate, point by point, the contents of the Masoliver talks, nor did it recall Papen, as it would have done if the encounter between the Spaniard and the ambassador had been completely unauthorized.[23] Berlin's bewildering behavior seems rather to have been due to the reaction in Spain, whose postwar position, according to Papen, was to be aggrandized. Franco's government was already under heavy Allied criticism for its pro-Axis stance, and the caudillo had no wish to allow the argument to deteriorate into a war. Germany's démenti on the Masoliver interview was probably intended to insure Spain's continued neutrality.[24] It was certainly not issued at the behest of Turkey, which refused Knatchbull-Hugessen's suggestion that the

21. Foreign Office Minute, 25 October 1941, P.R.O., F.O. 371/C11901/324/18.

22. Knatchbull-Hugessen to Foreign Office, 16 November 1941, P.R.O., F.O. 371/R9876/236/44.

23. Ribbentrop's mild rebuke to Papen can be read in Ribbentrop to Papen, 18 November 1941, A.A. 217/1287, and 19 November 1941, A.A. 217/1294; Papen to Ribbentrop, 19 November 1941, A.A. 217/1488.

24. Polish Embassy, Ankara, to Knatchbull-Hugessen, 28 November 1941, P.R.O., F.O. 371/R10387/236/44.

İnönü government request Papen's recall.[25] Finally, the German démenti was not meant to seriously impede Papen's overtures to the British. The ambassador contacted them again in December 1941, in Cairo, using a "highly reliable" courtier close to King Farouk. Again he threatened that Turkey would declare war unless discussions on his peace proposals, presented on this occasion in greater detail, were opened at once. According to the Egyptian informant, Britain must accept equitable division of Europe's raw materials; a Polish-Czechoslovak buffer state between Germany and Russia; revision of the Versailles treaty to conform to racial aspirations; abolition of all mandates; and the restoration of the former German colonies. Papen asserted that Hitler favored Egyptian independence but would not press for it or for the creation of an Arab federation. The Führer would ignore Italy's hope for overseas expansion. He had found Il Duce's army worthless and thought Mussolini had no penchant for colonial administration. Germany hoped to settle many of the Italian holdings on the Turkish Republic.[26]

These were generous terms and might have brought Turkey into the war. But they assumed that the rapid momentum of the German invasion of Russia would be maintained, which it was not, and they made no allowance for difficulties with the Soviet Turanians themselves. By the beginning of 1942, it became apparent that the Pan-Turanian sentiments propounded in the Turkish Republic were not universally shared by Turks in other countries. As previously remarked, many Russian Turks wanted to escape Soviet dictatorship, but by no means all saw their salvation in the Kemalist republic. German intelligence was disturbed to learn of a sizable group of Turanians living near the Soviet-Iranian frontier who detested Communism, but rejected modern Turkey at the same time. These people criticized Kemal Atatürk because he had disestablished the caliphate and they dismissed the Anatolian Turks as a disreputable hybrid of Albanians, Circassians, and Arabs—"Levantines" they derisively called them.

On the other hand, this Turanian faction fancied itself as

25. Knatchbull-Hugessen to Foreign Office, 21 November 1941, P.R.O., F.O. 371/R9990/236/44.

26. British Embassy, Washington, to Foreign Office, 10 December 1941, P.R.O., F.O. 371/C48/48/18.

racially pure and most closely akin to the original stock of the Ottoman invaders who came to Europe in the fourteenth century. Their leader and spokesman was Mehmet Emin Resulsade, a lifelong revolutionary, a former Menshevik, and a onetime friend of Joseph Stalin. Resulsade was now working for the creation of a "Greater Azerbaijan" to include territory then under the jurisdiction of the Soviets and of the Iranian shah. Resulsade proclaimed a program of indivisible independence for his new state, but he admitted that it would need foreign money and advice in its fledgling years. He was willing to receive aid from Germany and Turkey, although not exclusively, and intended to negotiate with all friendly powers. Under no circumstances, however, was he prepared to lease military bases in return for material assistance, a concession that the Germans regarded as a sine qua non for further encouragement.[27]

The Azerbaijan Turanians were the most outspoken in their anti-Turkish sentiments, but they were not alone in regarding Ankara ambivalently. The Germans heard murmurs of dissent from Georgia and Armenia, too. The Georgians informed German contacts that they had no confidence in the combat prowess of the Turkish army. It might occupy Georgia for a while but could not hold it permanently against a superior rival, particularly a resurgent Soviet Union. The Soviets might return and deal summarily with any of their former subjects who had wavered in their allegiance. The Georgians therefore preferred, or so the German reports alleged, occupation by the Wehrmacht. It would bring order and perhaps prosperity, which the Georgians were unwilling to predict of a Turkish restoration. Some Georgians even suggested offering their country to a succession of German field marshals, who would rule it as a kind of proconsular honorarium at the end of their military careers.

Some Armenians, too, desired that their country be assigned to direct German administration. The Germans had been in contact with the Armenian Revolutionary Federa-

27. Tippelskirch to Hentig, 28 January 1942, A.A. 691/VAA293. Resulsade had earlier worked for Germany's enemy, Marshal Józef Piłsudski of Poland. Resulsade was a member of the Promethean League, which the marshal used for anti-Soviet activities. On Resulsade, see Charles Warren Hostler, *Turkism and the Soviets: The Turks of the World and their Political Objectives*, pp. 172–73, 183, 189.

tion, the *Dashnagtzoutiun*, since spring 1940, when the Wehrmacht occupied Paris. Among the many Armenian conspirators living in the French capital were "generals" Dro and Papasian, guerrilla fighters who immediately offered their services to Germany in hopes of persuading Berlin not to sell out their country to the Turks in exchange for an alliance with Ankara. The Russian Armenians had no easy lot under Stalin, but it was no worse than what their kinsmen had suffered under the Young Turks during the First World War. Estimates vary, but approximately three-quarters of a million Armenians were liquidated by the sultan's government for "security reasons." Dro, Papasian, and their expatriate countrymen did not want to risk a recurrence of that slaughter and saw a clear threat of it in the rise of Pan-Turanianism. They insisted on complete independence from Turkey, guaranteed by the Axis new order. These Armenians would agree to join a Caucasian federation of which Turkey was a member, but never if Turkey were its head. Hentig, as chief consultant in Turanian affairs, found the *Dashnagtzoutiun*'s goals quite adaptable to the long-range aims of German policy. To Hentig, it was immaterial whether Azerbaijan and Georgia were consigned to Turkish control, but he felt strongly that Armenia should be given a special status. Armenia should not be surrendered to the Turks, however clamant Ankara's demands for it might become, but should be organized by the Germans as a buffer state against the Soviet Union. Hentig regarded the Armenians as a specially gifted people. He credited them with great intelligence, wide international connections, and a resilient toughness. Of all the Caucasian peoples, he recommended the Armenians most confidently for recruitment into the German ranks. They could be turned into first-rate partisan fighters whom, Hentig predicted, the Soviets would fear.[28]

After considering all this evidence, the German foreign ministry decided that, despite its brief flirtation with Pan-Turanianism, it could not continue to encourage Turkey's territorial ambitions in conquered Russia. Ribbentrop's office still recommended that Crimea might be thrown to Ankara as a sop, but any larger award would carry the risk of civil war between Turkey and her Caucasian kinsmen. The Wilhelmstrasse now found even the word *Turanianism*

28. Hentig to Woermann, 20 January 1942, A.A. 691/VAA 293.

objectionable. When referring to Turanian matters, German officials were henceforth instructed to use the term *Timorism* or *Daghestanism*. The first derived from a medieval Asian conqueror, and the second from the local name of a Russian province. The use of neither term gave any encouragement to the Turks, and this was exactly the effect the foreign ministry intended. The label *Turanian* was not to be applied to any of the three *Turkic* legions that the Wehrmacht considered manning with Russian Muslim prisoners of war. Instead, they would be named the *Tartar*, *Caucasian*, and *Georgian* legions. A fourth unit would be known as the *Armenian Brigade*. Hentig claimed to Woermann that the Turkish embassy in Berlin approved this nomenclature, but in fact Ambassador Gerede entered a protest and suggested that *Turkestan* might have been substituted for the four alternatives preferred by the Germans. The Turkish embassy argued that *Turkestan* was a traditional geographical term with no objectionable political overtones. But Hentig did not agree.[29]

Finally, German Pan-Turanian policy was muddled by the interference of the Ostministerium, specially organized to supervise the civilian population of conquered Russia and led by the Nazi party ideologue Alfred Rosenberg. Between Rosenberg and the foreign ministry, a jurisdictional conflict quickly developed. Generally speaking, the foreign ministry was more lenient than Rosenberg in its attitude toward the Turkic and non-Russian inhabitants of the Soviet Union. By the beginning of 1942, the Wehrmacht had taken about fifty-five thousand of these people prisoners and was preparing plans to use a select fifty-six hundred for intelligence work. But Rosenberg, who maintained that the Führer had made him solely responsible for the civilian administration of occupied Russia, balked at the army's plan, to which Ribbentrop gave tentative approval, and stood out for uniformly harsh treatment of all war prisoners. Many Kazakhs, Kirgizhians, Tatars, and Uzbeks were provisionally interned in the Ukraine, but it was planned to remove them because the climate was too cold. A group of about fifty Uzbeks petitioned Hitler personally to relocate them in a warmer climate, and the foreign ministry agreed to some more comfortable confinement. But Rosenberg held up the transfers, and many

29. Hentig to Woermann, 17 January 1942, A.A. 691/Pol. 1M.3713.

of these men died of pulmonary diseases. Later Rosenberg's department seems to have regretted its rigorous policy, and it began to pay the travel expenses and subsidize the education of some Turanians in Berlin. However, the Turkish government had heard about the fate of the Uzbeks and was not mollified by the educational gratuities that Berlin offered to the survivors of the earlier, harsh policy. It made the strongest protests to the Reich embassy in Ankara.[30]

The Bomb Plot of 24 February 1942 and Its Background

The İnönü ministry blamed Papen for Germany's callous treatment of the Turanians, though the record shows that the German ambassador had done much to shield the Turks from the full visitation of Hitler's and Ribbentrop's wrath. Papen was clearly pro-Turkish, though because of the circumstances described above he could not be pro-Turanian. The Turanian problem was making his office increasingly uncomfortable. The Turks were also annoyed that Britain had made no move to accept Papen's peace program or to invite Turkey to mediate a settlement based upon it. The ambassador deplored the draconian treatment of Turkish prisoners in German compounds, but he was unable to persuade Berlin to alleviate it. Instead, the Wilhelmstrasse's propaganda bureau only recommended that Papen start a whispering campaign to insinuate that, whatever the short-comings of German internment, Russian behavior was even worse. Soviet troops, it was to be asserted, were everywhere exterminating Turkish peoples near their lines. Sometimes, Papen was told to say, these mass murders would be preceded by kangaroo trials in which the Soviets would produce Jewish informers against the Turkish Muslim defendants.

The ambassador made little if any use of these propaganda directives. Instead, they were the occasion of a serious disagreement between Papen and the foreign ministry over how to handle Turkish public opinion. Contrary to Woermann's instructions, he refused to extol the blessings of Nazi rule in occupied Russia. Though the Stalinist regime was hardly guiltless of atrocities, Papen privately admitted as many crimes could be charged to the German side, and, he insisted, the Turks knew it. They had well organized missions

---

30. Hentig to Woermann, 28 January 1942, A.A. 691/no number.

abroad, too alert and perceptive to believe the kind of propaganda nonsense Berlin wanted its ambassador to disseminate in Ankara. Papen adamantly declined to propound the thesis that Franklin Roosevelt was mainly responsible for the Second World War and for prolonging it by his opposition to a negotiated peace. He argued that the Turkish leadership was too sophisticated to swallow any of this. He advised his superiors to admit Hitler's responsibility in the breakdown of international relations, though they could convincingly stress the provocations that the Versailles treaty offered the Fürher. They should also point out that Britain was letting her colonial dependents sustain some of the heaviest war casualties while she delayed Indian independence and repressed the legitimate demands of Egyptian nationalists. The Turks, he stressed, were interested in the political future of these Muslim peoples, not in boasts about the latest Wehrmacht heroics in France or Norway. Above all, the Turks should not be condescended to.[31]

This warning came too late, went unregarded in Berlin, and made Papen more unpopular than ever with the more rabid Nazi leaders. Their dislike of Papen must be borne in mind in view of the assassination attempt against him in late February. Moreover, Papen's admonitions could not avert a new quarrel between the Italians and Turks, which complicated the increasingly strained relations between Turkey and Germany. The question at issue between Rome and Ankara, rankling for about six months prior to February 1942, was the future of Yugoslavia and Albania in the Axis postwar reconstruction of Europe. Though he was sustaining heavy defeats in North and East Africa, Mussolini was confidently planning to convert Albania and the Yugoslav province of Croatia into hereditary possessions of the Italian crown prince. Mussolini had succeeded in forcing the Croatians to sign a customs union with Italy, but the rest of his scheme received only tepid encouragement from the Germans and provoked local Croatian political leaders to outright opposition. Chief among these leaders was the collaborationist Ante Pavelitsch, who admitted to Weizsäcker that he could not resist Il Duce militarily but, on the other hand, would be shot down by one of his own countrymen if he ac-

31. Braunstum to Ankara Embassy, 7 January 1942, A.A. 4721/72; Woermann to Papen, 14 February 1942, A.A. 2554/918.

ceded to any more demands from Rome. He begged for Berlin's backing, but the German authorities felt that their hands were tied. They did not want to abet Mussolini's chimerical ambitions in the western Balkans, but they were equally loathe to rebuff their ally publicly.

Turkish leaders had no such qualms. They of course opposed any long-term Italian occupation of either Croatia or Albania and argued that the Germans need not tolerate it, because neither area was strategically vital to the ultimate victory of the Axis. The Turks intimated that they were prepared to provide a neutral police force to maintain order in Croatia and Albania and so help the Germans to avoid an overt clash of interests with Il Duce's government. But the Wilhelmstrasse rejected Ankara's suggestion. It claimed that Croatia and Albania were honeycombed with dangerous Communist cells. Only the sternest military repression could eradicate them, and nobody in Berlin was prepared to turn the job over to the Turks. However, Foreign Minister Saracoğlu and his assistant Menemencioğlu depicted this Communist danger as exaggerated or nonexistent and persisted in meddling in Balkan affairs. Weizsäcker then had Papen remind them that any Turkish territorial claims in the Balkans would only induce the Soviet Union to raise compensatory demands along its frontiers with the Turkish Republic.[32]

This was a hard truth, but coming close upon the disappointment of their Turanian ambitions, the Turks would not accept it with silent resignation. They vented their spleen on Papen. When some Italian newspapers ridiculed the İnönü ministry, and one, *Le Monde Arabe*, published in French, even described Turkey as a "small nation" that should be wiped from the map, the Ankara police clamped down on the Arab journalists who worked for Papen's embassy. The police deported three Arabs employed by the German news service (DNB). Another court action was begun against Margarete Kruse, a German-born reporter for the DNB, who was reputed to be the chief coordinator of all Arab confidential informers in the pay of the Reich's Ankara embassy. When Papen protested, the Turkish foreign ministry cited British pressure to excuse its actions, but the real motive was long-smoldering Turkish resentment against the

32. Papen to Ribbentrop, 28 February 1942, A.A. 51/324; Weizsäcker to Papen, 4 March 1942, A.A. 51/131.

Arab nationalists, whose territorial ambitions Germany and Italy still seemed to be patronizing, or at least had not definitively repudiated, as they had all but done with the Turanian and Balkan dreams of the Turks. The Ankara government had not ceased to complain to Berlin and Rome for allowing the grand mufti to shuttle at will between those two cities, and the Turks took real pleasure in expelling the grand mufti's nephew from their country, though Papen tried to hold up the eviction. Consequently, Papen found relations between himself and Saracoğlu and Menemencioğlu becoming increasingly cool and access to their offices harder to obtain. In better moods, these Turks had often described him as "the last knight of the German Empire." Now they frequently declined to talk to him.[33]

Good relations with the Turkish government had never been more important than at the beginning of 1942, because at that time Germany's steadily depleting stockpile of raw materials was starting to worry the ambassador and his colleagues. Turkey produced sixteen percent of the world's chromite, from which was processed chromium, an alloy used to make high-grade steel. In 1940, the British government negotiated a clever agreement, contracting to receive from the Turks fifty thousand tons of chromite in 1941 and again in 1942, along with some undesirable, perishable agricultural produce, on condition that no chrome would go to the Germans during that time. The Reich felt the chromite pinch immediately, but Papen's embassy looked forward to negotiating an end to the British monopoly in late 1941 or early 1942. Even though the monopoly was damaging to the Germans, it was not entirely satisfactory to the Allies. The Turks put an outrageously high valuation on their agricultural exports and insinuated that the British would not trade the best heavy industrial equipment to Turkey for fear that she might become economically independent of the Western Powers after the war. The Americans sympathized to some extent with these Turkish charges, but Secretary of State Cordell Hull thought that, on the whole, Turkey was always an extortionate bargainer where her chromite was concerned.

---

33. Jenke to Foreign Ministry, 22 January 1942, A.A. 4723/112; Seiler to Ankara Embassy, 3 February 1942, A.A. 4723/41; Braunstum to Ankara Embassy, 3 February 1942, A.A. 4723/194. Papen to Foreign Ministry, 2 February 1942, A.A. 51/167.

Both London and Washington roundly criticized Turkey's trading procedures, and therefore it was not altogether surprising that Ankara signed with Berlin a formal agreement to resume chromite trading, dated 9 October 1941.[34] As had been expected, the Turks tied the sale of chromite to acceptance by Germany of many less desirable farm commodities that were glutting the Anatolian market. For this reason, the German foreign ministry was not entirely satisfied with the October accord and expected to negotiate the elimination of the objectionable provisos as soon as possible. In the meantime, Papen was not willing to wait until the beginning of 1943, when the first chromite consignments for Germany would be shipped, and, since he could not bargain directly with Saracoğlu and Menemencioğlu, decided to initiate schemes to get illegal private consignments of chromite out of Turkey. In the end, the German government gained nothing by this surreptitious approach, but to Papen's discomfiture, the Turks found out about it.[35]

Other than Papen, Kurt Zimmermann, a German exporter with Middle Eastern contacts, was the chief proponent of a private, piecemeal approach to the solution of the chromite shortage. On the basis of his own travels throughout Turkey, he advised Berlin that most Turkish mining concerns did not support the export monopoly that their government had conceded to Britain in 1940. The local producers wanted a return to a free market, especially if they could convince the Germans to employ native Turks to bid for the chromite and arrange for its packing and shipment. Zimmermann's Turkish contact was Satvet Lütfü Tozan, who agreed to head the cooperating syndicate and proposed a delivery route starting at Bursa, going through the Straits, and ending in Salonika, whence German carriers would take the chromite to the Reich. Zimmermann and Tozan agreed that the ore

34. Resumés of these commercial controversies are found in Kennedy to Hull, 22 June 1940, *FRUS, 1940*, vol. 3, pp. 944–45; Hull to MacMurray, 28 August 1940, *FRUS, 1940*, vol. 3, p. 950; Hull to MacMurray, 21 September 1940, *FRUS 1940*, vol. 3, p. 951; MacMurray to Hull, 15 October 1940, *FRUS, 1940*, vol. 3, p. 957; Steinhardt to Hull, 6 March 1942, *FRUS, 1942*, vol. 4, pp. 680–81; Matthews to Hull, 24 March 1942, *FRUS, 1942*, vol. 4, pp. 688–89. See also Robert E. Sherwood, *Roosevelt and Hopkins: An Intimate History*, p. 658. Weisband, *Turkish Foreign Policy*, pp. 101–5.

35. Papen to Foreign Ministry, 7 August 1941, A.A. 2554/2778. Krecker, *Deutschland und die Türkei*, pp. 179–81.

could be camouflaged enough to bring it past Turkish inspection in the Dardanelles, and Tozan even intimated that
some highly placed Ankara officials were ready to ignore rumors of this illicit traffic. What the Turks most wanted, Tozan
contended, was not to honor their chromite contract with
Britain but instead to procure German nails, screws, rail-
road tracks, and locomotive equipment, materials the British
were niggardly in supplying them. Turkey needed these
items as desperately as Germany needed the ore. Some local
Wehrmacht commanders in Greece believed in Zimmermann's proposals enough to finance his reconnaissance tours
of Turkey with German army funds. The skeptical foreign
ministry, persuaded by Papen, allowed Zimmermann to ply
his contacts with Tozan, but the Turkish police intercepted
the German businessman on one of his trips. He was expelled from Turkey, and Papen was held accountable.[36]

Within a fortnight, the Turkish ministers raised even more
serious grievances with the German envoy. From their London embassy, they had heard rumors that Germany was
fundamentally reevaluating her Middle Eastern policy. Previously, the Turks had assumed that Hitler would award
them territorial additions in exchange for their alliance.
Now they heard Hitler had changed his mind in favor of
direct German occupation of certain strategical positions in
Iraq and on the Persian Gulf. Rauf Orbay, the Turkish ambassador in London, who had his information from Anthony
Eden, thought the Führer was considering this new policy
as a reaction to the whirlwind of Japanese expansion in
eastern Asia. German documents show, and Eden correctly
assumed, that Berlin was awed by Japan's smashing success
at Pearl Harbor and then both exhilarated and frightened
by the rapid Japanese advance over Singapore, Sumatra, and
Borneo. German foreign ministry experts began to speculate
that Japan might achieve permanent superiority in the
Arabian Sea and the Indian Ocean, depriving the Reich of
naval bases in both areas. Such developments were not to
Hitler's liking, but he did not trust Turkish or Arab assistance to stem the Japanese tide. Hitler spoke of introducing
not only German colonists but also Scandinavian collabora-
tionists into the Middle Eastern area. Their presence would

36. Woermann to Ribbentrop, 21 January 1942, A.A. 1369/no number.

draw a western limit to Japan's Greater East Asian Co-Prosperity Sphere.[37]

This settlement program was of course never carried out, and the Germans probably overestimated Japan's military and industrial capacity to extend her hegemony. But the British government apparently shared Hitler's apprehensions, if Orbay's account of Eden's remarks can be accepted as accurate. Throughout the late winter and early spring of 1942, the foreign secretary returned to the threat of Japanese strategy with the Turkish diplomat. Eden professed to expect a Japanese landing in the Bay of Bengal, a withering aerial bombardment of Ceylon, and, unless the American Navy could be persuaded to start a diversionary action in the Pacific, recalling the Japanese fleet to its home waters, a British retreat to the port of Muscat on the Gulf of Oman. The Indian army would stage a holding action at Muscat, but Eden appeared doubtful of its success and did not exclude as a possibility the surrender of Aden, Yemen, and Hadhramaut to the Japanese.[38] This was a very glum assessment of Britain's situation, but it might not have been a completely truthful one. Eden might have deliberately planted these pessimistic remarks with Orbay for conveyance to the Germans. A seasoned negotiator, the Englishman could well expect them to create anxiety in Germany and to unsettle German relations with the nations of the Middle East, which the Axis new order had never definitively assigned to either the German or the Japanese sphere of influence.

Whether valid or feigned, Eden's forecast could not have drawn a prompter response from Saracoğlu. He summoned Papen and declared that he too thought the British were finished in the Far East. They would be compelled to forfeit everything east of the Burmese-Indian frontier to the Japanese emperor. However, in that case, Saracoğlu predicted that Britain would hold on more tightly to her remnants of empire in Iraq and Egypt. Both countries had achieved a measure of independence before the war, but, he suspected, in a negotiated peace with the Axis, Britain would be allowed to reduce them from semiautonomy to total subju-

37. Woermann to Papen, 14 February 1942, A.A. 1369/7.
38. Papen to Foreign Ministry, 19 February and 24 April 1942, A.A. 2554/no numbers.

gation. It was not likely, the Turk now thought, that Germany would help Turkey to share, much less to supplant, Britain's old primacy in the Middle East. Papen discountenanced these qualms, but he could never entirely dispel them.[39]

The implications of Japanese imperialism were still under discussion when the German ambassador was almost assassinated on 24 February 1942. On that morning, at about ten o'clock, a bomb exploded behind Papen and his wife as they walked to work along Ankara's main boulevard. The couple was knocked to the ground and their clothing torn, but they were not otherwise injured. A woman who was standing near them was killed by the explosion, and of the assassin, who seems to have set off his device while perched in a tree, nothing remained but one of his shoes. The front wall of an adjacent apartment house, in which members of the British embassy staff lived, was blown in. Within minutes, Turkish police were running all over the boulevard, and before the hour was up, both Saracoğlu and Menemencioğlu called on Papen to express their regrets and assert no Turk was involved in the crime. President İnönü's wife also spent several hours with Frau von Papen trying to calm her down. The Turkish president immediately offered to call in foreign police to work with his own investigators until all the conspirators were hunted down and the innocence of Turkey irrefutably demonstrated.[40]

All this sympathetic efficiency puzzled Papen, because at first he had not even remotely doubted the innocence of the Turks. Ribbentrop also found the Turkish government excessively solicitous. He omitted congratulating Papen on his escape but recalled him to Berlin with the observation that the Turks' Pan-Turanian aspirations were probably at the root of the recent violence.[41] Gerede, the Turkish ambassador in Berlin, hardly concerned himself with the assassination attempt at all. On his first visit to Weizsäcker after the explosion in Ankara, he made only the most perfunctory inquiry about Papen's health and then launched

39. Papen to Ribbentrop, 22 February 1942, A.A. 51/206.
40. Papen to Ribbentrop, 24 February 1942, A.A. 51/288, and 25 February 1942, A.A. 51/289.
41. Papen to Ribbentrop, 26 February 1942, A.A. 51/319; Ribbentrop to Papen, 24 February 1942, A.A. 51/342.

into an attack on Nazi policy toward Bulgaria. Gerede complained that he had heard the Germans were using Bulgarian units in the Russian campaign, while they refused to allow the Turks to serve as a neutral police force in Croatia and Albania. Could Germany be planning, Gerede asked, to repay Bulgiria by extending her frontiers at the expense of neighboring Turkey? Weizsäcker rejected Gerede's assumptions.[42]

Only four days after the bomb exploded, the Turks claimed to have established the assassin's identity. Despite their first protestations, the assassin turned out to be a Turk, after all. His name was given as Omer Tokat, a Turkish citizen though born in Yugoslav Macedonia. According to the police, Tokat was one of a gang recruited by the Russians to kill not only Papen but also Ribbentrop. It was alleged that Tokat and his associates had been taught marksmanship and demolition techniques by Soviet experts in the basement of the Russian consulate in İstanbul. However, the Turks would not permit any member of the German embassy staff to listen to the court depositions or to read the court stenographer's transcripts. Papen got all of his information from a police declaration. Meanwhile, the Turkish foreign ministry ordered the Soviet consulate in İstanbul surrounded by a whole infantry battalion. The entire consulate staff, over the protests of the Soviet ambassador, surrendered to the besieging soldiers. After interrogation of the consulate personnel, the Turkish police satisfied themselves that they had apprehended a few accomplices in the bomb plot. But, Papen was regretfully informed, the ringleader had already escaped to Syria.[43]

On 10 March 1942, *Izvestia* circulated a version of the assassination attempt that made the Germans themselves responsible for the crime. The Soviet newspaper recalled that bombs seemed always to have played a prominent part in Papen's career. As a young diplomatic attaché during the First World War, he had been expelled from the United States after being implicated in a scheme to blow up American military hospitals. Now the Gestapo, or someone even higher in the German government, were giving the ambassa-

42. Weizsäcker to Ribbentrop, 26 February 1942, A.A. 51/118.
43. Papen to Ribbentrop, 28 February 1942, A.A. 51/323, 5 March 1942, A.A. 51/350, 6 March 1942, A.A. 51/351, and 11 March 1942, A.A. 51/374.

dor a taste of his own medicine. The Nazis, the Soviet account concluded, wanted a pretext to occupy Turkey, and Papen was chosen by his old enemies in Berlin as the most expendable *casus belli.* Ribbentrop immediately denied these Soviet charges, though they remain somewhat plausible, because the enmity between Papen and some of the Nazi party leadership was well known and long-standing. Yet, a few weeks after the assassination attempt, Woermann was writing to a colleague in the Wilhelmstrasse that Germany could on no account undertake the invasion of Turkey. Its terrain and the Wehrmacht's already overextended line of operations put such a venture out of the question.[44]

Hans Kroll, Papen's second-in-command, wrote the German rebuttal to the Soviet account. Kroll pointed out that Stalin had been pleading with the British and Americans to open up a second front in the west to relieve the German pressure on his own lines. When Churchill and Roosevelt did not accommodate the Soviet dictator, Stalin indicated his displeasure by recalling his ambassador to Britain, Ivan Maisky. But, Kroll argued, if the Soviets contrived Papen's murder, the German Reich would be obliged to invade Turkey to avenge the ambassador's death. Hitler would be compelled to transfer some of his troops from the Russian to the Turkish front; the strain on Stalinist forces would be reduced, and they would then be more likely to make some headway in the recovery of White Russia and the Ukraine.[45]

There were overtones of irony in both the Soviet and German explanations of the Ankara bomb plot. The Germans were accused of scheming to invade Turkey, while they privately knew their resources to be unequal to such an operation. The Russians, on the other hand, desperately wanted an end to the hammering still being given their forces by the Wehrmacht, but hardly at the cost of converting Turkey into a war zone whence the Red Army could be outflanked. Certainly the Soviet ambassador, Vinogradov, made frantic efforts to avert a break between his country and Turkey. Vinogradov turned up the name of "Wulff," a

44. Ribbentrop to Papen, 14 March 1942, A.A. 51/275; Woermann to ———— [probably Ribbentrop], 12 March 1942, A.A. 63/176.

45. Kroll to Foreign Ministry, 31 March 1942, A.A. 51/484. Krecker, *Deutschland und die Türkei,* pp. 202–3. Krecker accepts Kroll's analysis because, until 1944, the Soviets strenuously insisted on Turkish participation in the war.

Gestapo agent who supposedly gave orders to Omer Tokat and his accomplices. The Turkish police traced this lead to American intelligence operators on the staff of the United States' ambassador, Lawrence Steinhardt. Steinhardt, however, in an astonishing display of Allied disunity, declared the existence of Wulff to be mere hearsay and rebuked his Soviet colleague for attempting to use it as evidence.[46]

The humiliated Vinogradov might well have asked for his passports at this moment. Moreover, if the Turks genuinely suspected his guilt, it is odd that they never demanded his recall. Pierson Dixon, the Foreign Office expert who followed the Ankara revelations for Anthony Eden, wrote that probably neither the Soviets nor the Germans were behind the attempted assassination of Papen. Dixon thought that in surrounding the İstanbul consulate, the Turks staged "an unnecessarily provocative precaution" to deflect suspicion from themselves.[47] The Foreign Office could not comprehend Turkey's ultimate motives, but the Ankara explosion immediately set in motion a Russo-German peace move. Turkish diplomats, expecting such a peace to yield territorial advantages, had always urged it with words. Perhaps on 24 February 1942 a Turkish agent had attempted to urge it with bombs. Only Omer Tokat knew the truth, and his own bomb had reduced him to a mass of gore. The British and Germans always wondered how Tokat became his own victim. The Turkish police alleged that the assassin believed his bomb to contain a delaying mechanism that would enable him to make his escape.[48] But such a mechanism would have also enabled Papen to escape injury. The German ambassador dared not say so, but he could not have thought the Turkish police proceedings other than a transparent fraud.

A Separate Peace Probe

When a Turkish judge indicted two Soviet citizens for conspiracy to murder Papen, the chagrined Vinogradov

46. Steinhardt to Hull, 31 March 1942, *FRUS, 1942*, vol. 4, pp. 828–29.

47. Dixon to Sargent, 14 March 1942, P.R.O., F.O. 371/N1360/693/38.

48. Morgan to Foreign Office, 24 February 1942, P.R.O., F.O. 371/R1266/1266/44. Papen to Ribbentrop, 4 March 1942, A.A. 51/no number.

protested and demanded their extradition. The Turks refused him, went ahead with the trial, and sentenced the two
men to jail terms of twenty years apiece. The court also gave
two Turkish henchmen each ten years in jail. Papen com-
plimented the Turkish judiciary for their expeditiousness,
but privately he admitted that the verdicts did not reassure
him and that he was afraid of further attempts on his life.
Some newsmen in Damascus, where Turkish censorship
could not curb them, circulated stories that the German
ambassador had had a nervous breakdown and become a religious fanatic.[49] There is no reliable evidence, however, that
the bomb plot affected Papen's mind. Still, it had at least
shaken the convictions by which he had conducted his embassy to Ankara in the past. Papen continued to believe that
an allied Turkey was vital to Germany in her fight against
Britain and the Soviet Union. But after the assassination
attempt, he became more inclined to argue that the war
had gone on long enough and should be ended by negotiation. In the process of bargaining for terms, it might no
longer be advantageous for Germany to insist on the in-
violability of the Turkish frontiers, much less on their extension.

In this new frame of mind, Papen became the focus of
several peace maneuvers. To Ulrich von Hassell, the former
German ambassador in Rome and later a member of the opposition to Hitler, Papen claimed that the Führer himself
favored a separate peace with Russia and had commissioned
the Ankara embassy to work for it. Despite their differences,
Hitler, according to Papen, continued to describe Stalin as
a great man. Hassell did not accept his colleague's assurances
at face value, but he was convinced that Papen favored Hitler's deposition by a military clique and the reorganization
of the German government under some prominent generals.
Above all, Hassell thought Papen aspired to formulate the
diplomacy of these generals, whether as official foreign minister or as an expert behind-the-scenes. In Hassell's words,
Papen wanted "to take German foreign policy in hand."[50]

To that end, the ambassador endorsed a Soviet peace probe

49. Papen to Ribbentrop, 18 June 1942, A.A. 51/916; Clausner to
Kroll, 17 July 1942, A.A. 4724/no number.
50. Ulrich von Hassell, *The von Hassell Diaries, 1938–1944: The
Story of the Forces Against Hitler Inside Germany. . .* , pp. 208, 216–17.

in early March. In neutral Ankara, it was not uncommon for newspapermen from opposing sides to sit down together over a cup of Turkish coffee. On 9 March 1942, just such an encounter occurred between Paul Schmitz, a reporter for the German news agency Transozean, and a Soviet correspondent from Tass, Anatole Valuiskiy. Valuiskiy was intimately associated with Vinogradov's embassy, and so the German journalist carefully noted everything he had to say. The Russian asserted that Stalin was confident that the Red Army would clear the Soviet homeland of the German invader, but the Kremlin leadership was less certain that it could keep title to Poland and parts of the Balkan Peninsula after the war. Stalin expected an Anglo-American coalition to block his way west and reckoned that continuing full-scale mobilization would be necessary to overcome it. The Soviet dictator, according to Valuiskiy, was reluctant to strain the resources of his country much longer, especially if he were offered compensation in the Middle East.

That whole area, Stalin held, was ripe for Communism. In Iran, any notion of leadership or national resistance against Soviet infiltration had departed with the exiled shah. The British might continue to work the Iranian oil fields, but already they were troubled with mechanical failures and strikes, all engineered, Valuiskiy boasted, by Communist agitators. The same pattern of subversion, he predicted, would appear if the British ever tried to impose full-scale mobilization on India in the face of a Japanese attack. As for Turkey, Valuiskiy described the white-collar workers, the junior army officers, and even the common soldiers as fed up with İnönü's government and ready to follow a Communist summons to overthrow it. To accelerate the collapse of the İnönü regime, the Soviet Union would be prepared to reach a secret understanding with Germany, acknowledging Turkey to be part of Stalin's sphere of influence. In return, Stalin would repudiate his alliance with Britain; its chief recommendation had always been, in the Kremlin's view, to open up inroads for Communist agents in the Middle East.[51]

Papen quickly forwarded Schmitz's memorandum to Berlin, together with his personal opinion that this was not a

51. Memorandum by Schmitz, Ankara, 9 March 1942, A.A. 2554/Geh. Rs. 145.

private digression, but an authentic pronouncement of the Soviet government, originating with Vinogradov and sanctioned by Stalin. This dispatch was soon followed by others detailing Stalin's ambitions in Iran. The Russian leader was currently associated with the British in the provisional occupation of Teheran to prevent the city from being used as an Axis listening post. But neither the Allies nor the Axis doubted that the Soviets wanted to convert their provisional tenure in Iran into a permanent one. The Red Army was recruiting an occupationary force for Iran, largely composed of Polish prisoners of war who had been interned in the Soviet Union since 1939. About forty-two thousand Poles were designated for this assignment, and Gen. Władysław Sikorski, head of the Polish government-in-exile in London, had approved it on the understanding that his countrymen would get better clothing, larger rations, and eventual liberty to return to their homeland. But Stalin never defined these benefits in a formal agreement, nor did he accept Sikorski's suggestion that an Anglo-American team periodically inspect the welfare of the Poles. The Poles, being assembled in Tashkent for transport to Teheran, heard of the dictator's attitude and mutinied. The mutineers were quickly disposed of by Soviet firing squads, but Papen urged Berlin quickly to offer Stalin Iran by treaty, since it appeared he would have difficulty taking the country by force of arms.[52]

In the end, Stalin did not take Iran at all. In November 1943, with the governments of Britain and the United States, he solemnly affirmed the integrity and independence of the country. But before he yielded this declaration, he managed to despoil Iran of much of its grain crop and to form the Tudeh party under Soviet Communist auspices. Papen reported that Stalin's confident aggressiveness at Teheran had a paralyzing effect on the Turks. It deepened their anti-Communism, but to a level of numbness and pessimism that seemed to debilitate them for an active alliance with Germany. Saracoğlu had even begun to extol the Russian soldier, whom he said could fight on a handful of bread, while his family at home could survive on hot water tinctured with tea. The Turk remarked that he had once hoped for a

52. Erdmannsdorff to Papen, 31 March 1942, A.A. 2554/434; Papen to Ribbentrop, 13 April 1942, A.A. 2554/502.

counterrevolution against Stalin, but the course of the war had convinced him that the Russian masses were loyal, however irrationally, to the regime.

This reasoning probably was crucial to Saracoğlu's decision to reshuffle the personnel of a number of Turkish embassies throughout Europe. He substituted pro-Allied diplomats for predecessors of a neutralist or pro-German persuasion. One of these new appointees, Foat Tugay at Madrid, even avowed himself a Leninist. This was too much for the Wilhelmstrasse, and Papen and Weizsäcker demanded that Tugay be replaced. Saracoğlu refused, observing that Turkish public opinion was now too aroused against Germany to permit even the smallest concession to the Wilhelmstrasse. Many Turks suspected that Germany was draining off not only Turkish raw materials but also the very food from Turkish tables. Inflation was out of control and grain very scarce, but the public willfully forgot that Britain as well as Germany had bought large consignments of Turkish farm produce since 1939. When Saracoğlu talked of cutting the rations of certain army units, Papen concluded that the Turks might not have the stamina, even if they had the spirit, to fight with Germany against Russia. It was therefore best to view Turkey as a spoil in a Russo-German peace.[53]

It was bad enough that Turkey's value as a future German ally had all but vanished by the spring of 1942. It was still worse, however, that the Reich's actual allies—Bulgaria, Rumania, Italy, and Japan—were giving the Germans only minimal and declining support. The first three had become general nuisances by this time. Bulgaria and Rumania lodged territorial claims against each other, and the latter was rumored to be in secret contact with Moscow. Mussolini, on the other hand, was as vociferous an enemy of Communism as he had ever been, but he never tired of intriguing against the Germans. In regard to Ankara, his only concern was to urge the Wilhelmstrasse to share more of the Turkish export market with Italian entrepreneurs. However, his complaints were mild compared with Japan's increasingly domineering

53. Kroll to Papen, 28 April 1942, A.A. 2554/no number; Ettel to Foreign Ministry, 15 July 1942, A.A. 745/no number; Papen to Foreign Ministry, 2 May 1942, A.A. 2554/675; Stohrer to Ribbentrop, 31 May 1942, A.A. 51/2949; Papen to Foreign Ministry, 7 August 1942, A.A. 2554/4075.

and exigent attitude toward Middle Eastern affairs. As indicated, the Axis powers steadily declined to underwrite the
demands of Arab nationalism and treated the exiled mufti
and his companion in misfortune, Rashid Ali al-Gailani, as
little better than pariahs. By the spring of 1942, the pair had
convinced the Wilhelmstrasse to furnish them with private
letters assuring Italo-German support for the independence
of all Arab countries under the British yoke. But the Japanese suddenly interfered and insisted on a declaration of
their own proclaiming Arab independence from all colonial
control, not merely British, but French, Italian, and Portu-
guese, too. Furthermore, Tokyo wanted a similar pledge giv-
en to India. The Germans were appalled, and Ciano's first
deputy, Marchese Lanza d'Ajeta, declared that they and
the Italians must immediately close ranks to set a limit to
Japanese imperialism in the Middle East. Yet a month later,
Mussolini personally approved the Japanese address to
India. Germany, however, refused to subscribe the Japanese document. The Japanese in turn charged that Berlin
was failing to treat them as a fully equal ally and blamed
Weizsäcker for this policy. A year later, Tokyo's ambassador
in the German capital, Hiroshi Oshima, tried unsuccessfully
to have Papen recalled for defeatism. In Ankara, meanwhile,
the Japanese military attaché told Papen that his government
had no intention of coordinating its strategy to assist the
German offensive in North Africa. Japan would move against
British forces in India only when she chose, but when she
did, she would go all the way to the Persian Gulf. To this
threat, Papen thought the best answer was an immediate end
to the war.[54]

54. Papen to Foreign Ministry, 4 May 1942, A.A. 2554/679; Macken-
sen to Foreign Ministry, 15 April 1942, A.A. 63/1219. Woermann to
Weizsäcker, 1 May 1942, A.A. 63/296; Papen to Foreign Ministry, 12
May 1942, A.A. 2554/2629. See also Karl Heinz Abshagen, *Canaris:
Patriot und Weltbürger*, p. 367.

Chapter 7

Turkey at the Turn of the Tide, 1942–1943

Turkey the Bill Collector

Nothing came of the Valuiskiy peace proposal, though it had some supporters on the German general staff and at the foreign ministry. Extremists in the Nazi party, on the other hand, tried to use it to have Papen dismissed. In June 1942, the Auslandsorganisation, a rival of the foreign ministry led by Gauleiter Ernst Wilhelm Bohle, sent a special delegate to Ankara to censure the ambassador in public. The Auslandsorganisation was formed in 1931 to develop relations between Berlin and German ethnic groups overseas. But it meddled more generally in foreign affairs and frequently collided with Ribbentrop. When Papen accepted the Turkish post in 1939, he made it a condition of his acceptance that the Auslandsorganisation would never be allowed to interfere with him or his staff. There were no incidents between him and Bohle's people until the spring of 1942, when an AO man named Friede turned up in Ankara, convened the city's German community, and pointedly stated that anyone who practiced private diplomacy or deviated from the Nazi party line should be shot. Papen protested to Ribbentrop, who supported him against Bohle; Admiral Canaris, chief of German counterintelligence, and Gen. Wilhelm Keitel also interceded on the ambassador's behalf. Papen was empowered to exclude Friede from all embassy premises, and his staff was forbidden to have any official or social contact with the man. Friede left the Turkish capital, and the ambassador stayed on the job, continuing to work for peace with Russia.[1]

But events in the Mediterranean area outdistanced his efforts and made them seem premature. Rather unexpectedly, the Turks resumed their old pro-German stance and amiability, though Papen now regarded both as counterfeit

1. Franz von Papen, *Memoirs*, trans. Brian Connell, p. 445; Papen to Ribbentrop, 9 June 1942, A.A. 51/867; Weizsäcker to Ribbentrop, 22 June 1942, A.A. 51/402. (For list of abbreviations, see p. 221.)

and unreliable. Developments in Egypt and in the Soviet Union brought about the change. A few months before, the Turkish leaders had had the satisfaction of seeing their old enemy King Farouk humiliated by the British. On 4 February 1942, the British ambassador, Lampson, decided to shatter the glassy cordiality between himself and the king by going to Abdin Palace in Cairo with a tank escort and demanding that Farouk dismiss his Italian servants and bring the Wafd and its leader, Nahas Pasha, to power. Confronted by the towering British diplomat, Farouk broke down. Had he not submitted to Lampson's terms, the ambassador was prepared to force his abdication. Churchill thought Lampson should have pushed for the abdication, but the ambassador relented and accepted Farouk's promises to fire the Italians and cease his pro-Axis intrigues. Thereafter, however, Miles Lampson seemed to lose his drive and thrust. He had scored a great diplomatic victory, but apparently at the cost of too much personal anxiety. He confided to Foreign Secretary Eden that if there were to be future rows like the last one, it would be better if the Egyptian political opposition took the lead against the king. However provocative the king's behavior, he feared his own hectoring would arouse support for the slippery Farouk. He recommended that Eden might try to influence the king's policy through the Egyptian ambassador in London, but Eden replied that the ambassador had recently been recalled to Cairo for a holiday—before he could be summoned to the Foreign Office.[2]

Obviously, Eden was no more eager than Lampson for another confrontation with the Egyptian king. Moreover, both the foreign secretary and his ambassador were beginning to have doubts about the Wafd, of which they had earlier held high hopes. Nahas affirmed his belief in an Allied victory and said he hoped that the destinies of Egypt and Britain would always be closely intertwined. He had Easter gifts sent to all British troopers in Egypt. Nevertheless, Lampson wondered whether it was really in Britain's interest to strengthen any one Egyptian political party so much. There was no guarantee against the Wafd's becoming as difficult as the king. The British thought Nahas was more trustworthy

2. Lampson to Foreign Office, 13 March 1942, P.R.O., F.O. 371/J1191/38/16. Lampson to Foreign Office, 27 March 1942; Eden to Lampson, 30 March 1942, P.R.O., F.O. 371/J1446/38/16.

than most of his countrymen, but he was not immune to nepotism, and his wife, who was known to influence him, was a notorious social climber.[3]

This was a weakness ready for Farouk to use. Several members of Nahas's cabinet, though perhaps not the prime minister himself, wanted to be elevated to the Egyptian nobility. The king dangled before Nahas the possibility that he would ennoble them in return for certain concessions. To Lampson's annoyance, Nahas agreed to some of Farouk's terms. The king was allowed to appoint a number of members to the Egyptian senate, even though his choices were not sympathetic to the Wafd program and had no convictions other than the king's convenience. Farouk was also permitted to form a well armed bodyguard separate from the regular Egyptian army and accountable to the king alone. Most irritating to Lampson, Farouk cut all contact with him and Nahas in May 1942 by moving to a remote villa in the Sinai Peninsula. Lampson admitted, at one point, that he was not even sure of Farouk's whereabouts. But Nahas was in mediocre health and shrank from ordering the king back to the capital. Nor did Lampson have the nerve to issue such an order. He told the Wafd leader that difficulties on the home front must be avoided at all cost while the British army prepared to counterattack Rommel in the Western Desert.

To Eden, he speculated that further compromise with the king might be timely. Perhaps Farouk could be encouraged in his ambitions to assume the caliphate and the leadership of the Arab unity movement. Neither of these issues was as important as a decisive victory over Axis forces in North Africa. Farouk was allowed to hear about Lampson's change of mind, and when he returned to Cairo, he was in an extraordinarily amicable mood. He encouraged the British to plan to use Egyptian units in combat against Rommel. No definite commitment to this end was accepted by the British in 1942, but the Turks objected to this Anglo-Egyptian rapprochement and the rumored concessions behind it. They did not know that Lampson was to gird himself for future struggles with the king, and in their apprehen-

3. Lampson to Foreign Office, 24 February 1942, P.R.O., F.O. 371/J1107/38/16; 21 March 1942, P.R.O., F.O. 371/J1353/38/16; 1 April 1942, P.R.O., F.O. 371/J1578/38/16.

sion they again drew closer to the Germans. They abruptly recalled their ambassador from Cairo.[4]

The growing momentum of German operations in the Soviet Union also influenced the Turks. A few months before, the Turks, and the German generals themselves, thought the Russian campaign foredoomed to failure. The Wehrmacht had overrun almost all of the Crimea and taken Kiev, but, though they had reached the suburbs of the city, they had not captured Moscow. Hitler had never given high priority to the capture of Moscow. He preferred to concentrate his resources on a drive to the Caucasian oil fields. But his generals argued that without the seizure of the Soviet capital, the German invasion would become a drawn-out and eventually futile affair. Hitler did not agree, and Rundstedt, Leeb, and Bock, the commanders of the three original army groups, tendered, and Hitler readily accepted, their resignations. Gen. Walter von Brauchitsch, the commander in chief, was also dismissed, and Hitler himself assumed the functions of his office. Rundstedt was said to have urged the complete evacuation of Russian territory, but Hitler would not hear of so extreme a plan. He was somewhat sobered by the appearance of unexpected reserves of Soviet manpower, yet he planned confidently for a renewed offensive in the spring of 1942. The Führer began by replacing Rundstedt with Reichenau, Bock with Kluge, and Leeb with Küchler. When Reichenau died unexpectedly in January 1942, Hitler restored Bock to command but dropped him finally in July.

Meanwhile, Hitler worked out a new plan of attack, highly unorthodox and to his generals deeply disturbing. The Wehrmacht was to advance, though not as a unit. The southern flank was to proceed rapidly toward the Caucasus and Stalingrad, while the northern flank moved on Leningrad at a slower pace. The center, despite professional objections, Hitler kept relatively immobile. This feature of the plan was the most controversial and persuaded even the new echelon of commanders to protest to the Führer. Nonethe-

4. Lampson to Foreign Office, 25 March 1942, P.R.O., F.O. 371/J1429/38/16; 6 April 1942, P.R.O., F.O. 371/J1619/38/16; 21 April 1942, P.R.O., F.O. 371/J1918/38/16; 10 May 1942, P.R.O., F.O. 371/J2204/38/16; 15 May 1942, P.R.O., F.O. 371/J2363/38/16; 20 May 1942, P.R.O., F.O. 371/J2364/38/16; 16 July 1942, P.R.O., F.O. 371/J3219/38/16. Ribbentrop to Papen, 8 April 1942, A.A. 51/390; Seiler to Ankara Embassy, 29 June 1942, A.A. 2554/12.

less, he remained fixed on the oil of the Caucasus as his primary goal, and with the spring thaw came a series of victories that silenced his critics. In May, the German Eleventh Army under Erich von Mannstein besieged and captured the Soviet naval base of Sevastopol. A few weeks later, Bock overran the Ukraine with eight German armies. Before autumn, Voroshilovgrad, Rostov-na-Donu, Maikop, and Novorossisk were all to fall into German hands.[5]

As a result, Hitler was never more confident, though he might have been troubled, as his generals were, by Germany's increasing dependence on Rumanian, Hungarian, and Italian auxiliaries. He began to plan naval operations in the Black Sea to match the advance of his armies along its shore. The Führer now wanted to bring his U-boats into action against the Soviet Black Sea fleet. He hoped to destroy it or, as he put it to the Turkish government, to protect the Turkish merchant navy against Soviet attack. Hitler was also anxious to curtail suspected Turkish violations of neutrality in favor of the Allies. It was reported to him that a Soviet merchant ship that appeared off Montevideo, Uruguay, had been passed through the Straits by the Turkish authorities, though so many machine guns were visible on its deck that it could have been classed as a vessel of war. Hitler of course anticipated that the Turks would invoke their neutrality to exclude his submarines from the Black Sea. Therefore, he briefly considered a scheme to dismantle the U-boats at Linz, Austria, send them down the Danube on freighters, and then reassemble them at the Rumanian port of Constansa, well behind the Turkish barrier at the Straits. But he soon rejected this project as too time-consuming and decided upon a direct diplomatic bid to Ankara. Papen did not encourage this approach and advised that the most that should now be required of Turkey was neutrality, so that the Wehrmacht's flank in Russia would be protected. However, Hitler ordered a propaganda offensive, and the ambassador was directed to assure Saracoğlu that Hitler still contemplated a leading place for Turkey in the Axis new order and did not exclude some territorial rectifications for her.[6]

---

5. An excellent account of the war on the Russian front is found in Liddell Hart, *History of the Second World War*, pp. 241–51.

6. Ritter to Ribbentrop, 1 May 1942, A.A. 708/no number; Papen to

The Turks jumped at this hint and immediately informed Papen that they wanted to buy 400 million Reichsmarks worth of tanks, antitank guns, pursuit planes, and submarines. This was to be a credit transaction, repayable over a ten-year period in semiannual installments. Hitler was at first inclined to accept this arrangement, for several reasons. He wanted the Turks to allow German submarines into the Black Sea. His need for Turkish chromite was becoming critical. And in July 1942, he appeared to glimpse a possibility for influencing a favorable change in the Turkish government. Early in that month, Refik Saydam, the prime minister, died. He was a political nonentity, without influence compared to İnönü and Saracoğlu, though, having been trained as a physician in Germany, he was favorable to that country. However, with his passing the German leadership thought it could gain a stronger supporter by replacing Saydam with an "honorable general" who would realign Turkish foreign policy and ally with the Axis.[7]

According to Saracoğlu, the Turks wanted German armaments only for defensive purposes and to maintain their neutrality against all challengers. This was only partly true. Saracoğlu still had Pan-Turanian ambitions. About the time that he presented his list of weapons to Franz von Papen, a much publicized visit of Turkish journalists to the Russian front occurred. This delegation was led by Necmeddin Sadak, a popular feature writer, a parliamentary deputy, and a close friend of Saracoğlu and other cabinet ministers. Papen credited Sadak with a very sharp intelligence and warned against any attempt to hoodwink him. The Turks' tour was well planned and went smoothly for the Germans, except at the end, when Sadak and some of his colleagues insisted on bringing up the political future of the Turanian peoples. The Germans, caught off guard, were not ready for their questions and refused to discuss the problem.[8]

Before these difficulties surfaced, Ribbentrop suggested an exchange ratio for the delivery of German submarines. He

Ribbentrop, 9 May 1942, A.A. 51/703; Ritter to Papen, 16 June 1942, A.A. 2554/Geh. Rs. 373.

7. Papen to Ribbentrop, 8 July 1942, A.A. 51/1005, and 11 July 1942, A.A. 51/1012; Memorandum by Rintelen, 8 August 1942, A.A. 2554/ no number.

8. Papen to Foreign Ministry, 17 July 1942, A.A. 2554/no number, and 18 August 1942, A.A. 2554/A4350.

proposed that the Reich sell one submarine to Ankara of every two that the Turks let through the Straits. This proposal was addressed to the Turkish general staff as well as to Saracoğlu's foreign ministry. The army advised Saracoğlu that the entry of German submarines into the Black Sea was desirable but would have to be delayed until the heavily mined Straits could be cleared and some extensive cable netting removed. In the meantime, the Turks were ready to take possession of any submarines the Germans wanted to sell, accepting delivery at the port of Alexandretta. They further advised Papen that the German government should not let the question of the entry of the submarines into the Black Sea delay the conclusion of a general arms agreement. Turkey promised to intern all Soviet warships rather than permit any to escape through the Straits. This assurance hardly addressed the tactical aim that Hitler was trying to achieve. Nor could the Führer accept Saracoğlu's observation that matériel ought to be delivered to Turkey without a quid pro quo, because her neutrality was the greatest benefit that Turkey could offer Germany in exchange. Saracoğlu argued that as long as Turkey was not belligerent, she could make more difficult the bombing of the Rumanian oil fields and the joining of the British and Soviet armies.[9]

General Keitel, with Hitler's concurrence, announced that no further consideration would be given to furnishing the Turks with German arms under these circumstances. This decision might have been final, had not Saracoğlu responded with an adroit diplomatic ploy. While they talked trade with the Germans, the Turks leaked details of these negotiations to the British and Americans. This was strictly within their rights as neutrals, but the disclosures had the effect of laying Germany's economic prestige on the line. The British quickly opened up an office of the "United Kingdom Corporation" in Cairo. Its business was to supply the Turks with war matériel and bid competitively for their raw materials. The Americans cooperated with promises of large allotments of lend-lease equipment to Turkey. Saracoğlu maximized the effect of American participation when he talked to Papen. He told the ambassador that the Turkish envoy recently recalled from Egypt would be transferred to Washington, where he could assess American productive capacity. If that capacity was a reality and not a bluff, the Turkish envoy was to negotiate a series of trade agreements that would largely preempt Britain's place as a supplier of Western goods to Turkey.[10]

The threat of American competition made Hitler decide to reverse himself. He did so grudgingly and with considerable distaste but, as he told Keitel, Turkey had always been as much a political and propaganda problem as a military and economic one. Menemencioğlu, Saracoğlu's deputy, must have known of the Führer's misgivings, for he brazenly remarked to Papen that Germany must satisfy Turkey even while straining every nerve to beat Russia. If Germany withheld delivery of matériel, Menemencioğlu suggested, it would betray to the world a lack of confidence in the ultimate victory of the Axis new order over Soviet Communism. So the Germans agreed to receive a Turkish commercial delegation, led by Faik Hozar, in Berlin. They abandoned further attempts to get their submarines into the Black Sea, but they still hoped to obtain sizable allotments of chromite in return for their weaponry and machines. They managed to force the Turks to reduce their aggregate demands from 400 million to 100 million Reichsmarks of goods. But repayment, though the Germans wanted a shorter-term reckoning, was to be strung out over ten years. The Turks also insisted that they would take only the newest equipment, nothing damaged or obsolete. Only when the first consignment of German goods arrived at their Turkish destinations would Ankara promise to dispatch the items on the German want list. Furthermore, the Reich had to agree to take the first installments of the Turkish repayment in perishable commodities like raisins, hazel nuts, eggs, and vegetable and linseed oils. Part of Ankara's indebtedness was also to be liquidated in Turkish state bonds. The most vital allocations—chromite and copper—would still not follow until the latter part of 1943.[11]

10. Papen to Foreign Ministry, 2 June 1942, A.A. 2554/833; Ripken to Ankara Embassy, 4 June 1942, A.A. 2554/Ha. Pol. 3056. See also David L. Gordon and Royden Dangerfield, *The Hidden Weapon: The Story of Economic Warfare*, pp. 122ff.
11. Wiehl to Ripken, 9 August 1942, A.A. 2554/no number; Papen to Foreign Ministry, 20 August 1942, A.A. 2554/1176; "Proposal of a Credit Treaty," 27 August 1942, A.A. 2554/no number.

Originally, the Germans had been led to believe that Turkey had 4,000 tons of copper for sale, but later Faik Hozar pleaded a miscalculation and declared only 1,000 tons could be delivered to the Reich. Similarly, the Turkish foreign ministry had once indicated that the German loan might be repaid with as much as 120,000 tons of chromite, but the amount under discussion in Berlin was whittled down to 90,000 tons. The Turks claimed that their total annual chromite production would hardly reach 120,000 tons, and some of this would be required by domestic industries. But German agents secretly reconnoitering the Anatolian chromite deposits reported to Berlin that the total annual production was well in excess of the 120,000 ton figure. At one point, Faik Hozar, confronted with this information, argued that Turkey had to withhold some chromite with which to appease the Allies, who were trying to coerce her into a declaration against the Axis. Moreover, the wily Turk assured his German counterpart, Dr. Karl Clodius, that some chromite could be channeled into neutral Sweden, which supplied Hitler's war machine with high-grade steel. The evidence suggests that the German negotiating team did not accept these explanations easily, but they were forced to agree to them by a further Turkish threat to reveal the whole course of the negotiations, with all the compromising details, to the international news syndicates. At all cost, the Germans wanted to conceal the extremity of their supply problems from the enemy. Therefore, they took what they could get from the Turks. About 45,000 tons of chromite were delivered to Germany in late 1943.[12]

The Turco-German credit treaty of 100 million Reichsmarks was signed on 5 September 1942, though neither Hitler nor Ribbentrop was satisfied with it. Papen, on the other hand, held that it was a fair price for Turkish neutrality, which he now valued as highly as Turkish chromite or active collaboration in the war. Hitler had promised himself a propaganda advantage from the accord, but at first he seemed to be disappointed even in this. When Refik Saydam died,

12. Ripken to Ribbentrop, 3 August 1942, A.A. 2554/Ha. Pol. 4430; Ripken to Schnurre, 5 August 1942, A.A. 2554/Ha. Pol. 4482; Gordon and Dangerfield, *The Hidden Weapon*, p. 122; Edward Weisband, *Turkish Foreign Policy, 1943–1945: Small State Diplomacy and Great Power Politics*, pp. 113–15.

Saracoğlu took over as prime minister, while briefly continuing to hold the portfolio for foreign affairs. He then relinquished the latter office to Numan Menemencioğlu, who began his tenure by treating the international press to a series of pro-Allied pronouncements. He asserted that the Wehrmacht's failure to break Soviet resistance in the summer offensive of 1942 meant that Germany had lost the war. The new foreign minister also predicted that Rommel would be unable to prevent the Allies from landing in North Africa. Four days later, on 7 November 1942, Allied vanguard units poured ashore at Casablanca, Oran, and Algiers and proved him right.

Papen protested the Turkish minister's behavior, but Menemencioğlu cited the recent commercial treaty to prove that his heart was still with the Germans, even though he had to make comments that might suggest otherwise to placate the badgering British and American ambassadors. According to Papen's report, he even hinted that chrome deliveries to Germany could be accelerated if Hitler would sign an agreement ceding Syria to Turkey at the conclusion of the war. This was an extraordinary suggestion, since Menemencioğlu had just been implying in public that the Germans were barely in shape to hold their own territory, much less to give away that of other countries. But these persistent irredentist probings were well in line with the whole record of Turkey's wartime diplomacy. Just a few months earlier, Menemencioğlu suggested to Papen that a "third power" should be brought in to arbitrate and guarantee territorial discussions between Turkey and Germany. Ribbentrop rejected this proposal, fumed at Menemencioğlu's audacity, and threatened to recall Papen, whom he suspected of having encouraged it.[13]

One benefit alone seems to have accrued to Germany from the credit treaty of September. It may well have ruined the

13. Ripken to Wiehl, 5 September 1942, A.A. 2554/Ha. Pol. 5223; Ribbentrop to Papen, 12 September 1942, A.A. 51/1104; Kroll to Foreign Ministry, 21 October 1942, A.A. 2554/A.5535; Woermann to Ankara Embassy, 3 November 1942, A.A. 2554/1553. The Allied invasion of North Africa gave another example of Papen's extraordinary political durability. Ribbentrop recalled Eberhard von Stohrer, Germany's veteran ambassador to Spain, because he had failed to predict this invasion. See Carlton J. H. Hayes, *Wartime Mission in Spain, 1942–1945*, p. 129.

visit to Turkey of Roosevelt's emissary, Wendell Willkie, which took place in the same month. The onetime Republican presidential contender was scheduled to spend two days in Ankara. He was charged to urge the Turks to continue their neutrality, if he sensed they could not be persuaded to enter the war on the Allied side. Willkie was also supposed to emphasize the superiority of the American industrial plant to Axis resources. Finally, he wanted the Turkish government to pledge that it would never use any lend-lease consignments from the United States against Soviet Russia. But the Turks were impassive and noncommittal about all these points, breaking their reserve only to object that some of the supplies at first promised to them had been rerouted to the British forces in Egypt. President İnönü arranged to be out of town and pointedly returned just after Willkie's plane departed from Ankara airport. Though he met the American envoy, Menemencioğlu was uncommunicative and out of sorts. He was troubled by a gastric ailment that shortly was to require a German surgeon to be flown to him in Ribbentrop's special plane.

As a result, Willkie's mission, Papen crowed, had been a failure and his reception "second-class." Even the British ambassador, Knatchbull-Hugessen, concurred in this opinion, surprisingly not without a hint of self-satisfaction. The Englishman thought Roosevelt had made a poor choice in Willkie. Admittedly, Willkie was friendly and enthusiastic, but at times also maladroit and rather uninformed. He affronted the British contingent by overemphasizing the American industrial contribution to the war effort, and he bewildered the Turks when, in answer to their questions about the opening of the Second Front, he responded that it already existed in Egypt. When pressed by the Turks about a Second Front in Europe, Willkie said he did not know and "anyhow his opinion wasn't worth much." Finally, he called anybody who still believed in an Axis victory, as many Turks still did, a "sucker." Knatchbull-Hugessen found this kind of language too lacking in ceremony. Knowing as well as he did the astute and devious character of Turkish diplomacy, he might also have said that this statement was too far from the truth.[14]

14. Helm to Foreign Office, 11 September 1942, P.R.O., F.O. 371/R6202/6202/44; Knatchbull-Hugessen to Cadogan, 11 September 1942,

Turkey the Obstacle

The Anglo-American landings in North Africa soon showed how high a price the Germans had paid for the latest credit arrangement with Ankara. It had renewed Turkish neutrality but had not made it more benevolent. In the ensuing weeks, the neutrality instead became obstructive and pernicious. The German High Command was now faced with the prospect that Rommel's Afrika Korps, together with the German military forces in Tunisia under General von Arnim, would be wedged between the Allied invaders of French Morocco and the British Eighth Army advancing from Egypt behind Gen. Bernard Montgomery. At first, the Germans had the advantage and managed to reinforce Rommel with fifteen hundred men a day brought in by air transport from Europe. Montgomery's supplies were brought by the slower and more tortuous route round the Cape and up the Red Sea. But the material imbalance would gradually be redressed, and the Germans in the meantime had to find ways to recover the initiative or at least hold the line. Haj Muhammad was quick to offer his help. His exile in Europe was not a happy time for him, and though misfortune made the mufti and Rashid Ali al-Gailani companions, it did not make them friends. Al-Gailani had been deposed from power, but the German government continued to honor him as a former head of state. It treated him to all the perquisites of office, while the mufti, who was never an official political leader, though he claimed adherents and influence around half the globe, had to settle for a more hand-to-mouth existence. He soon quarreled with the Iraqi premier over precedence and rank, and the Germans declined to clearly favor one man over the other. But with Rommel on the defensive, Haj Muhammad hoped to exploit the situation and come out ahead of his Iraqi rival. He urged the Wilhelmstrasse to recognize him as official head of the Pan-Arab movement and then fly him to North Africa where

---

P.R.O., F.O. 371/R6241/6202/44. Lampson to Foreign Office, 11 October 1942, P.R.O., F.O. 371/J4183/38/16. Papen to Ribbentrop, 11 September 1942, A.A. 51/1285. Admiral Leahy and Secretary Stimson also took a dim view of Willkie's capacities as a diplomat. See William D. Leahy, *I was There: The Personal Story of the Chief of Staff to Presidents Roosevelt and Truman. . .* , p. 154; Henry L. Stimson and McGeorge Bundy, *On Active Service in Peace and War*, p. 308.

he would use his influence on the bey of Tunis. To that po-
tentate, he would deliver an Axis declaration of independence for Tunisia and the other French dependencies along
the Mediterranean. The bey in turn would rouse his nation
for the Axis and furnish Rommel, the mufti estimated, about
one-half million auxiliaries to combat the Anglo-American
coalition.[15]

The proposals were not new, except in one very important
respect. Haj Muhammad no longer talked about absolute
independence for the Arab countries. He now asserted that
they needed, and indeed wanted, European guidance and
capitalization. His conception of Arab nationalism, he informed the German foreign ministry, was therefore completely compatible with the long-term lease to the Reich of
air bases, oil wells, and sundry industrial concessions. He
recommended the Anglo-Egyptian Treaty of 1936 as the
pattern for German postwar influence in North Africa,
despite the fact that this treaty enabled the British to domi-
nate all military vantage points along the Nile, throttle the
Egyptian economy, rig the country's legislature, and browbeat Egypt's king as though he were a juvenile lackey. If
Ribbentrop would not publicly endorse these proposals, Haj
Muhammad later added that he would be ready to travel
to Tunis with only a private letter of encouragement for the
bey. In that case, he asked that Admiral Canaris accompany
him to make the gesture more official and, perhaps, to protect the mufti's life. Canaris seems to have favored the trip,
which both he and Haj Muhammad felt would result in
the creation of a barrier to the joining of Montgomery's and
Eisenhower's armies.[16]

This time the mufti's schemes tantalized Ribbentrop, especially since German military planners expected the Allies
to enlist North African Arabs by promising them eventual
independence. But the Nazi foreign minister found that prior
commitments denied him latitude. As was to be expected,
Italy protested against pandering to the mufti, as did Spain.
Yet, according to the Wilhelmstrasse's chief regional experts,

15. Mackensen to Foreign Ministry, 9 September 1942, A.A. 63/3418;
Memorandum to the Abwehr, unsigned, 27 November 1942, A.A. 63/5214.
16. Abwehr Memorandum to OKW, unsigned, 9 December 1942, A.A.
63/no number; Weizsäcker to Ribbentrop, 12 December 1942, A.A.
1171/728.

the main risk to be avoided was the offense German association with Haj Muhammad might give to Turkey. Except for Admiral Canaris, and his opinions on the matter were not consistent, the mufti now had almost no German advocates. Fritz Grobba might have spoken out for him, but the veteran orientalist recently had quarreled with Haj Muhammad over the pettiest of differences. Grobba attended a bit too closely on Rashid Ali to suit his Palestinian rival, but he always denied that he tried to set one man against the other. After all, it was German protocol that al-Gailani should be given precedence over Haj Muhammad. But the mufti was irrationally sensitive about such matters and soon accused Grobba of being a dabbler in Arab affairs. Grobba might understand Iraq, the mufti said, but he had no larger comprehension of Arab problems. Furthermore, his behavior raised doubts about Germany's ultimate intention toward Arab nationalism.

After the most cursory investigation, Ribbentrop and Weizsäcker found against Grobba and replaced him with Curt Prüfer, former German ambassador to Brazil. The choice was strange, because Prüfer did not mince words or hedge his opinions about the mufti and Pan-Arabism. He characterized both as "foggy" and warned that Germany should have nothing to do with them for fear of antagonizing the Turks into joining the Allies. Prüfer insisted that Turkey was the only Muslim state that could harm Germany. Her continuing neutrality must be assured at any cost. Otherwise, the Wehrmacht's flank in southern Russia would be laid open to Allied counterattack and the Balkan underbelly of Europe exposed to aerial bombardment. Ribbentrop accepted this analysis. Apparently, his aim was not to render Grobba justice, but, consistent with his policy, to use him as a scapegoat to appease the Turks.[17]

Whatever opportunity there was for a North African insurrection to impede the Anglo-American advance, the Germans now threw away. The Wehrmacht was training an Arab army corps at Cape Sounion near Athens to be sent to assist Rommel on their home ground. But Berlin now

17. Prüfer to Woermann, 3 December 1942, A.A. 63/no number; Woermann to Ribbentrop, 16 December 1942, A.A. 63/819; Prüfer to Weizsäcker, 17 February 1943, A.A. 1171/11.

decided that these men would no longer be maintained as a unit and would go instead to the Soviet Union. Rather ironically, Canaris was chosen to tell the mufti that he would have no influence or control over these recruits, as well as that the Reich would not henceforth welcome his political interference and in fact had had evidence for some time that made them doubt the wisdom of it. Canaris was alluding to a secret Gestapo appraisal of Haj Muhammad that minimized his importance in the Arab world and judged the information gotten from his contacts to be no better than, and in some cases even inferior to, intelligence taken from less well paid espionage sources. These contentions, which Ribbentrop accepted at face value, may have been true. If they were, the foreign minister was entitled to break completely with the mufti, which even now he did not do. Haj Muhammad kept begging, and when Ribbentrop definitely canceled the mufti's Tunisian trip on 15 December 1942, he asked to be permitted to go and proselytize for the Axis among the nine hundred thousand Muslims of Croatia, Bosnia, and Herzegovina. He thought he could incite them to begin partisan activities for the German military command or at least dissuade them from enlisting in the partisan companies of Marshal Tito. Ribbentrop agreed, merely because, as he said, he had refused the mufti in so much else. Haj Muhammad was secretly landed in Yugoslavia in April 1943. Far from his home ground, he was ineffective, though he spoke of going on to work among the Muslims of the Russian Caucasus. In either area, he was a provocation to the Turks and did the Germans no good whatever. They simply continued to pay his bills. The Italians did not even do that and emphatically sealed Albania to the mufti's Balkan peregrinations.[18]

The jealousy of the mufti had always been an obstacle to a fruitful relationship between the Axis and the court of Cairo. With Haj Muhammad sinking deeper into political limbo, rapprochement between the Wilhelmstrasse and King Farouk should have been possible, but instead Turkish opposition prevented it. Throughout most of the summer

18. Mackensen to Foreign Ministry, 17 September 1942, A.A. 63/3524; Sonnleithner to Weizsäcker, 15 December 1942, A.A. 1171/no number; Weizsäcker to Woermann, 4 March 1943, A.A. 63/142; Mackensen to Foreign Ministry, 9 June 1943, A.A. 63/2732.

of 1942, Farouk professed his belief in an Allied victory, but behind the scenes the king was mending his political fences and conspiring to subvert the British war effort once again. He loathed Ambassador Lampson irreconcilably, and whatever friendliness he showed the British envoy was a feint, imposed not only by superior British military strength but also by domestic threats to the monarchy. The most dangerous of these was not the Wafd party, with its public membership and bourgeois program, but the Muslim Brotherhood, with its secret affiliates and equalitarian goals. In August 1942, as the British later learned, Farouk made his peace with Hassan al-Banna. With the connivance of Nahas Pasha, the palace began to subsidize the Muslim Brotherhood, probably because the king and his prime minister had discovered that al-Banna was already receiving monies from foreign sources.

Reliable informants told Farouk that the Persian, Afghan, and Japanese governments had the Brotherhood's leader in their pay, and Farouk himself turned generous to neutralize these potentially dangerous benefactors. The king also permitted al-Banna to resume political campaigning. Just before the battle of El Alamein, the Brotherhood's leader hailed Rommel and called for his triumph over Montgomery's army. Meanwhile, his followers organized anti-British demonstrations in Cairo. They jeered British army personnel in the streets, while pointedly applauding any Free French army units passing by. Members of the Muslim Brotherhood burned an oil refinery at Suez, and Farouk apparently hoped, and the British feared, they would go still further. It all depended on the Germans:

> He [al-Banna] was waiting on instructions from the Germans to put his sabotage plans into effect; the attitude of the Ikhwan to the Germans depended on German reciprocity, for unless the movement were given a dominant place in Egyptian politics the Germans would learn its real strength to their cost. It is suspected that his [al-Banna's] expressed desire to cooperate with the Wafd and concentrate the activities of his association on religious reforms are insincere, and reports of sabotage plans continue to be received.[19]

19. Lampson to Eden, 24 December 1942, P.R.O., F.O. 371/J245/158/16. Charles de Gaulle, *War Memoirs*, vol. 2, *Unity, 1942–1944*, pp. 15–17.

Just at this time, in preparation for the supreme effort against Rommel at Alamein, Ambassador Lampson ordered Farouk to prepare for the evacuation of his government to the Sudan or South Africa. Remembering the fate of the shah of Iran, the monarch refused, and this time his whole princely family supported him. With one exception, his uncles, who were usually jockeying for the succession, now urged their royal nephew to hold fast to his throne and stand up to the British. The Egyptian people were behind him, too. Food was scarce, prices high, and British management everywhere unpopular and held in contempt. American military personnel, who the British accused of wanting to steal their empire, made matters worse by brawling with His Majesty's forces in Cairo bars. Nahas Pasha was unable to keep Britain's critics in the Egyptian parliament quiet, and Lampson was thinking of dropping him in favor of a not-too-promising substitute. Farouk therefore made contact with the Germans through an envoy, Lutfil Barudi, in Istanbul. Barudi informed German intelligence that the Egyptian army had sixty thousand men, tough and battle-ready, since most had been in the ranks for five years or more. The Egyptian envoy insisted that it was not necessary for the Germans to consider doing any Egyptian campaigning themselves, because the climate would be too extreme for them, while the native troops were well up to it. All they needed was a signal from Berlin and modern German equipment flown to them.[20]

This operation would seem to have been feasible, because the High Command was then airlifting supplies to Rommel's troops; the same method could have been used to arm Egyptian confederates. But Berlin at once looked for the difficulties rather than the dividends of such an investment. The Wilhelmstrasse listened not only to Lutfil Barudi but also to an Egyptian pilot, Mohammed Raduan, who had fled across Rommel's lines. He advised the Germans to put their money on an Egyptian revolt but not to let King Farouk hold their bets. According to young Raduan, Farouk was a selfish "Turk" who thought nothing of the common people's welfare and advancement. The Wafd party was no better, top-heavy with superannuated British toadies and reeking with corruption.

20. Ettel to Woermann, 8 August 1942, A.A. 737/no number.

The young officer recommended that the Germans establish a military dictatorship in place of the monarchy but merely succeeded in confusing Ribbentrop. Raduan made a few Arabic recordings for the Nazi propaganda ministry and then was flown back to Rommel's lines, leaving German confidence in Farouk severely shaken. But the Wilhelmstrasse was still more profoundly unsettled when it discovered that the Turkish diplomatic missions in Alexandria and Cairo had detected the liaison between Farouk and the German foreign ministry and were disclosing all its details to the British. The king tried to restore German confidence by still further appeals, but the Turks riddled all security measures, with the Italians probably abetting them. When Mussolini again raised his old claims to primacy in Egypt, Ribbentrop responded that Il Duce could not debar German forces from using the economic and military resources of the country as they saw fit. Then he ignored King Farouk, while the battle of El Alamein, begun on 23 October 1942, marked the start of Rommel's retreat from Egypt. Clearly, the Italians were no longer a problem, but the Turks were.[21]

If the German foreign ministry was unable to establish lasting contact with Muslim sympathizers like Haj Muhammad and King Farouk, who were easy to reach, it is perhaps not surprising that no productive links were forged with pro-Axis politicians in the Far East. Again, the fault was largely Germany's, but Turkey had a hand in the final failure. In April 1941, Subhas Chandra Bose, chief of the pro-Axis "Forward Bloc" of the Indian Congress party, came to Berlin and sought material aid from Hitler and an Axis declaration for Indian independence. The Führer and the Wilhelmstrasse both agreed at that time to avoid this kind of commitment but later appeared to have regretted the decision. Bose turned from Berlin to Tokyo, where he went as a petitioner in 1942. The Germans then heard from him only sporadically, and finally not at all. During the battle of El Alamein, they tried to reestablish communications, because

21. Tismer to Kramarz, 31 July 1942, A.A. 745/Pol. VII 6706g; Ettel to Rintelen, 25 August 1942, A.A. 737/no number; Wiehl to Clodius, 10 October 1942, A.A. 737/Ha. Pol. 6037g. Just how precarious the British position in Egypt was is suggested by the account of Arthur Bryant, *The Turn of the Tide: A History of the War Years Based on the Diaries of Field-Marshal Lord Alanbrooke, Chief of the General Staff*, pp. 356–64.

they knew that much of Montgomery's muscle came from Australian and New Zealand contingents, which the Berlin High Command would have liked to see recalled or tied down in pro-Axis diversionary operation in India or Afghanistan.

Canaris's organization could not break through to Bose but did negotiate for a time with the fakir of Ipi, an Afghan religious leader. The fakir posed as an ascetic mendicant, but he was really a combination of huckster and robber. He informed the German representative in Kabul that he would spark a rebellion for one hundred thousand Reichsmarks and sustain it for additional monthly payments of forty thousand Reichsmarks. Furthermore, he was confident that his followers could be smuggled across the Indian frontier and reach the leaders of the Indian "Forward Bloc." The Germans had failed to reach these leaders by radio transmitter from Kabul, because the Afghan government, fearful of British reprisals if it violated its neutrality, jammed the circuits. But before he began, the fakir demanded Berlin's guarantee that Afghanistan would not be made a Turkish protectorate (such schemes had apparently been discussed in his circle), nor allowed to slip into the equally obnoxious Japanese Greater East Asian Co-Prosperity Sphere. The fakir denounced the Turks as atheists who had foresworn Islam and the Japanese as vicious brutes who mutilated their prisoners of war. However, Ribbentrop was as unresponsive to the fakir as he had lately been to Haj Muhammad and King Farouk. The foreign minister's decision must have had its critics, because a year later Nazi counterintelligence agents had contacted Indians who would be capable of servicing German submarines operating in the Bay of Bengal. Considerable money was advanced to these people, but in the end it was a waste because Canaris could never be sure of his communications through Afghanistan or count on even local disturbances in India itself.[22]

As a result of these repeated German rebuffs, Muslim leaders finally and permanently succumbed to feelings of insult and alienation. In the late summer of 1942, German blunders allowed the Soviets to convene an Islamic congress in the southern Russian town of Ufa. A succession of speakers

22. Pilger to Foreign Ministry, 12 September 1942, A.A. 737/627; a summary account of the fakir's activities is in Pilger to Foreign Ministry, 3 May 1944, A.A. 694/136.

averred their loyalty to Stalin and the compatibility of the Prophet's teachings with the Communist regime. Some of the enthusiasts called for a *jihād* against Hitler's Reich. Of course, none was ever proclaimed, but the Ufa meeting was not without repercussions. A few months later, King ibn-Saud of Saudi Arabia, an old but unsuccessful suitor for the Wilhelmstrasse's support, proclaimed that the best hopes for Arab independence lay with the Allies, despite their association with the irreligious Soviet dictator. Neither the Saudi king nor the Russian ulama of Ufa can have believed that a triumphant Stalin would respect their religious liberties and jurisdictions, but the necessities of war compelled them to espouse ideological paradoxes. In the Ufa congress and in the palace of ibn-Saud, irreconcilable ideas were being born, with Turkey playing midwife at the birth and Nazi Germany its witness.[23]

Turkey the Troublemaker

For the reasons discussed, few German leaders believed by the beginning of 1943 that the Turkish Republic was still a genuine neutral. Franz von Papen insisted that such was the case, but Ribbentrop, as has been shown, had a variety of evidence from widely diverse areas that suggested the contrary. The foreign minister now argued that even if the Turks sincerely wished to preserve their neutrality, the strategical situation would not permit them to do so. The Wehrmacht was locked in the mammoth battle of Stalingrad and had diminishing control over the Black Sea coast. American supplies and men were piling up in Syria, poised, the Germans believed, to invade Turkey from the south. On Cyprus, there was intensifying British activity, portending an amphibious landing on Italian-held Rhodes. Finally, there were the inflation and commodity shortages in Turkey itself. Even the sanguine Papen admitted that these might bring down the newly installed Saracoğlu cabinet. Turkey's old enemies were quick to feed Germany's fears and cast the policy of Ankara in the most sinister light. The Bulgarian prime minister told the German embassy in Sofia that İsmet İnönü no longer felt able, either materially or morally, to resist Allied pressure to enter the war.

---

23. Schweinitz to Papen, 12 August 1942, A.A. 4723/635.

Uppermost in the Turkish president's mind was now fear of Russia. Once the battle of Stalingrad had been decided in Moscow's favor, Ankara officials expected the Red Army to advance rapidly on the Straits. The only recourse left to save the Straits from Russia was to cast Turkey's lot with the Anglo-American partnership in hopes that it could keep the Soviets under control. The Bulgarians believed there was an even chance of Anglo-American altruism prevailing against Soviet ambition, but at the price of locations in the Anatolian hinterland being turned into Allied air bases for raids on Sofia and Salonika. The Bulgarian leadership maintained that it was only a question of time, and probably a short time at that, before the Turks declared war on the Reich and its European satellites. Orders had therefore been issued for the evacuation of the government archives, the administrative offices, and the officials' families from Sofia into the countryside.[24]

The offenses that the Turks had so far committed against the Reich were covert and indirect; Ribbentrop was prone to magnify and Papen to minimize them. But in January 1943, the foreign minister thought Ankara had offered him the most irrefutable of insults when it allowed Winston Churchill to land in Adana. The British prime minister had come, simply enough, to persuade Turkey to enter the war. Churchill's colleagues in London did not think he would succeed and advised against the trip. His reception at Adana was in fact very disconcerting. Upon meeting him, Saracoğlu said all Turkey was delighted at his visit. Churchill asked how that could be, since it was supposed to be a strict secret. In fact, Turkish security measures were almost offensively lax. A German engineering team was working near Adana, but no attempt was made to remove it. During one of the conference sessions, it rained heavily, and Churchill's Turkish guards scurried for cover, heedless of the safety of their British guest. Also, Marshal Çakmak appeared to have no conception of modern warfare. Çakmak had to consult his subordinates constantly on details, and Churchill found it impossible to keep up an uninterrupted conversation with him.

The Englishman's oratory was, as ever, masterful, but it failed to move the mundanely logical İnönü and Saracoğlu.

24. Koecher to Foreign Ministry, 31 January 1943, A.A. 52/238.

He did not try to coerce them into war, but he spoke ominously of a developing world situation that might oblige Turkey to take sides. In that event, the prime minister offered to supply Ankara with all the modern weaponry of war. In the meantime, which Churchill intimated must be short, the British government would be content with Turkey's neutrality, conjoined, Churchill hoped, with a growing Turkish confidence in Russia.[25]

It was precisely these remarks about the Soviet Union that were least convincing to the Turkish leadership. To all Churchill's offers of military largesse, İnönü posed the reminder that İstanbul was a city of wood, a tinderbox that a modern air force could in moments make little more than a memory. Against the threat of Russian expansion, the Turkish president wanted protection more sinewy than Churchill's promise to write persuasive letters to Stalin. Saracoğlu also rejected Churchill's contention that the United Nations would guarantee Turkey against future Soviet imperialism. Saracoğlu said most of Europe would become Communist whether occupied by the Red Army or not and so could be expected to vote Stalin's line in any international assembly. In short, Churchill came away from Adana without any binding promises from the Turkish leaders, though he was convinced he had made İsmet İnönü his warm friend.[26] But İnönü's friendship, like that of humbler men, was strongest when never brought to the test.

Curiously, the Adana meeting caught Papen completely off guard, and the German ambassador was not aware of it until it was already in progress. Ribbentrop was amazed and angry at his envoy, especially because Papen tried to depict the encounter between Churchill and İnönü as harmless. To the contrary, the Nazi foreign minister agreed with Count Ciano, who declared that Turkey had violated her neutrality by even permitting Churchill to touch her soil. Nor was Ribbentrop mollified when he heard Menemencioğlu's version of the Adana talks. According to this account, when Churchill alluded to the problem of supplying the Soviet Union by air transport over Turkish territory,

25. Winston S. Churchill, *The Second World War*, vol. 4, *The Hinge of Fate*, pp. 696–712; Bryant, *The Turn of the Tide*, pp. 467–68.

26. Şevket S. Aydemir, *İkinci Adam: İsmet İnönü*, 2:255–57; Churchill, *Hinge of Fate*, pp. 709–11.

the supply method he thought was least objectionable to the Ankara government, Menemencioğlu retorted that not only did he oppose such traffic, but he would have any British planes attempting it shot out of the sky. As to the question of Stalin's postwar ambitions, Menemencioğlu contented himself with the less vituperative observation that Ankara knew Soviet military attachés in the Allied capitals all opposed the delivery of lend-lease materials to the Turkish government.[27]

Menemencioğlu tried to convince Papen that Churchill spent almost as much time railing against Mussolini and his African empire as he did discussing the terms of the Turkish intervention. This may have been true, and Churchill's outpourings against Il Duce may have been a spontaneous eruption. But it is more probable that the Turkish foreign minister, or one of his colleagues present at Adana, deliberately gave the British leader his opening to discuss territorial rectifications. It is quite likely that the Turkish delegation alluded to the postwar status of the Dodecanese islands, which Italy had taken from the Ottoman Empire in the Tripolitan War of 1911. The Young Turks and then the Kemalist Republicans had always wanted to recover these areas, and Churchill could reasonably have encouraged their hopes.

Just before the Adana conference, Rauf Orbay, the Turkish ambassador in London, sounded Emmanuel Tsouderos, the Greek prime-minister-in-exile, about the reversion of certain Mediterranean islands to Ankara's jurisdiction. Orbay did not actually use the term *Dodecanese*, and he disclaimed any authorization from İnönü, but Foreign Office experts were certain that he had these islands in mind, and they were unable to reassure the Greeks, who wanted to dispossess the Italians of the Dodecanese after the war. Ribbentrop believed annexation of the Dodecanese islands was Ankara's price for participation in a Second Front to be opened in the Balkans. Such an operation would knock Italy out of the war, force the German High Command to divert some of its troops from the Russian front, and set a barrier

27. Papen to Foreign Ministry, 2 February 1943, A.A. 52/167. On Papen's surprise at the Adana meeting, see also Knatchbull-Hugessen to Foreign Office, 3 February 1943, P.R.O., F.O. 371/R1024/1016/44, and 6 February 1943, P.R.O., F.O. 371/R1119/1016/44.

to the Red Army's advance toward the Straits. Ever since the First World War, Churchill had advocated one of his favorite strategies, a stab at Europe's soft Balkan underbelly; Ribbentrop believed his adversary in London might now implement such a plan.[28]

Papen denied this, or as Ribbentrop put it, would have had the officials at the Wilhelmstrasse believe that Churchill and the Turks talked only about the weather at Adana. This jibe at the ambassador was quite unfair. What Papen emphasized was that Turkish public opinion would not support whatever intentions the Ankara government had for a Second Front in the Balkans. To prove this, he cited riots in Smyrna when news of Churchill's visit appeared in the local newspapers. Against Papen's moderate counsels, Ribbentrop set the latest rumors from German embassies throughout Europe. These reported that Churchill at Adana had offered not only the Dodecanese but also northern Syria to the Turks as payment for their alliance. The British denied there was any discussion of Syria, but their archives suggest that second-string British diplomats did speculate with their Turkish counterparts about a change in the status of the northern Syrian districts of El Jezireh and Aleppo.[29]

What troubled Papen was not so much the question of whether these reports were reliable, but rather the larger thesis that he feared Ribbentrop was trying to drive home by continually adducing them. The foreign minister, it was becoming ominously clear, was mounting a campaign to justify war against Turkey. At this stage of the fighting, such a war would have been a tremendous risk for the Reich. But the opening of a new front might also have been a strain sufficient to break the Soviet army's encirclement of General von Paulus at Stalingrad. It would also have put an end to the mischief-making power of Turkey, which had now thoroughly exasperated the Nazi foreign minister. He was not able to prove that an accord between the heads of state had issued from Adana, but he had fairly convincing evidence, some of it relayed by the "dovish" Papen, that har-

28. Palairet to Howard, 6 January 1943, P.R.O., F.O. 371/R214/214/67; 14 January 1943, P.R.O., F.O. 371/R464/464/19. Ribbentrop to Papen, 3 February 1943, A.A. 52/167.

29. Spears, Beirut, to Foreign Office, 10 February 1943, P.R.O., F.O. 371/E845/27/89; Huene to Foreign Ministry, 4 February 1943, A.A. 52/360.

monious collaboration existed between Turks and Britons in lower echelons.

Though İnönü, if not Churchill, had conducted himself with relative reserve at the recent conference, neither man required such deportment of their representatives in foreign capitals. This was especially true of the military attachés and the members of the Turkish and imperial British ministries of war. İnönü, Saracoğlu, and Menemencioğlu could all truthfully deny that Allied contingents were being permitted to encamp on Turkish soil. Nor were Anatolian airfields being made available to service Allied planes. But there were American and British flight instructors, construction engineers, and tactical experts at-large at Turkish army bases. In Syria, American firms were helping the British to build hangars to accommodate over four thousand planes. These structures were of the latest type, and the Turks were reported to be unobtrusively slipping over the frontier to study and copy their design. Growing bolder against possible German objection, they later invited the American engineers to come to Smyrna to survey the ground for future landing sites.[30]

A German agent, bypassing Papen and reporting directly to Berlin, saw a number of what appeared to be British work gangs in the Smyrna area in May. The cut of their clothes, which sometimes consisted of random articles of British military issue, and their English speech gave them away. Yet Papen insisted that the men in question were all Turks, sporting British uniforms that they had picked up in local rummage sales. The ambassador could not have believed this. Air Marshal Sholto Douglas, who supervised delivery of British aircraft to Turkey, later asserted that his men took few pains to conceal their nationality. They did not wear service uniforms, but the equally telltale flannel trousers and sport coats of English cut. Any German spy could have spotted them.

Ribbentrop's further charge that the Turkish army was

30. Papen to Foreign Ministry, 17 February 1943, A.A. 52/248; Sonnleithner to Papen, 4 February 1943, A.A. 52/253. Anthony Eden, *The Reckoning: The Memoirs of Anthony Eden, Earl of Avon*, p. 240; Raymond de Belot, *The Struggle for the Mediterranean, 1939–1945*, trans. James A. Field, Jr., p. 241.

delivering meteorological data to the British, Papen did not deny but made light of. Such collaboration, he argued, was motivated by anti-Communism, not by anti-Nazism. According to the German ambassador, the Turks felt that the danger of Communist infiltration had become more insidious than ever, since the Soviets had switched their tactics from terror and assassination to generosity and gentleness in Iran. Through the offices of the Tudeh party at Teheran, the Soviets were passing out money and free food and thus gaining more adherents every day. The Turkish foreign ministry believed that if a plebiscite were held among Iranians, the majority would vote for federation with the Soviet Union. Under such circumstances, Papen insisted, the Turks were entitled to take whatever countermeasures they wished. And as for preventive war against Turkey, the ambassador thought it would be a suicidal dissipation of Germany's resources.[31]

In provoking Berlin, the Turks of course knew the risks they were running. They could depend on Papen's sympathetic advocacy, but they also worked so that he would not be their sole recourse in a crisis. They dared not attack the Axis; they could and did undermine the dispirited members of the Tripartite Pact, Bulgaria, Rumania, and Hungary, allies of Germany since 1941. The Turks may have been following the example of the United States. The American State Department had recently posted its former envoy to Bulgaria, George Earle, to İstanbul as naval attaché. While appraising Turkey's matériel needs with a view to filling them from American stockpiles, Earle was to mediate outstanding problems between Sofia and Ankara and to encourage defections from Axis-occupied Europe. The Wilhelmstrasse soon heard that the Turkish embassy to Hungary was actively cooperating to make Earle's mission successful. The British Foreign Office also detected signs that the Turks and Hungarians were hatching an anti-Axis intrigue in Budapest. It called for the creation of a Balkan Grand Alliance of Hungary, Rumania, Bulgaria, and Turkey. The members would pool their troops to resist Soviet encroach-

31. Papen to Foreign Ministry, 6 May 1943, A.A. 52/663; William Sholto Douglas, *Combat and Command: The Story of an Airman in Two World Wars*, p. 543.

ment on the Balkans, impressing on Germany that this goal was as urgent as the prosecution of the Wehrmacht's campaign within the Soviet Union.

If Berlin did not agree with this viewpoint, the Balkan confederates would simply desert the Axis and sue for a separate peace with Britain and the United States. The Hungarians apparently did not think they were guilty of any breach of faith toward Hitler. They argued that their talks with Ankara were a way of bringing Turkey closer to the Axis. But since the Germans found out that Turkish emissaries had been negotiating, since the beginning of the year, with representatives of the Balkan governments-in-exile in London, which had avowed their dedication to the total destruction of the Axis, this Hungarian sophistry was hardly believable. Stranger still was the role of Franz von Papen. When Berlin questioned the Hungarian foreign ministry about its connection with the Turkish détente, the ministry expressed surprise that the German government had any doubts about its motives. It had informed Papen of Turkey's projected Balkan coalition, and he had approved its goals and promised that he would inform the Wilhelmstrasse of all the details.[32]

Papen did not inform his ministry or even consider the consequences of Turkey's Balkan pact until approximately 16 March 1943. Nearly three months were allowed to slip by before Berlin was sufficiently informed to consider measures to stop Ankara's conspiracy. When Papen finally reported the matter to Berlin, he attempted to represent it as a purely economic union. As such, he had discussed it with Menemencioğlu, warning him that he must never allow these negotiations to serve Britain's ends. And he had reminded the Turkish foreign minister, as he had Under Secretary Woermann in Berlin, that a confederation of these Balkan countries could never achieve economic independence from Germany and should not waste time trying to do so. That these states might become not merely commercial competitors of

32. Woermann to Papen, 22 February 1943, A.A. 52/305; Ribbentrop to Papen, 12 March 1943, A.A. 52/385; Jagow to Foreign Ministry, 13 March 1943, A.A. 52/449. Knatchbull-Hugessen to Foreign Office, 24 June 1943, P.R.O., F.O. 371/R5836/55/44. Almost a year earlier, the British had intelligence that Turkey was trying to align the Balkan states against the Axis. See Hoare, Madrid, to Foreign Office, 13 May 1942, P.R.O., F.O. 371/R3135/24/44.

the Reich, but its military foes, was a possibility the ambassador did not address. He deliberately ignored the prospect of their defection to the Anglo-American Allies, entailing the establishment of Balkan bases from which Nazi industrial centers in central Europe could be bombed. Woermann, however, was not so oblivious. Twenty-four hours after receiving Papen's bland analysis of Ankara's latest intrigues, he wired back an unequivocal reprimand. There was no mistaking, he held, that Turkey's Balkan pacts were more anti-Axis than anti-Communist.[33]

Actually, the thrust of Turkish diplomacy at this time was both anti-Axis and anti-Communist. As Papen pointed out in his own defense, Bulgaria stood directly in the Red Army's line of march and for months had been begging Berlin for additional German troops to bolster her defenses. But the High Command decided that none could be spared from more critical theaters of the war and, instead of sending in German recruits, sent a few hundred collaborationist Greeks to Bulgaria as "territorial police." These were supplemented by some overage German noncombatants who did nothing to build the Bulgarians' confidence against the Soviet threat. In fact, Bulgaria demanded the recall of the Greek territorial police. They were regarded as not only inefficient, but, in light of the decades of territorial wrangling between the two countries, as insulting to Bulgaria's national honor. Berlin subsequently considered assigning additional German units, ranked as second-rate, to the Bulgarian sector. But the High Command moved with deliberate slowness, because it realized it was in a quandary. If the Wehrmacht's presence in Bulgaria were increased, the Turks would charge that the Reich was planning a sneak attack on their frontiers and therefore prosecute their defectionist designs all the more intensively. Yet if more German help were not sent to Bulgaria, the ministers in that country would seek their own road away from the Tripartite Pact. In İstanbul, the Allies had thrown open many doors to fugitives from the Axis.[34]

Ribbentrop ordered Papen to keep a sharp eye for the whereabouts of these fugitives and, in the meantime, to remind Menemencioğlu that his policies were, to say the least,

33. Woermann to Papen, 20 March 1943, A.A. 3969/420.
34. Beckerle to Foreign Ministry, 20 April 1943, A.A. 52/619.

not consonant with the Turco-German Friendship Treaty of 1941. But the foreign minister did not trust solely to his ambassador's vigilance, which seemed to have become deliberately if not treasonously myopic, and appointed Hans Kroll, Papen's first deputy, to supervise counterespionage work in İstanbul. The Turkish foreign ministry was now saying that the Balkan states had taken its peace offensive too seriously and made more out of it than was ever intended in Ankara. In any case, Menemencioğlu's office claimed to have received few inquiries from Budapest, Bucharest, and Sofia; and the time for them, it asserted, was now past. Whatever had been done, the Turks claimed, had been intended to help Hitler at a period when his lines in Russia were slackening. Turkish policymakers now professed to consider them much firmer and to believe that Germany would win the war.

Papen reported that his own investigations tended to support the truth of Menemencioğlu's remarks. As far as he could find out, only the Bulgarian emissary had visited İstanbul in December. Since that time, according to Papen, he had not returned. His name was Puljew, he was left-leaning or Communist, and did not represent any highly placed body of official Bulgarian opinion. But an Abwehr countercheck disclosed that the ambassador was misinformed. Puljew had returned several times to the city, on each occasion meeting with George Earle at a place arranged by the Turkish secret police. It is not clear whether he was a Communist, but he was certainly no maverick. If Bulgarian liberal and leftist elements wanted peace, so too, Berlin discovered, did the hitherto staunchly Germanophile King Boris. The monarch would have preferred to probe for peace with the British ambassador, Knatchbull-Hugessen. However, London's envoy recommended the king's agent to George Earle. Boris was described as morbidly afraid of losing both his throne and his life. He hoped that a quick deal with the American naval attaché would save him from his Communist—and his Fascist—enemies.[35]

Further leads, none of them emanating from Papen's embassy, showed that Rumania had sent a negotiator to İstan-

35. Kroll to Foreign Ministry, 2 April 1943, A.A. 3969/467. Knatchbull-Hugessen to Foreign Office, 7 May 1943, P.R.O., F.O. 371/C5246/699/18; Helm to Central Department, 15 May 1943, P.R.O., F.O. 371/C6397/699/18.

bul in late February. He was Savel Radulescu, former under secretary in the Bucharest foreign ministry and presently a member of the state petroleum commission. A Yugoslav spokesman arrived about 12 March and was very favorable when Menemencioğlu speculated that they might all merge their foreign policies, armies, economies, and monetary systems. Menemencioğlu mentioned that he had begun his endeavors just after his return from the Adana conference. Yet he boasted that Churchill had not given him his cue and that British money would not underwrite the agreements between Turkey and her neighbors. Rather, his goal was independence of all the Great Powers, Germany of course included. The only skeptics at these conferences appear to have been members of the Hungarian delegation, though that country, as has been seen, was originally most responsive to Turkey's proposals. However, Menemencioğlu rebuked the Hungarians and asked them if they wanted to slide back under "a revived Hapsburg hegemony" or some other kind of Teutonic control. The Hungarians must have acceded, because the Turkish foreign minister appears to have anticipated no internal difficulties and even went so far as to reassure the Soviet Union that his coalition posed no threat to it. In view of post war events, that assurance appears to have been premature, arrogant, and foolish all at the same time.[36]

But to Hitler's war effort in 1943, the self-confident attitude behind Turkish foreign policy was considered dangerous. Ribbentrop thought the situation demanded the occupation of Turkey before she openly disavowed her neutrality. Papen stalled him, thereby sparing the Republic much human and material loss. Papen did this by steadfastly depicting Menemencioğlu, Saracoğlu, and İnönü as men of good faith and as valuable informants about activities in the enemy's camp. However, Hans Kroll, who was becoming Papen's nemesis, was also fully aware of the ulterior drives of Turkish foreign policy and, unlike his chief, unequivocally disapproved of them. He informed Berlin that Ankara wished Germany no good, if only because she was still the ally of the detested Italians. Kroll likewise frowned on the visit of Air Marshal Sholto Douglas to Ankara in March, and of General Sir Henry Maitland Wilson to the city in April.

36. Ribbentrop to Papen, 28 May 1943, A.A. 52/790.

To receive Churchill's supreme Middle Eastern commander, the Nazi diplomat charged, was to bend Turkish neutrality beyond the breaking point. Here Kroll exaggerated, though he was unaware of it. Maitland Wilson approved delivery to Turkey of three hundred and fifty tanks, three hundred antiaircraft guns, five hundred antitank guns, and about ninety-nine thousand various small arms in 1943.

But to Wilson's exasperation, the Turks did not use this equipment to anything like Britain's idea of maximum advantage. They did not improve their harbors, strengthen their railroads, or ever find enough locomotive coal to take this matériel to inland army bases. Edwin C. Hole, the British consul general at İzmir and an eyewitness of this Turkish mismanagement, wrote of:

> lines of army cars here which were brought down on trucks without even the wheels being chocked up, and sustained heavy damage in the process. They have been left standing in the open for weeks on end with no attention, without the engines being turned over or the weight taken off the tyres. The Turk has very little mechanical sense and all this valuable material will shortly be useless.

At another point, Hole said the Turks had the mechanical aptitude of "Neandertal Man." But Alexander Cadogan, the Foreign Office under secretary, suspected the Turks were more than just stupid. He accused them of being deliberately obstructive. Kroll, though he did not know of Britain's difficulties in detail, put his finger on one reason for them. Maitland Wilson talked about a Balkan campaign to liberate Greece and evict the Italians and Germans from the Dodecanese islands. The British would then schedule a plebiscite to determine the postwar possession of the islands. Kroll knew that the Turks were afraid the vote would go to the Greeks. It would be much harder, Ankara feared, to recover the Dodecanese from a liberated Athens than from a beaten Rome. For that reason, Kroll believed, the İnönü government was ambivalent toward a Second Front in the Balkans and not out of any genuine friendship for Nazi Germany.[37]

37. Kroll to Foreign Ministry, 26 April 1943, A.A. 52/616. Hole to Knatchbull-Hugessen, 8 July 1943, and Foreign Office commentary, P.R.O., F.O. 371/R6831/55/44. Further reactions to the difficulties of lend-lease operations in Turkey are found in Matthews to Hull, 14

As might have been expected, the Italian foreign ministry shared Kroll's dim view of Turkey's intentions. Il Duce's ambassador to Bulgaria, Magistrati, returned to Rome in the middle of April and reported that Bulgarian agents had detected a large buildup of Turkish armed forces along the Thracian frontier. These were suspected of being the spearhead of a projected Anglo-Turkish drive into central Europe. The Bulgarians were calling for Turkey to be "judged by her actions," and Magistrati was perfectly ready to echo these pleas at the Palazzo Chigi. The Italian diplomat thought that only the presence of Fevzi Çakmak as chief of staff held the Turks to their neutrality. But the British were working for his replacement by the pro-Allied Asım Gündüz. The latter's appointment would be followed by Ankara's declaration of war on the Axis, which Germany had best prepare for as quickly as possible.

Ribbentrop decided to put Menemencioğlu to a peculiar test. In July and again in August, he ordered Papen, at an appropriate social function, to confront the Turkish foreign minister with a draft treaty stating that Ankara would automatically call for the Wehrmacht's intervention if the Allies attempted to land on Turkish soil. Ribbentrop did not think the Turk would accept on the spot, but he wanted Papen to observe his first facial reactions very closely. If there was anything sheepish or suspicious about them, the Wilhelmstrasse would judge accordingly. But the German ambassador twice refused to contrive this little episode. He thought it was enough that the Turks were delaying delivery of British lend-lease matériel, and, at any rate, considered it senseless to attempt to formulate future policy on the twitch of a muscle or the quiver of flesh.[38]

Papen had his way, and Ribbentrop restrained his anger, perhaps because an additional factor gave him pause. As they had done several times before, the Japanese intervened to take an unexpected and disturbing interest in Turkish affairs. Though the Wilhelmstrasse had always regarded

March 1943, *FRUS, 1943*, vol. 4, p. 1098; Winant to Hull, 25 May 1943, *FRUS, 1943*, vol. 4, pp. 1130–32; Hull to Winant, 29 May 1943, *FRUS, 1943*, vol. 4, pp. 1132–33; Kelley to Hull, 5 November 1943, *FRUS, 1943*, vol. 4, pp. 1149–50. Weisband, *Turkish Foreign Policy*, pp. 157–59.

38. Mackensen to Foreign Ministry, 16 April 1943, A.A. 52/1776; Ribbentrop to Papen, 10 July 1943, A.A. 52/1072, and 2 August 1943, A.A. 52/1149. Papen to Foreign Ministry, 14 July 1943, A.A. 52/1029.

Sofia as a diplomatic backwater, it was astonished to learn that the Japanese had made it a nerve center of their intelligence work and their most important listening post in the Balkans. Their Sofia embassy was directed by Akira Yamaji, known to some members of the German foreign service from his earlier assignments in Berlin and Vienna. He was a very unusual, and potentially dangerous, Japanese. He spoke fluent German and workable Bulgarian. His staff was highly expert, all its members competent in one or more Balkan or central European languages.

Furthermore, all these Japanese were outgoing and popular, not least Yamaji's wife, who dressed and entertained in the Western manner. An accomplished hostess, she made many friends for her husband. He flattered the Bulgarians by referring to them as "the Japanese of the Balkans," visited even their second-rate towns, and was made an honorary citizen by many of the communities. Yamaji gave large sums of money to charitable institutions, but what so disturbed the Wilhelmstrasse was that he spoke of giving away the territory of Germany's allies or satellites. He encouraged the Bulgarians to make irredentist claims against Yugoslavia and the Yugoslavs to demand land from Albania. In the process, he not only affronted the Italians but worked with Communists and Jews. He disapproved of Nazi anti-Semitism, and one of his attachés rented property from a Jewish landlord. Worst of all, Yamaji seemed to be encouraging Bulgarian defeatism, coordinating his efforts with the maneuvers of the Turkish foreign ministry, His liaison man to Ankara was Dimitri Dragneff, a Bulgarian newspaperman who had lived a long time in Turkey. Ribbentrop was not always sure whether these defectionist maneuvers were officially sanctioned by Tokyo or only the work of unlicensed subordinates. But a few months later, he and the Italians had Japanese journalists generally excluded from Albania. Those in Turkey were put under close watch. Beyond that, the Nazi foreign minister decided it was best not to antagonize Japan, and for this and the other reasons suggested, he suspended consideration of a preventive war against Turkey.[39]

Meanwhile, an event occurred that permanently put all

39. Memorandum for Ribbentrop, "Japan's News Network in Southeast Europe," unsigned, 17 March 1943, A.A. 350/2678; Chief of Security Police to Foreign Ministry, 22 June 1943, A.A. 350/3267 Geh. Rs.

such Nazi plans out of the question. On 24 July, a few days after the first bombing of Rome, the Fascist Grand Council voted Mussolini out of power. The next day, the king of Italy arrested him and assumed command of the armed forces. Marshal Pietro Badoglio, who had been feuding with Il Duce since the days of the Abyssinian campaign, formed a new government and opened peace negotiations with the Allies. These terminated on 8 September, when Italy withdrew from the war. Rather unrealistically, Badoglio asked the Turkish government to mediate and secure better terms from the Allies. Menemencioğlu refused. Knatchbull-Hugessen analyzed the Turk's policy as follows:

> There is no doubt that he [Menemencioğlu] and the Turkish government as a whole have welcomed the fall of the Italian dictator, partly for itself and . . . perhaps because events may shape themselves in such a way as to enable Turkey, without any risk to herself, to help to play the role of policeman in the Balkans. . . . There are indications that his subordinates in the Ministry have been toying with dreams of some sort of a compromise peace in which Italy might occupy a neutral buffer position not unlike that of Turkey. But if such ideas were ever entertained by M. Menemencioglu himself, he was astute enough not to oblige Signor Guariglia [the Italian ambassador] by offering himself as the intermediary for bringing them to fruition. He no doubt realized that to do so would probably ruin whatever chances he may have later on of exercising his influence in his chosen sphere—Bulgaria, Roumania and Hungary.

Later, the British diplomat predicted that Turkey would not rest content as policeman of the Balkans. She would demand to be possessor of the Dodecanese, too. As an inspired article, published in *Tanin* on 10 September, put it, "Italy's surrender means her departure from the Balkans [and] the restitution of the Dodecanese to their legitimate owners."[40]

Yet the Germans were not idle. They occupied the Po Valley, rescued Mussolini from his confinement in the Abruzzi Apennines, and took direct control of Rome. The king and Badoglio were driven to Bari, while Marshal Rommel, in a new assignment, became virtual master of Italy. But by this time, the Anglo-American Allies had conquered all

---

40. Knatchbull-Hugessen to Eden, 2 August 1943, P.R.O., F.O. 371/R7416/55/44, and 13 September 1943, P.R.O., F.O. 371/R9066/55/44.

Sicily and, in the middle of August, crossed to the mainland. The Wehrmacht now had a new front to defend and quickly funneled massive reinforcements into the peninsula. According to British estimates, the Turks hoped the belligerents would bitterly contest every foot of Italian soil, permanently destroying the country's economy and forever eliminating Italy as Turkey's competitor in the Mediterranean.[41] The Turks waited to see how devastating the destruction would be. For the present, they could be sure the day had passed when the Reich could consider a punitive operation against Turkey. It was a major accomplishment of Ankara's diplomacy that it had successfully dodged the German menace until that day arrived.

41. Madrid Embassy to Foreign Office, 10 July 1944, P.R.O., F.O. 371/R11216/11216/44.

Chapter 8

The End of Papen's Mission

The fall of Mussolini opened the last phase of intrawar relations between Berlin and Ankara, posing new goals to both governments. The end of Il Duce's reign was the beginning of Germany's death throes. After losing major battles, Hitler's armies were still capable of making surprising comebacks, though the significance of their efforts was debatable at the time and proved only temporary in the long run. But in any case the Wehrmacht could no longer successfully shoulder the additional burden of coercing the satellites and intimidating the neutrals. For instance, in early 1944, Finland and the Soviet Union engaged in separate peace negotiations, which ultimately broke down. But the Reich could only be glad of the issue of those talks; it could not have forced it. In a short time, the Nazi government's supreme task would be to keep Germany's heartland intact against invaders. To hold on to the periphery of empire would soon be beyond her means. For Turkey, on the other hand, the latter part of 1943 was a time of relief and renewed confidence. The Turks always respected Mussolini more as an enemy than Hitler did as an ally. Consequently, Il Duce's passing seemed to remove a great obstacle from the path of Turkish greatness and awaken old territorial ambitions. Yet the Turks could not achieve these alone or arbitrarily. For if Italian pressure had disappeared, that of the Allies to enter the war descended on Ankara more heavily than ever. Until July, İnönü's government had had to parry threats of retaliation from Ribbentrop, sometimes abetted by Ciano. Now it was Hull, Eden, and Molotov against whom the Turks had to take their precautions.

Turkish diplomats actually never stopped talking about the return of the Dodecanese islands and Mosul. Depending on the political situation at the time, they just varied the decibel level of their demands.[1] As has been said, British

1. Knatchbull-Hugessen to Foreign Office, 9 July 1943, P.R.O., F.O. 371/R6011/55/44, discusses these territorial aspirations and the Turkish press campaign supporting them. (For list of abbreviations, see p. 221.)

military missions to the Turkish capital were accorded cool receptions and unsatisfactory hearings.[2] But the Turks used these visits to demonstrate to the Germans their growing international prestige. Papen and Kroll were assured that Gen. Maitland Wilson would not be allowed to bully Turkey into war. At the same time, it was made clear to the German embassy that the Republic must be compensated for its neutrality, since the British general thought it important enough to attempt to alter. Menemencioğlu liked to make vague, disquieting allusions to the mountain of lend-lease matériel that the British were stockpiling for the Turks in the warehouses of Alexandria. He made no threats, but he could be irritatingly unaccommodating to representatives of the Axis. When the Italian ambassador paid Menemencioğlu a farewell call after Mussolini's deposition, the Turk said he hoped Italy could still hold the line against Montgomery's and Patton's troops, who were then advancing up the peninsula. He added that he did not think the defense of Albania should be permitted to distract Italy from her main efforts. The Italian diplomat agreed and suggested that Albania might be included in Turkey's Balkan Federation. He hoped that the new Italy would be invited to join, too. Yet Menemencioğlu gave him no encouragement on the latter point, not even as a parting courtesy. Nor would he accredit a new Turkish representative to Mussolini when the Germans, having sprung Il Duce from captivity, set him up as the head of the small, Fascist Republic of Salo in the Milanese lake country.[3]

To the Allies, the Turks were almost equally independent. Gen. Maitland Wilson recommended an invasion of the Balkans to parallel Allied operations in Italy. The Americans did not want this, because they feared it would siphon strength from their preferred "Operation Overlord," the cross-channel invasion of France. But Churchill regarded the Balkan scheme as warmly as ever, and Stalin believed Turkey should be engaged in the fight against Germany in some way. Nevertheless, the İnönü government refused to issue

2. Knatchbull-Hugessen to Foreign Office, 14 June 1943, P.R.O., F.O. 371/R5466/55/44; 15 July 1943, P.R.O., F.O. 371/R6830/55/44. Kroll to Foreign Ministry, 20 April 1943, A.A. 52/589.

3. Papen to Foreign Ministry, 29 July 1943, A.A. 52/1096; Steengracht to Weizsäcker, 20 October 1943, A.A. 52/488.

a declaration of war against the Axis, though it hinted one might be forthcoming in return for precise territorial incentives. When Knatchbull-Hugessen demanded that Turkey fulfill her alliance pledge of 1939, Saracoğlu replied:

> Turkey has no intention of abandoning neutrality to enter the war, but she does not consider herself neutral vis-a-vis Britain and America. He [Saracoğlu] asked that it should be understood that the term neutrality was employed only in order not to bring about complications with other powers. The Prime Minister then said that if Germany evacuated the peninsula, she [Turkey] would collaborate in any Anglo-American initiative directed towards restoring Balkan order.

Of Saracoğlu's stand, the Foreign Office expert, George L. Clutton, minuted that "Mr. John Bunyan would have called the Turkish Prime Minister Mr. Facing Bothways. I have rarely heard of such desperate juggling with words."[4]

In the middle of August, Menemencioğlu began to complain that Radio Moscow was encouraging the Arab unity movement in its Arabic transmissions to Iraq and Syria. What particularly irritated the Turkish foreign minister was that Britain took no steps to quash these broadcasts. He protested to Knatchbull-Hugessen that a compromise on the Arab area must have been hatched between the Kremlin and Churchill's government because, so far, the latter had been unable to stage the Second Front that Stalin demanded.[5] The British ambassador denied these allegations and assured the Turk that the Arab question would be solved to mutual advantage after the war. But Knatchbull-Hugessen and his colleagues in the Foreign Office did not really believe that they could allay Turkish suspicions or modify Turkey's anti-Arab policy. Maurice Hankey, chairman of the Colonial Research Council, wrote:

> The fact is that Turkey is against an Arab Federation, or even a Syrian Federation, and no doubt an effective and strong

4. Knatchbull-Hugessen to Foreign Office, 29 August 1943, and Memorandum by Clutton, 31 August 1943, P.R.O., F.O. 371/R8163/55/44.

5. Thompson, Baghdad, to Foreign Office, 19 August 1943, P.R.O., F.O. 371/E4930/506/65; Knatchbull-Hugessen to Foreign Office, 22 August 1943, P.R.O., F.O. 371/E5010/506/65.

Arab power to the south would offer stronger opposition to Turkish claims on Syria or Iraq for territorial changes.[6]

With equal vehemence, Menemencioğlu castigated the policy of the Bulgarians. He described them as pro-Communist at heart, unwilling affiliates of the Axis, and ready to double-cross it if the Allies made suitable territorial concessions. The government in Sofia, he charged, aspired to play the "gendarme" of the Balkans and was indifferent whether it did so under Nazi or Soviet auspices. Menemencioğlu hinted that Ankara would like to be named as Hitler's policeman in the Balkans, but Papen countered that Berlin had no reason to suspect the good faith of the Bulgarian King Boris.[7] A few weeks after this conversation, that monarch died under mysterious circumstances. The Turks expressed their official sympathies but also used the obsequies to arouse German apprehensions about Bulgaria's course under Boris's successor, the child king Simeon, and the newly installed regency. Ankara warned of a separate peace and Allied beachheads established at Burgas and Varna, unless more pro-Axis forces were stationed in Bulgaria. As has been indicated, the Turks cannot have had German detachments in mind, because these posed a danger to their own sovereignty. But they might have been ready to detail their own units west of the Maritza frontier, as a nonaligned and anti-Communist "peacekeeping" force. With greater issues at stake among them, it could be hoped in Ankara that neither the German, British, nor Soviet governments would find it worthwhile to evict the Turks after the war.

A Bulgarian diplomat told the German embassy that his superiors regarded a Turkish invasion as imminent. He thought it would nominally be conducted in behalf of the Allies, but he had no doubt that Ankara's troops could vanquish any opposition Sofia could muster and thereafter organize a long and effective occupation. Evidently the Germans agreed, because the Army High Command wanted to

6. Thompson, Baghdad, to Foreign Office, 27 August 1943, and Memorandum by Hankey, 30 August 1943, P.R.O., F.O. 371/E5129/506/65.

7. Papen to Foreign Ministry, 5 August 1943, A.A. 52/1138. Menemencioğlu made similar remarks about Bulgaria and about Turkey policing the Balkans to the British ambassador. Knatchbull-Hugessen to Eden, 29 August 1943, P.R.O., F.O. 371/R8531/55/44.

send a full general to the Turkish capital to offset the visits of the British military and conduct staff talks on future Balkan operations. Marshal Fevzi Çakmak looked forward to receiving Gerd von Rundstedt for this purpose, but Papen decided that the deputation should be called off. He argued that it was unnecessary because, if not in Bulgaria, then irredentist aspirations elsewhere would force the Turks to declare themselves. Prodding from the outside, on the other hand, might act as a check on their chauvinistic minds.[8]

The ambassador thought that the Dodecanese islands would act as the irresistible bait and cited articles by Necmeddin Sadak as proof. The journalist, recently returned from Germany, had never regarded an Axis victory as a foregone conclusion. But now he recommended that Hitler support a strong Balkan bloc to buttress the new order in southeastern Europe. To Turkey, he assigned the leading role but argued that she could not effectively fulfill it unless the defenses of İstanbul and of the Anatolian coast were deepened. To achieve the first, Necmeddin Sadak demanded border rectifications from Bulgaria; for the second, Italy would have to be forced to surrender the Dodecanese islands to the Turkish Republic. Ankara raised this issue as soon as Mussolini fell from power. The Churchill ministry wanted to exploit the confusion attending the transition from Il Duce to Marshal Badoglio by sending an amphibious force to the Dodecanese. The prime minister, consonant with the 1939 treaty between London and Ankara, expected Turkish assistance either in the form of servicing ships of the Royal Navy or participating in the landing operations themselves. But he would not discuss the question of postwar sovereignty in the islands, and the Turks abstained from further involvement in the venture. Instead, strictly interpreting their rights as neutrals, they threatened to confiscate any landing craft beached on their shores and to intern all accompanying personnel. A month later, Knatchbull-Hugessen pressed for their assistance again. Refusal, he threatened, would bring curtailment of further lend-lease supplies and exclusion from the peace conference at the end of the war. The envoy was especially emphatic on this occasion because it was rumored that failure to carry his point would cost

8. Papen to Foreign Ministry, 29 August 1943, A.A. 52/1243, and 14 September 1943, A.A. 52/1322.

him his job. But Menemencioğlu remained adamant.[9] He
knew that he had the undeniable moral ascendancy of the
Balkan Peninsula, because the neighboring states were de-
featist and the Allies hampered by rivalries among themselves. Besides, he hoped to get better terms from the other
side.

Though it was late in the war, Papen was ready to bargain.
He recommended to the Wilhelmstrasse that Badoglio be
petitioned to cede the islands to lighten the burden of
Italian defense against the invading Allies. But it was soon
evident that the marshal was not interested in assuming
that burden in whole or in part; instead, he was secretly
haggling for a capitulation to Gen. Mark Clark's army.
Toward Mussolini, ensconced in his puppet domain under
Wehrmacht guns, Ribbentrop took a strictly legalistic attitude. The Reich would continue to honor his title to the
Dodecanese and to work for the full restitution of Fascist
authority over the Italian Empire. Nonetheless, the Turkish
foreign ministry was not discouraged, though Ribbentrop's
rather irrelevant respect for treaties caused it to be more
careful of its own pledged word to the Allies. The next bid
for the Dodecanese did not come from Menemencioğlu or
his under secretaries, but rather from members of the Turkish secret service. One of them delivered an ultimatum for
the islands to Ambassador von Papen at the end of September. The agent, hinting at impending British landings, gave
Germany only twenty-four hours to answer affirmatively.
However, Ribbentrop was not interested in neutralizing the
eastern Mediterranean at this price; nor did he like the
method. He found the ultimatum outrageous and the secret
service man an inappropriate courier, especially since Ribbentrop was expected to return his acquiescence through the
officially accredited representative of the Reich. Finally, he
again invoked the legal rights of Mussolini and with that,
turned the Turks down flat.[10]

9. Schellenberg to Foreign Ministry, 31 July 1943, A.A. 52/no number; Papen to Foreign Ministry, 26 September 1943, A.A. 52/1370.
Knatchbull-Hugessen to Eden, 29 August 1943, P.R.O., F.O. 371/R8530/
55/44. Knatchbull-Hugessen to Foreign Office, 31 August 1943, P.R.O.,
F.O. 371/R8281/55/44; 2 September 1943, P.R.O., F.O. 371/R8373/55/44.
10. Papen to Ribbentrop, 16 September 1943, A.A. 52/1332; Ribbentrop to Papen, 29 September 1943, A.A. 52/1534; Papen to Ribbentrop,
30 September 1943, A.A. 52/1391.

The Turkish leaders were so angry that they then made an informal agreement with the British ambassador. Though Turkish troops would not participate in assault operations on the Dodecanese themselves, the leaders promised to supply the British personnel who did with fresh meat and vegetables.[11] Churchill was sufficiently encouraged to order General Wilson to attempt landing on Rhodes in autumn 1943. He described the times as right for "daring, improvising, and playing high." But the British invasion of Rhodes was ignominiously repelled by an Italo-German force, and the Germans then went on to capture Cos, Leros, and Samos, where Wilson's command had maintained outposts since the beginning of the war. The Germans hoped to take sizable numbers of prisoners, but the defenders managed to execute another Dunkirk. Using the same Turkish caïques that brought in their victuals, the British now evacuated several hundred of their troops, together with some Italian auxiliaries, their commanding officers, and a Greek archbishop.[12]

The Turkish cabinet kept abreast of the operation, and consequently the German foreign ministry ordered Papen to register the strongest of protests against this violation of Turkish neutrality. Nonetheless, the German ambassador deferred action and advised Ribbentrop that Turkish cooperation with General Wilson's troops was largely the policy of only one man, Prime Minister Saracoğlu, who barely overcame the objections to the plan made by the neutralist or pro-German members of the government. Papen believed Saracoğlu had scored his last success. The prime minister was described as widely unpopular with his countrymen, who blamed him for inflation, food shortages, and administrative corruption. Other ministers were demanding Saracoğlu's resignation and intriguing for his job, foremost among them Foreign Minister Menemencioğlu. Papen argued that Menemencioğlu would be able to oust Saracoğlu from power if he first achieved a major diplomatic success at the foreign ministry. The German ambassador urged the Wilhelmstrasse to confer such a success upon him by ceding to Turkey the Dodecanese islands.[13]

11. Ribbentrop to Papen, 29 September 1943, A.A. 52/1535.
12. Winston S. Churchill, *Closing the Ring*, (Boston, 1951), pp. 203–25, has a narrative of the Dodecanese fighting.
13. Papen to Ribbentrop, 25 October 1943, A.A. 52/1526.

The supreme crisis in Turco-German relations, Papen held, had been reached. This was the best opportunity to bring Menemencioğlu into power and the Turks into the war against Russia to destroy the Red Army in a flanking movement. The German envoy was probably right in his assessment of the Turkish domestic situation,[14] but wrong in his forecast of its strategical consequences. The turning point of the war had come at Stalingrad, and it was some months since General von Paulus and his men had been encircled and interned by Soviet troops. Yet hindsight makes the significance of Stalingrad clearer than it was to the men of the time. It should be remembered that Stalin's forces were not able to clear the Crimea until April 1944, and another full month elapsed before the Germans surrendered Sevastopol. These victories were very costly, and Soviet commanders were acutely aware that much of their equipment was technically inferior to German armaments. Two armies invading the Crimea, one under Tolbukhin descending through the Perekop isthmus and another led westward from Kerch by Yeremenko, sustained nearly one hundred thousand casualties. Even Stalin could not have justified such losses indefinitely, and any new weight, even as relatively light as that of Turkey, thrown into the balance against him might have prodded the Soviet dictator to attempt a separate peace with Germany. In June 1943, Molotov and Ribbentrop had secretly conferred behind German lines to end the fighting on the eastern front. Molotov insisted on the restoration of Russia's prewar frontier, and the talks broke down.[15] But the possibility remained that such negotiations might be resumed.

Yet even if a separate peace with the Soviet Union could not be achieved, Turkish intervention on the side of the Axis could most conceivably have shaken the alliance between

14. Some months before, Knatchbull-Hugessen had reported Saracoğlu's leadership to be unpopular for the same reasons as those cited by Papen. But the British envoy thought Saracoğlu might stave off the collapse of his ministry by using police terrorism against his opponents, especially those from minority groups. Knatchbull-Hugessen to Eden, 19 May 1943, P.R.O., F.O. 371/R4490/7/44; 2 June 1943, P.R.O., F.O. 371/R5698/55/44. Knatchbull-Hugessen to Foreign Office, 16 June 1943, P.R.O., F.O. 371/R5310/55/44.

15. On the Molotov-Ribbentrop talks and the liberation of the Crimea, see Liddell Hart, *History of the Second World War*, pp. 488, 574–76.

Stalin and the Anglo-American coalition. If, as Papen wished, Ribbentrop had offered the Dodecanese islands and the Turkish Republic had accepted them, then the Soviet Union would most probably have protested the alteration of the Mediterranean power balance and intervened militarily to redress it. The British would hardly have tolerated a Soviet invasion of Turkish territory. In October 1943, Foreign Secretary Eden, together with his American opposite, Cordell Hull, had met in Moscow with Commissar Molotov. They agreed about general war aims but not about Soviet aspirations in the Balkans. Eden was extremely reluctant to concede Yugoslavia to the Soviet sphere of influence. He specifically objected to Russia's supplying the pro-Communist Tito with some of its lend-lease equipment.

In the end, the British government decided to tolerate the Soviet presence in Yugoslavia, but the Foreign Office soon served notice on Soviet missions that London would not accept the extension of Moscow's hegemony over Turkey. Knatchbull-Hugessen reported that Vinogradov, Stalin's envoy at Ankara, had inquired about the possibility of putting the eastern vilayets of Turkey under the "protective custody" of the Red Army, as had been done in Iran. The Soviet ambassador also put in a claim to the Dodecanese or some other eastern Mediterranean base and to the Italian navy. Knatchbull-Hugessen rebuffed Vinogradov on all counts and cautioned Eden to prepare countermeasures.[16] Papen found out about these disagreements and reported additionally that Stalin was afraid the quarrel would degenerate into a war between the erstwhile allies. According to Papen's informants, Stalin had begun to remark that Turkish air bases, which could be used to mount attacks on the Rumanian oil fields, could serve equally well for raids on the Soviet refineries at Baku. Furthermore, Knatchbull-Hugessen was said to be urging the threat of such raids to deter the Soviet Union from aggressive movements against eastern Anatolia.[17]

Knatchbull-Hugessen had a chance to press these ideas on Eden when he and Menemencioğlu were invited to meet with the British foreign secretary in Cairo in early November 1943. Eden wanted to brief and reassure the Turkish

16. Knatchbull-Hugessen to Eden, 17 November 1943, P.R.O., F.O. 371/R12267/55/44.
17. Papen to Ribbentrop, 24 November 1943, A.A. 52/1600.

minister about the results of the recently concluded talks in Moscow. In preparation for his trip to Egypt, Knatchbull-Hugessen drafted a lengthy paper entitled "A Long-View of British Turkish Policy." As will be seen, a copy of this paper was purloined from the British embassy by a German agent and delivered into Papen's hands. The paper argued that the Soviet Union was out to wreck the Montreux Convention and deprive the Turks of any control over traffic passing through the Straits. Russia would propose that the right of unrestricted egress accrue to all the Black Sea nations, but since she had the only significant battle fleet, Russia would obviously profit most from this change in the regulation of Straits traffic.

Furthermore, the British ambassador alleged that the Soviets wanted to convert Turkey into a permanent neutral like Switzerland or like Belgium in the early nineteenth century. By international agreement, Ankara would be forbidden to contract alliances and, in effect, would be perpetually vulnerable to Soviet dictation. Vinogradov was said to have remarked that this kind of arrangement would be preferable to an outright Soviet annexation of Turkish territory, but Knatchbull-Hugessen did not think even annexation out of the question once Stalin had recouped his losses in the war. The envoy expected the Turks to place little reliance on British support. Instead they would try to make trouble between Britain and Russia. One of Menemencioğlu's deputies was already saying that the Turks would accept a Soviet commissioner at the Straits if the British were prepared to include a Russian in the regulation of the Suez Canal and Gibraltar. Knatchbull-Hugessen dismissed this compromise as preposterous and again recommended a stout attitude toward the Soviet bully.[18]

These and similar reports about Anglo-Russian tensions, together with memoranda about the Cairo and Teheran conferences, came to Ribbentrop as part of the "Cicero Papers." Partly for this reason, the Nazi foreign minister failed to give these papers their full due and to apply them to the formulation of German political and military policy. "Cicero" was the code name of an Albanian spy who worked as valet to the British ambassador in Ankara and pilfered his secret papers in return for large payments from the Gestapo.

18. Papen to Ribbentrop, 5 November 1943, A.A. 52/1603.

Cicero told the Germans he hated the British because an English aristocrat had killed his father, also in domestic service, in a hunting accident. Cicero offered his first microfilm of top secret documents to a member of Papen's staff for twenty thousand pounds about 30 October 1943. This began an association with the German embassy of approximately three months duration. Cicero had ample opportunity for theft because Knatchbull-Hugessen was cavalier and even careless about security precautions. During this time Berlin paid Cicero three hundred thousand pounds for data concerning Allied technical personnel in Turkey, types of armament being shipped to Russia, and agenda for the inter-Allied conferences.

But from the start, the Wilhelmstrasse was suspicious of these documents. Ribbentrop complained about Cicero's fees, even though he saw to it that about two-thirds of the money was paid in counterfeit currency. He also feared that the spy was a British "plant," because a strange set of fingerprints was detected in the margin of one of the documents, suggesting that Cicero had an accomplice who held the papers while he photographed them. And, finally, the whole intrigue was conducted under Gestapo rather than foreign ministry auspices. A Gestapo representative on Papen's staff sent the papers directly to Ernst Kaltenbrunner, Himmler's deputy in Berlin, without letting Papen, his nominal superior, see them first. Ribbentrop received them only after Himmler and Kaltenbrunner had read them through.[19]

Papen was vexed because information in the documents stolen by Cicero bearing on Turkish domestic problems would have helped him in his representations to the İnönü government. Ribbentrop was disgruntled because the procedure itself was an affront to his ministerial prerogative. After an interoffice fight with Himmler, the Gestapo was persuaded to allow Papen to see the Cicero papers before they were forwarded to Berlin. But Ribbentrop never got over his initial distrust of their source. Several times, Papen had to reassure him about the authenticity of the documents, and on at least one occasion, the foreign minister inquired

19. L. C. Moyzisch, *Operation Cicero*, trans. Constantine Fitzgibbon and Heinrich Fraenkel, pp. 40, 56–64, 78–79, 133. William Sholto Douglas, *Combat and Command: The Story of an Airman in Two World Wars*, p. 544.

whether the Ankara embassy had considered measures to liquidate Cicero if the need arose.[20] In the meantime, suspicion in Berlin was so thick that it obscured the opportunities at hand in Ankara and Cairo. The correspondence between Eden and Knatchbull-Hugessen was ignored, the status of the Dodecanese islands remained unchanged, and the Allies proceeded with a series of high-level conferences that arranged the total destruction of Hitler's Reich. With inter-Allied postwar rivalries now always simmering just below the surface, these talks were usually strained and difficult. But they were not failures, partly because the Germans had bungled their opportunity to bring those rivalries to a boil.

The Cairo meeting for which Knatchbull-Hugessen prepared his précis occurred between 5 and 8 November 1943. It was intended to be the first of two between top ministers from London, Washington, and Ankara. The second conference, scheduled for the following December, was to include President İnönü as well as Foreign Minister Menemencioğlu. Churchill and Eden hoped that their Turkish counterparts would agree in the second Cairo Conference to proposals that had been sketched for them in the first one. Eden did not like Menemencioğlu, whom he considered pro-Axis, but on the whole he approached his task optimistically. But Menemencioğlu was not to be coerced by just a brave show. Eden confronted the Turkish foreign minister with two proposals. The first was that Turkey furnish the Allies with airbases. The second was that Turkey declare war on Germany and fight her with the Allies. Eden would have preferred not to press the second proposal at Cairo, because he thought it more likely that Turkey would fulfill her alliance commitments in stages. Molotov, on the other hand, had already made it clear at the Moscow Conference that he thought the lease of bases alone was a waste of time that would not directly aid Russia's war effort. Molotov pressured Eden to push for full Turkish participation in the war. Averell Harriman, the American ambassador in Moscow, thought Molotov was himself subject to pressure from Soviet army commanders. Harriman wrote:

20. Wagner to Papen, 27 December 1943, A.A. 52/1803; Sonnleithner to Papen, 18 January 1944, A.A. 52/111.

Without coming to Moscow it is hard to appreciate how differently they view the war from the British and ourselves. The Russians have the primitive view that they have suffered and bled to destroy Hitler and see no reason why the Turks should not do the same if it can help shorten the war. They honestly believe that the entry of Turkey will force the Germans to move a considerable number of divisions from the eastern front. In posing this demand they are entirely indifferent to any moral or actual obligation to assist the Turks in fighting the Germans.[21]

Menemencioğlu may have guessed that the impetus behind Eden's program came partly from the Soviets, which would only have made his refusal more inevitable. He remarked that Eden's two proposals were in reality the same, because both entailed the clear danger of German retaliation, for which Turkey was not prepared. Yet Menemencioğlu dealt with the British proposals separately. He rejected the first one outright but promised to refer the second to Ankara for further consideration. Though pleading the defenselessness of his country, he insisted she be allowed to undertake a full and active role in the fighting rather than merely opening aircraft facilities to the Allies. "*Again and again* Numan repeated that Turkey would never agree to play a passive part" (my italics). And, the Turk continued, the British foreign secretary must make clear all the political ramifications of Turkish intervention.

Menemencioğlu did not say precisely to what questions the term *political* referred, but he hinted broadly. According to the version of this conversation given by the British embassy in Washington to the State Department, Menemencioğlu observed that Britain and the Soviet Union seemed already to have reserved for themselves territorial bounties to be claimed at the end of the war. Britain had intervened in strength in Iraq, Russia was claiming Moldavia and Transylvania, and both powers had occupied Iran. The Turkish minister was implying that Ankara should have a share of the spoils, but Eden refused to be pinned down. He ex-

21. On Molotov and the Red Army, see Harriman to Roosevelt, 6 November 1943, *Foreign Relations of the United States: The Conferences at Cairo and Tehran*, p. 158. The quotation is taken from Harriman to Roosevelt, 4 November 1943, *The Conferences at Cairo and Tehran*, p. 153. Herbert Feis, *Churchill, Roosevelt, Stalin: The War They Waged and the Peace They Sought*, pp. 228–31.

plained that Iraqi independence was guaranteed by a treaty
and that the occupation of Iran was only a temporary wartime measure. About Soviet policy, he could not comment.
And never once did he refer to the Dodecanese. Among the
British delegation at Cairo, only Gen. Henry Maitland
Wilson raised the possibility of utilizing Turkish troops to
recapture the Dodecanese. But the general said nothing about
Turkey receiving control of the islands permanently. Without the prospect of such concessions, Menemencioğlu would
not commit himself. At the end of the talks, he left Eden
weary and exasperated. The Turk appeared to be hard-of-
hearing, but Eden suspected his deafness was feigned. In
his memoirs, the foreign secretary wrote that no one can be
so deaf as a Turk who does not wish to be persuaded.[22]

About one point in the conversations, Eden was particularly puzzled. Though London was far behind schedule in
delivering planes, tanks, and antiaircraft installations to
strengthen Turkey's arsenal, Menemencioğlu refrained from
criticizing Eden and instead requested 134,000 tons of boxcars and locomotives in addition to the offensive weaponry.
This request may have been merely a delaying tactic, but
Papen, who was excellently informed about details of the
Cairo conferences, thought it had a further significance.
Planes and tanks, he commented, were ideal for a descent
on Syria and Iraq where rail networks were rare, but Bulgaria and adjacent Balkan areas were tolerably well served
with railways. If the Turks intended to penetrate further
into the peninsula, their primary problem would be to increase Turkish capacity to use existing Balkan lines. To solve
this problem, Papen thought, was one of Menemencioğlu's
goals in his exchanges with Eden.[23]

After the first Cairo Conference, the British and American

22. Alling to Stettinius, 9 November 1943, *The Conferences at Cairo
and Tehran*, pp. 164–67. This is based on a report furnished by William
Hayter, first secretary of the British Embassy in Washington. See also
Kelley to Roosevelt, 10 November 1943, *The Conferences at Cairo and
Tehran*, pp. 174–75; Combined Chiefs of Staff Minutes, 24 November
1943, *The Conferences at Cairo and Tehran*, pp. 330–34. Anthony Eden,
The Reckoning: The Memoirs of Anthony Eden, Earl of Avon, p. 485.

23. Alling to Stettinius, 9 November 1943, *The Conferences at Cairo
and Tehran*, p. 165. Papen to Foreign Ministry, 18 December 1943, A.A.
52/1845.

leaders moved on to Teheran for talks with Marshal Stalin. They pondered the question of Turkish intervention several times, and from their remarks several points ought to be recalled. Churchill said the Turkish army would have been considered a good army at the end of the First World War but had begun to appear deficient when Bulgaria started to import more modern weapons from France. Churchill's observation appears to be faint praise or even a veiled slight unless it is viewed in the context of other events at the Teheran Conference. It should be remembered that Stalin, in his very first remarks to Roosevelt, admitted the war situation was still very bad for Russia. The Red Army held the initiative but, according to Stalin, could take the offensive nowhere except in the Ukraine. The Soviet leader still emphatically wanted Turkish intervention.

Later, at the second Cairo Conference, Roosevelt was more unequivocal in his praise for the Turkish army. He thought the Turks had a fine infantry and a very good artillery that could make real headway in land operations. He agreed that their aerial arm was deficient, but, taken as a whole, there was no question that the Turkish army was much stronger than the Bulgarian army. At Teheran, Churchill attested his steady conviction that Turkey should be in the war. Gen. Sir Alan Brooke, chief of the imperial general staff, agreed. Both Englishmen reiterated that an allied Turkey could force a redeployment of German troops, intimidate Rumania and Bulgaria into leaving the war, and forward more supplies to the Soviet Union. But throughout the Teheran proceedings, Churchill made it clear that he would not offer Turkey anything more than material assistance and the promise of a place at the peace conference at the end of the war. If Turkey proved obdurate, he threatened to support a change in Turkey's regulatory powers at the Straits. And he enjoined his staff never to raise the matter of the Dodecanese islands in any subsequent conferences with President İnönü. To reassure Turkey and facilitate her entry into the war, Stalin volunteered to pledge that if Turkey declared war on Germany and the pro-Axis Bulgarians in turn attacked the Turks, then the Soviet Union would declare war on Bulgaria and immediately cross her frontiers. The Russian intended his move to forestall all possible

Turkish reservations. Instead, Menemencioğlu later used it as a reason to multiply those reservations.[24]

At the second Cairo Conference, 2 to 7 December 1943, Menemencioğlu, supported by İsmet İnönü, resumed his obstreperous maneuvering. This time his argument with Eden concerned the improvement of Turkish aircraft facilities prior to the issuance of a Turkish declaration of war. The British wanted permission to introduce about seven thousand technical and military personnel into Turkey to build and service airfields to protect İstanbul and İzmir from Axis bombardment. Only when these facilities were complete and ready to receive British squadrons, about 15 February 1944 by military estimates, would Turkey be expected to declare war. But Menemencioğlu argued that the Germans were liable to declare war before that target date arrived. He feared they would dispatch their bombers as soon as they discovered Allied personnel filtering into his country. Eden replied that Germany would not necessarily find out about this collaboration, and if she did, would probably not have the forces to spare for retaliatory action. Menemencioğlu retorted that he could not be so sanguine about the future, that the admission of seven thousand foreigners was excessive, and that he would have "to take up *political matters* in another direction" (italics mine).

Eden and Air Marshal Sholto Douglas offered to reduce the number of Allied personnel in Turkey to about two thousand men, but Menemencioğlu rejoined that he could not say whether that number was too many or too few, since

---

24. For Churchill on the Turkish army, see Bohlen Minutes, Tripartite Meeting, 1 December 1943, *The Conferences at Cairo and Tehran*, pp. 586–93. For Stalin on the war situation, see Bohlen Minutes, Roosevelt-Stalin Meeting, 28 November 1943, *The Conferences at Cairo and Tehran*, pp. 483–86. Roosevelt on the Turkish army, see Agreed Minutes, Third Tripartite Meeting, 6 December 1943, *The Conferences at Cairo and Tehran*, pp. 740–47. Brooke on Turkish intervention, Combined Chiefs of Staff Minutes, 29 November 1943, *The Conferences at Cairo and Tehra*n, pp. 514–28. Churchill on the Straits, see Bohlen Minutes, Tripartite Meeting, 1 December 1943, *The Conferences at Cairo and Tehran*, pp. 586–93. For İnönü and the Dodecanese (that is, Rhodes), see Bohlen Minutes, Tripartite Meeting, 1 December 1943, *The Conferences at Cairo and Tehran*, pp. 586–93. For Stalin's pledge about Bulgaria, see Bohlen Minutes, Tripartite Meeting, 1 December 1943, *The Conferences at Cairo and Tehran*, pp. 586–93. Sir Ernest Llewellyn Woodward, *British Foreign Policy in the Second World War*, 2:600. Feis, *Churchill, Roosevelt, Stalin*, pp. 265–66.

he had no military or technical advisers in his delegation. Eden finally asked Menemencioğlu what he had in mind by political matters, and the Turk answered that he meant the Russian guarantee covering Bulgaria. He wished to discuss it further, though to what end he left unclear.[25] Surely Menemencioğlu could not have wished to define Russia's obligation more extensively. Rather, it seems reasonable to conjecture that he wanted to limit Russia's scope for action or nullify it altogether. Menemencioğlu, as well as the Allied leaders, was fairly sure the Bulgarians could not maintain their frontier against a Turkish attack, but he could entertain no such illusions if the Red Army were to take up stations there.

In his conversations with Churchill and Roosevelt, İsmet İnönü was not only difficult, like Menemencioğlu, but also defensive. He reproached the Allies for harboring suspicions about Turkish policy, though this somewhat surprising interjection can only have aroused more suspicions. The Turkish president shared his foreign minister's anxieties about a German attack during the preparatory period and thought Turkey could not be ready for war by 15 February 1944, no matter how large the consignments of matériel delivered by the Allies. Throughout the talks, he was loathe to discuss technical details because he had come without any Turkish army officers to advise him, an omission that his auditors could well have regarded as both singular and inexcusable. Roosevelt wondered aloud why the Turkish president was now so apprehensive about the admission of Allied personnel, when these, without objection, had been trickling into Turkey for a year previously. İnönü had no explanation but did not become more accommodating.[26] Churchill tried to cajole him, but the wary Turk treated the British leader as if he were tainted.

Churchill, fresh from his meeting with Stalin at Teheran, was quick to assure İnönü that no binding decisions about the Balkans had been taken in the Iranian capital. But the

25. Agreed Minutes, Hopkins-Eden-Menemencioğlu Meeting, 5 December 1943, *The Conferences at Cairo and Tehran*, pp. 726–33.

26. On İnönü's defensiveness, see Agreed Minutes, First Tripartite Meeting, 4 December 1943, *The Conferences at Cairo and Tehran*, pp. 690–98. For Roosevelt's reaction to Turkish objections, see Agreed Minutes, Third Tripartite Meeting, 6 December 1943, *The Conferences at Cairo and Tehran*, pp. 740–47.

Turk did not believe him and drew off, more and more frequently, into Roosevelt's company. This annoyed the British prime minister, and he bluntly told the Ankara delegation that if Turkey did not enter the war, all further lend-lease supplies would be cut off. Roosevelt was more sympathetic and more ready to accept Turkey's unpreparedness, as İnönü and Menemencioğlu depicted it, at face value. But he confided to his son that he suspected the Turks wanted lend-lease equipment not so much to fight in the Second World War as to maintain superiority in the eastern Mediterranean when it was over. If a German account can be believed, Lawrence Steinhardt, American ambassador to Turkey, was even harder on İnönü. He was alleged to have called the Turkish president "dim-witted" and to have compared his character and policies to those of the openly pro-Axis caudillo of Spain, Francisco Franco. Perhaps İnönü heard such remarks. Menemencioğlu told Papen that had the Turkish president known how he was going to be treated at Cairo, he would never have gone.[27]

The experiences of the conferences undoubtedly disconcerted İnönü, but they may have affected Winston Churchill even more. At the end of the talks, the Turks promised to enter the war in principle but without accepting any date for intervention or any precise preparatory program. The nature of their contribution to the Allied war effort was still not clear. It was now clear, however, that there would be no further expansion of Allied activities in the Mediterranean. The November 1943 Teheran Conference, where all the Allied leaders agreed to mount a cross-channel invasion of France as quickly as possible, much diminished the prospects of such Mediterranean activities, in any case. But though Churchill was committed to the Normandy operation, some of his closest associates believed that until the time of the second Cairo Conference, he still wanted to postpone or modify it. At Cairo the Turks frustrated his long-cherished scheme of striking Europe's "soft under-belly." General Brooke commented that this was the point when Churchill lost the predominant position he had held from the beginning of the Anglo-American dialogue. A few weeks later,

27. Elliott Roosevelt, *As He Saw It*, pp. 148–49. Papen to Foreign Ministry, 13 December 1943, A.A. 52/1804, 1805.

Churchill suffered a severe bout of pneumonia at Carthage.[28]

Menemencioğlu described the rest of December as a time of "stormy crisis," during which he did not rule out the possibility of a British surprise attack to seize Turkish air bases. He was taking all precautions to forestall this danger. The foreign minister ordered all British military and technical personnel to be shadowed night and day by detectives, and any Englishman thought to be involved in intelligence work was to be watched especially closely. Any unannounced British aircraft, he threatened to have shot down immediately. And, in the event of a British landing, he would have all Turkish stocks of fuel and ammunition destroyed within forty-eight hours. If Eden and his staff chiefs attempted the invasion of Turkey, Menemencioğlu vowed it would "cost them their necks." In the meantime, the İnönü government forbade further construction on a British radar network in European Turkey, which was to be used in conjunction with air raids on the oil fields of Ploesti, Rumania. Knatchbull-Hugessen argued about this matter with Menemencioğlu but got nowhere.[29]

Yet the British did not implement their threat to curtail lend-lease deliveries to Turkey. Instead they offered to make available at the earliest possible time all the locomotives, boxcars, track, and lubricants that the Turks had recently requested. They did not delude themselves that these items would buy Turkish intervention or even shorten the war. They were fairly certain they would be used in some internecine Balkan struggle totally unrelated to the overall Allied strategical aims just agreed upon at Cairo and Teheran. George L. Clutten, the Foreign Office expert on Turkish affairs and a frequent critic of İnönü's ministers, urged his superiors to deny all further aid to Ankara and to call Turkey's bluff. He wrote:

> The Turkish Foreign Minister puts it abroad that Turkey considers herself in danger of attack from Bulgaria. Turkey is

28. Trumbull Higgins, *Soft Underbelly: The Anglo-American Controversy over the Italian Campaign, 1939–1945*, pp. 129, 131, 134, 138. Frederick E. Morgan, *Overture to Overlord*, pp. 279, 284–85. Feis, *Churchill, Roosevelt, Stalin*, p. 304.

29. Papen to Foreign Ministry, 18 December 1943, A.A. 52/1842, 24 December 1943, A.A. 52/1875, and 3 January 1944, A.A. 52/1.

not in any such danger but to say that she is may be very useful cover for her own military preparations.

But Alexander Cadogan, under secretary of the Foreign Office, thought Britain had no other option but to placate the Turks to some degree. He replied to Clutten:

> We do not wish to break with the Turks altogether. That is to say, we do not want an abrupt cessation of activity, which would be a clear indication to the Germans that we had given it up as a bad job, and that they need no longer fear any threat from that direction. . . . Our object is still to get Turkey into the war as early as possible and in any case to maintain a threat to the Germans from the eastern end of the Mediterranean until Overlord is launched.

Cadogan still hoped that British squadrons would be able to fly into Turkey on 15 February 1944, but he admitted the timetable could not be regarded as set and might be varied by "the progress of events."[30]

By the beginning of 1944, British and German relations with the Turkish Republic had thus reached a state of impasse and immobility. Neither belligerent coalition had lured the Ankara government into the war. According to informants of the German embassy, President İnönü was eager to break the deadlock and invited Eden to come to the Turkish capital to talk again about the postwar status of Bulgaria. The foreign secretary did not respond to this invitation, if indeed it was ever extended.[31] Nor did Papen any longer encourage Turkish irredentism. Instead he resumed and intensified his efforts to reach a separate peace with one of the Allies. Success would obviate the need for alliance with the Turks or for concessions to them.

The origins of Papen's peace offensive may be traced to August 1943. Analyzing the recent fall of Mussolini, Papen frankly told Ribbentrop it happened because the Fascist party was a closed syndicate of old hacks. It had long needed younger members and fresh ideas, but a vain and purblind Mussolini had stubbornly excluded both. To avoid a similar catastrophe for National Socialism, the ambassador urged

30. Foreign Office to Knatchbull-Hugessen, 21 December 1943, and Memorandum by Clutten, 23 December 1943, P.R.O., F.O. 371/R13547/55/44.

31. Schliep to Foreign Ministry, 7 January 1944, A.A. 52/9.

that the party leadership be changed and that traditional Christian values be incorporated into the party program. If these things were done, Papen believed, the papacy would be ready to mediate a peace between the Reich and the Allies and to use its influence to spare the German people the consequences of unconditional surrender.[32] Papen never once mentioned Hitler by name. Perhaps he had in mind only the reconstitution of the lower echelons of the Nazi hierarchy. Apparently because Hitler's position was not explicitly challenged, Ribbentrop was emboldened to present Papen's suggestions, which he characterized as being supported by many German Catholic bishops, to the Führer. But, according to a report from the Swedish legation in Berlin to British intelligence, Hitler fell into a rage before the discussion went very far and accused both Ribbentrop and Göring of treason. The Führer forbade any peace bids from Ankara but failed to take the obvious step of recalling his envoy in that city.[33] Even Ribbentrop did not castigate the German ambassador. He merely advised him to maintain the standard propaganda line about Germany's inevitable victory[34] and to describe all Wehrmacht retreats in Russia as "planned withdrawals."

But Papen, neither reproved nor removed, said what he pleased. He discussed peace terms with the German communities of Ankara and İstanbul and with neutral newspapermen in his embassy. On one or two occasions, he even exchanged views with Allied journalists whom he accidentally met during train trips. To all these audiences, Papen described what he called a "Catholic peace." This would entail the emergence of a new Germany, including the Rhineland, Bavaria, Austria, Hungary, and the Adriatic ports of Trieste and Pula. But Protestant Prussia would pass under inter-Allied control, and the government offices would be tranferred from Berlin to Vienna. In a generous bid for Russian endorsement, Papen recommended that the whole of Rumania and Bulgaria be relegated to the Soviet sphere of influence.[35]

32. Papen to Foreign Ministry, 18 August 1943, A.A. 2618/6407.
33. Foreign Office to Knatchbull-Hugessen, 5 September 1943, P.R.O., F.O. 371/C9241/55/18.
34. Ribbentrop to Papen, 26 August 1943, A.A. 2618/825.
35. Papen to Hencke, 11 January 1944, A.A. 52/12.

Despite Hitler's violent injunction against peace moves, Ribbentrop still did not obstruct or even restrain the ambassador. In fact, he apprised him that the German minister to Rumania, Manfred von Killinger, was broaching similar ideas with Russian contacts in Bucharest. Toward both men, Ribbentrop continued uncharacteristically benign, though he questioned whether Papen had sufficiently pondered the Turkish reaction to his activities. The İnönü government had often called for an early peace and offered to mediate between Germany and the Allies, but it could hardly be expected, the foreign minister pointed out, to endorse any program that relinquished to the Soviet Union the Bulgarian territory that Turkey coveted. Ribbentrop enjoined greater confidentiality on Papen, but his directive came too late and perhaps would have been unrealistic at any time.[36] In Turkey it was impossible to keep anything secret from Menemencioğlu and his alert and overactive secret police. Perhaps Papen was so resigned to leaks from his own and other legations that he made no serious effort to stop them. For whatever reason, he clearly underestimated how insidiously disruptive the opposition of Menemencioğlu could become.

Papen was particularly vulnerable to Turkish counterattack. That he was not a Nazi was well known, as was the fact that his embassy had become a haven for persons disaffected from Hitler's regime. Papen had recently approved the assignment to his staff of Erich Vermehren and his wife, née Countess Plettenberg, a distant relative of Papen's family. The Vermehrens were under suspicion in Germany for their liberal-democratic and Catholic-pacifist political convictions, and it was one of Weizsäcker's protégés, Adam von Trott zu Solz, a man who had been sounding the British about resistance against Hitler since 1938, who introduced Vermehren into the German foreign service.[37] Trott zu Solz was later executed for his part in the bomb plot against Hitler of 20 July 1944.[38]

The Vermehrens' removal to Turkey probably saved them

36. Ribbentrop to Papen, 25 December 1943, A.A. 52/1794.

37. Memorandum by Bieberstein, 5 February 1944, A.A. 52/no number.

38. For more information on Adam von Trott, see Harold C. Deutsch, *The Conspiracy Against Hitler In The Twilight War*, (Minneapolis, 1968), pp. 150–52, 359.

from arrest by the Gestapo, but it is not certain that Papen used his influence to facilitate their departure from Germany, as his enemies in Berlin later charged. The ambassador did personally issue their travel passes and for the last leg of their journey, from Svilengrad, Bulgaria, to İstanbul, made available his special courier plane. This was an unusual and, some critics later alleged, a suspicious courtesy to be shown a junior diplomat, but it was not necessarily clear proof that Papen instigated Vermehren's subsequent conduct. Vermehren's mother, who worked for Goebbels's propaganda ministry in Lisbon, was as rabid a Nazi as her son was a clamant critic of the regime, and Andor Hencke, under secretary for Middle Eastern affairs at the Wilhelmstrasse, cited the mother's allegiance to certify the son's reliability in his post at Ankara. Vermehren became the secretary of Papen's deputy military attaché.[39]

The new man was soon secretly petitioning the British embassy for political asylum. He offered to deliver to Knatchbull-Hugessen a complete list of all Abwehr agents in Turkey and of their contacts in the Turkish governmental offices. Yet the British discouraged Vermehren's attempts at defection several times. In the first place, they thought it would be of limited propaganda value. Since Vermehren and his wife were anti-Nazis of long standing, their flight would hardly demonstrate the growth of a German opposition to Hitler due to the recently worsening war situation. Second, the British expected the Turkish police to pursue any fugitives and, consonant with their rights as agents of a neutral state, to demand their surrender so that they could be returned to the Germans. Knatchbull-Hugessen wanted to avoid this kind of embarrassment. However, in early 1944, the Turkish government ordered its police not to meddle in any desertion from Papen's staff, and consequently they did nothing to impede the Vermehrens' escape to the British embassy and their subsequent removal to asylum in Syria.[40] A number of other defectors followed the Vermehrens' example and sought and were granted asylum in Turkey.[41]

As Menemencioğlu could have anticipated, indeed as he

---

39. Twardowsky to Hencke, 2 February 1944, A.A. 52/68.

40. Busk, Ankara, to Foreign Office, 22 February 1944, P.R.O., F.O. 371/R3825/7/44.

41. Papen to Foreign Ministry, 2 March 1944, A.A. 52/332.

probably planned, the flight of the Vermehrens incriminated Papen and brought him under sharp attack from extremist Nazis in Berlin. The ambassador was so compromised that it was now unlikely that he could bring to consummation the peace bids he had begun to circulate. Ribbentrop, to evade the consequences of any complicity he might have had in Papen's recent maneuvers, ordered the ambassador to justify himself to the Gestapo and lend their investigations every support. He also alerted him to prepare for his recall to Germany. The British tried to hasten that recall by circulating a story that Papen had been seen dining with the Vermehrens the night before their escape.[42] Yet the British were able to derive little more than Papen's discomfiture from the incident. Erich Vermehren denounced Hitler volubly, but he drew a distinction between the dictator and the German people. He refused to propagandize the German home front and in fact told the British that bombings from the air and reverses on the battlefield had only united the German people more solidly behind the Führer.[43] The British thought the Abwehr list a valuable acquisition, but they were very disturbed by the interpretation the Soviet government gave Vermehren's flight. The Soviets professed to believe that because the British gave Vermehren protection, they also accepted the ideas for peace associated with Papen's circle. Foreign Office counselors drafted an immediate dispatch to Moscow stating that Britain did not agree to the loss of Bulgaria to Russia's sphere of influence.[44]

The virtual dissolution of the Abwehr was a crippling blow to German diplomacy in Turkey. Nearly twenty Abwehr agents swiftly left the country to avoid arrest by the Turkish police. Most of them returned to Germany, but one agent, named Glentschkowski, surrendered to the British. Knatchbull-Hugessen's staff regarded Glentschkowski's desertion to be fully as important as Vermehren's. Glent-

42. Schmidt to Papen, 10 February 1944, A.A. 52/2558. Sterndale Bennett to Foreign Office, 10 February 1944, P.R.O., F.O. 371/R2861/7/44.

43. Moyne, Cairo, to Foreign Office, 25 March 1944, P.R.O., F.O. 371/C4393/103/18.

44. Kerr, Moscow, to Foreign Office, 13 February 1944, and Memorandum by Howard, 16 February 1944, P.R.O., F.O. 371/C2028/1912/18; Ministry of Information to Foreign Office, 7 March 1944, P.R.O., F.O. 371/C3165/1912/18.

schkowski was a specialist in maintaining surreptitious contact between Papen and the Russians, and though Berlin would certainly try to replace this agent, the British did not expect any successor to be able to work as effectively. Few Turks, they predicted, would now come forward to serve as liaisons between the German embassy and Ankara governmental circles. The danger of retribution from Menemencioğlu was simply too great. Consequently, Papen would be bereft of indispensable information, and his latitude to pursue secret diplomacy would be severely circumscribed.[45]

German evidence suggests that Papen would have agreed with the British appraisal. He asked Ribbentrop to be honorably recalled, but the German foreign minister insisted on maintaining him at his post. The Wilhelmstrasse managed to dismiss the Gestapo's charges of treason against Papen as unsubstantiated, and the ambassador was reprimanded for nothing worse than an error of judgment in having recruited Vermehren to his staff.[46] Thereafter, Papen's influence with Ribbentrop actually seemed to increase despite protests by the Gestapo. In March 1944, the Hungarian prime minister, Nicholas Kállay, dissented from the pro-Axis policy of Admiral Horthy, the regent, and took asylum in the Turkish legation in Budapest. The Gestapo wanted to remove Kállay from the premises forcibly, but Papen successfully intervened. The Germans decided to respect Turkish diplomatic immunity and made no further attempt to molest Kállay, who survived the war.[47]

Meanwhile, Menemencioğlu resumed his incorrigible insinuations about Bulgarian policy. The Turkish foreign minister complained about the increasing boldness of the Bulgarian Communist opposition to King Simeon's regency. He also charged that both Bulgarian monarchists and Communists were secretly angling for peace with the Allies. Papen did not doubt that Bulgaria's loyalty to the Tripartite Pact was insincere, but he was no more confident about Menemencioğlu's veracity and reported that he had fairly good evidence that Turkish agents were stirring up

45. Knatchbull-Hugessen to Foreign Office, 18 April 1945, P.R.O., F.O. 371/C5299/1912/18.
46. Papen to Ritter, 22 February 1944, A.A. 52/288.
47. Nicholas Kállay, *Hungarian Premier: A Personal Account of a Nation's Struggle in the Second World War*, pp. 436, 441–42.

dissension and discord at Sofia. They were still intent, he charged, on obtaining a piece of territory as a result of the war.[48]

Menemencioğlu admitted as much publicly in a speech that he gave after an official dinner on 28 February 1944. No Germans were invited to this function, but a member of Papen's embassy received a full report from a guest in return for a fee. In the course of his remarks, Menemencioğlu declared Hitler had made two great military mistakes. He had failed to prevent the British evacuation at Dunkirk and had been unable to mount a cross-channel invasion of the British Isles. But, the Turk continued, Hitler's political mistakes were even graver. The Führer had ineptly committed himself to maintaining the integrity of the French and Italian colonial empires, thereby burdening German diplomacy with a major encumbrance. In Menemencioğlu's opinion, these colonies should have been traded off long before to strengthen Germany's own strategical position.

Nevertheless, a last opportunity to do so, the foreign minister held, was now at hand. Vinogradov, the Soviet ambassador, had told him that the war would be over by April. He, however, thought the Germans would hold on until autumn and give the Allies such grueling opposition that a negotiated peace would be conceded to Berlin. Yet, to be successful at the conference table, Germany had to be supported by faithful and prosperous allies and benevolent power blocs. Menemencioğlu again proposed a Balkan federation under Turkey's aegis to arbitrate between Germany and "Pan-Slavic Europe," but he emphasized that this bloc must be industrially strong, economically self-sufficient, and permanently cleansed of irredentist rivalries if it were to maintain the balance for a lasting peace. It was in the interest of both the Axis and the Allies, the foreign minister insisted, to help the Balkan bloc to prosper. In conclusion, he asserted that Germany still had a chance to win the battle for Russia as long as she held sway over most of the Ukraine and the Crimea. He thought it did not matter if the northern and central sectors of the German lines collapsed or even if Red Army units stood on the German frontier itself. As long as the Wehrmacht controlled the south—Crimea and the Ukraine—Stalin would be deprived of important sources of fuel and

48. Papen to Foreign Ministry, 23 February 1944, A.A. 52/295.

foodstuffs. To recover these, Menemencioğlu speculated, the Soviet leader would be compelled to bargain with the German government, inducing his Anglo-American allies to concur in such negotiations or ignoring them if they did not.[49]

This dinner speech was not a realistic appraisal of the current military situation, but it was a frank admission of some persistent Turkish wishful thinking. It derived in part from an assumption to which Ankara doggedly clung, despite the withdrawal of German forces from southeastern Europe. According to a secret British intelligence report, İnönü and his ministers were convinced that the alliance between Russia and the Western Powers would not survive until the final rounds of the struggle against Nazi Germany. It would be sundered by an argument over the Polish Question. The Turkish cabinet simply could not believe that the British would tolerate the installation of a Communist regime at Warsaw. To combat it, the Turks expected that Churchill might have to compose his differences with the Germans so that their combined forces could be marshaled to keep Poland free. The fight against Stalinist imperialism, begun over Poland, the Turks believed would not end until the whole Balkan Peninsula was secured against Soviet encroachment. Under such circumstances, Ankara hoped that London would be quite ready to turn over the Crimea to German administration or, less objectionably, to a German deputy.[50] As late as the middle of May 1944, Menemencioğlu tried to obtain a guarantee from Germany that the Crimea, so dear to Turkish irredentists, would be held at all costs. Papen evidently gave some kind of assurance, though not a written pledge.[51]

But it was Bulgaria, as well as the Crimea, that was on Menemencioğlu's mind both before and after he made his dinner speech. Just a few days later the Turkish foreign minister again attempted to arouse German suspicions about the regency in Sofia. Through the Turkish secret police, he had Papen informed that certain circles in the Bulgarian capital had commissioned an emissary to meet with George Earle in İstanbul to discuss a separate peace. The Turk alleged that Bulgaria was ready to declare war on the Axis if King

49. Walther to Hencke, 10 March 1944, A.A. 52/96.
50. Bennett to Foreign Office, 10 February 1944, P.R.O., F.O. 371/R2861/7/44.
51. Ankara Embassy to Altenburg, 14 May 1944, A.A. 745/982.

Simeon's government were allowed to acquire a portion of eastern Macedonia from Yugoslavia and gain a corridor to the Aegean Sea through the Greek port of Dede Agach. Berlin had the greatest difficulty in verifying these rumors, and Papen's own investigation could establish only that a certain Sevoff, a professor of architecture close to Simeon's advisers, had traveled to İstanbul to confer with professional colleagues. He had not gotten clearance for his trip from the German embassy in Sofia, but there was no hard proof that he was carrying peace terms to Earle or any other Allied representative.

But, Papen suspected, the Turkish secret police set up the situation to make it appear that Sevoff did so. British intelligence was informed by the Turks of Sevoff's arrival in İstanbul, and a British agent broke into Sevoff's hotel room at 5:30 in the morning. The Englishman demanded to know what the professor's business was but got only the curt reply, "Not what you think." The next day, Sevoff moved into his country's İstanbul consulate, where his sleep was less troubled. After a few days, he returned home, but Papen did not think he had ever met with George Earle. Instead, it was the ambassador's opinion that the whole episode had been contrived by the Turks to incriminate the Bulgarians so that the Wehrmacht would retaliate and Bulgaria would be laid waste preparatory to a partial or total Turkish occupation. Papen advised Berlin to consider the Sevoff case closed.[52]

While Menemencioğlu tried to raise the ambassador's doubts about Germany's allies, the British and Americans reduced lend-lease deliveries to a trickle and deprived Turkey of virtually all imported oil. The İnönü government was advised that this decision would be reconsidered if Turkey stopped shipping chromite to the Germans and opened her bases to Allied aircraft. As a result of these measures, panic gripped the whole country; people began to hoard food, and those rich enough to contemplate emigration bought gold heavily.[53] Yet even now Menemencioğlu would not deviate from what Knatchbull-Hugessen flatly called his pro-German

52. Papen to Ribbentrop, 7 March 1944, A.A. 52/360, and 8 March 1944, A.A. 52/365; Beckerle to Foreign Ministry, 20 March 1944, A.A. 52/389.

53. Knatchbull-Hugessen to Foreign Office, 5 April 1944, P.R.O., F.O. 371/R6042/7/44.

policy. The foreign minister pled, as he had so often done before, that Germany was still too strong to be provoked. The British envoy shot back that Menemencioğlu exaggerated Germany's strength better than Papen could ever have done. It was a fiction invoked so that Turkey could avoid her obligations to Britain under the alliance treaty. But he admonished the foreign minister that "in London thoughts of the future were outweighed by thoughts of the present. All countries were judged according to the part they had played in the war. At present Turkey was actually helping Germany by her negative attitude."[54]

Yet there was a piquant irony in this situation of which Knatchbull-Hugessen may not have been fully aware. Menemencioğlu fulminated against the Allied lend-lease embargo as a kind of economic blackmail, even as he himself blackmailed the Germans to ease the deprivations imposed by the Allies' decision. He warned Papen that unless Berlin was prepared to see the benevolent İnönü government fall, it must supply Turkey with both agricultural and military equipment. Menemencioğlu demanded consignment of two thousand reapers and threshers, with an equal number of tractors soon to follow. Additionally, the Germans would be called upon to make up any Turkish deficiencies in oil because, according to the foreign minister, the fuel crisis alone would be enough to topple the regime and bring in a pro-Communist dictatorship. Papen did not encourage him to expect that any of these quotas could be met by the Reich, but, almost incredibly, the ambassador did support a request that thirty shining new streetcars be delivered to the municipal transport system of Ankara. Perhaps he agreed with Menemencioğlu's argument that no article was better calculated to bring home to the Turkish man in the street the Reich's unshakable confidence and undiminished will to victory.[55] Or perhaps, at this late date in the war, both men were dealing in fancies rather than facts.

Whatever Papen's illusions, they were rudely shattered on 20 April 1944, when Ankara succumbed to Allied demands and ended chromite shipments to Germany. The government's decision stunned Papen, who, like Ribbentrop, had

54. Knatchbull-Hugessen to Foreign Office, 8 April 1944, P.R.O., F.O. 371/R5703/3901/44.
55. Papen to Foreign Ministry, 13 April 1944, A.A. 52/571.

chosen to regard the chromite question as "nondiscussible" and bound by solemn contract. More surprising, however, was that the British embassy was caught equally unawares by Ankara's pronouncement, though Knatchbull-Hugessen had been lobbying for it for months.[56] A few weeks later, the Germans thought they had found an explanation for the general mystification. They learned that the chromite embargo was largely President İnönü's decision, while Menemencioğlu and several other members of the cabinet hotly disputed its wisdom.

İnönü ordered his foreign minister to present the chromite proposal for immediate ratification to the Turkish National Assembly, but Menemencioğlu omitted the customary advance notice to the press. He did this because he wanted to leave the British, as well as the Germans, in the dark so that neither could intimidate the parliamentary deputies. He then intended to introduce the chromite embargo as a question still open to further debate rather than as a *fait accompli*. He hoped to induce a majority of deputies to speak out for continuing commerce with Germany. But the foxy İnönü suspected what Menemencioğlu had in mind, alerted the Turkish secret police, and instructed them to circulate rumors in the National Assembly that Britain would declare war on the Republic within forty-eight hours and bomb Ankara if the embargo were not passed at once. This specter, the Germans believed, brought the deputies quickly into line behind their president and left Menemencioğlu isolated and confounded. İnönü then left the capital for a country vacation. He invited Saracoğlu and his wife to join him, a singular mark of favor indicating that the prime minister was soon to receive Menemencioğlu's portfolio in addition to his own.[57]

Menemencioğlu sensed that he had become expendable, but the evidence suggests that he was not easily resigned to the fact. Throughout May, he sought repeatedly to see İnönü and Saracoğlu but could never gain an interview of any great length with either man. The pair took frequent holidays from Ankara, undoubtedly to shield themselves from

---

56. Papen to Ribbentrop, 21 April 1944, A.A. 52/626; Knatchbull-Hugessen to Foreign Office, 21 April 1944, P.R.O., F.O. 371/R6329/6206/44.

57. Walther to Foreign Ministry, 2 May 1944, A.A. 2621/687.

the foreign minister's recrimination and complaints but also to avoid any public demonstrations against their regime. Both Papen's and Knatchbull-Hugessen's reports agree that commodity shortages and an unstable foreign policy had made the government leadership very unpopular, and neither envoy thought that the tenure of the pro-Allied Saracoğlu was much more secure than that of the Axis partisan Numan Menemencioğlu.[58]

A foreign policy success might still have secured Menemencioğlu in office, but the prospect of such a success went up in smoke when Allied aircraft bombarded and destroyed the bridge and railway network of southeastern Bulgaria. At the end of May, the bridge and tracks connecting Svilengrad, Bulgaria, with Edirne, Turkey, were smashed by bombers. Within a few days, twenty more bridges along or near the Bulgarian-Turkish frontier were blown up. Menemencioğlu protested to the British and American envoys and told Papen he did not think the raids would stop short of the Turkish border. He feared that Allied planes would bomb Turkish railway installations, though London and Washington would then claim the incidents were accidental and offer to pay damages. Whatever they gave, the Turk declared, would not put the Arda and Maritza bridges back into service for a long time to come. Menemencioğlu charged that the fault was Germany's. She was too lenient with the Bulgarians, had insufficient antiaircraft equipment in the area, and assigned only second-class troops to man it. The foreign minister was so concerned that he offered Turkish troops to cooperate with the Germans in aerial defense assignments on Bulgarian soil. Papen caught the spirit of urgency and pressed these proposals on Berlin, together with his own recommendation that Wehrmacht units be increased all over Bulgaria. But Field Marshal Keitel, speaking for the Army High Command, decided that no additional personnel could be spared from other operations, all of which Berlin judged to be more critical.[59]

The rupture of almost all rail communications between

58. Papen to Foreign Ministry, 17 June 1944, A.A. 745/3573. Knatchbull-Hugessen to Sargent, 19 June 1944, P.R.O., F.O. 371/R10200/789/44.

59. Papen to Foreign Ministry, 30 May 1944, A.A. 745/856, 1 June 1944, A.A. 745/865, and 3 June 1944, A.A. 745/876; Altenburg to Ribbentrop, 11 June 1944, A.A. 745/no number.

Turkey and Europe really ended the official careers of Papen and Menemencioğlu, though each man remained in his post a while longer. The broken bridges of Bulgaria turned the diplomat and the minister into caretakers of disillusioned hopes and outworn policies. For Papen, the advocate of the Turkish alliance and later of Turkish neutrality, neither goal was attainable now that the İnönü government, severed from the markets of central Europe, had become more than ever vulnerable to Allied blockade. If Ankara would have relief, it would have to pay the Allied price of first reducing Turkish trade with Germany still more and then of declaring war on her. For Menemencioğlu, who had aimed to bring Balkan Thrace and the Dodecanese islands under Turkish jurisdiction, the demolition of the railways turned his objectives into embarrassing phantoms that stalked the brief remainder of his term in power. For even if he had had German matériel and manpower for a Bulgarian offensive, he now no longer had quick transportation to bring Turkish troops to the Thracian front. Menemencioğlu had gambled for renown and lost. He had now to await his dismissal.

It occurred because of a dispute about the interpretation of the Montreux Convention. According to its provisions, commercial ships of belligerent nations had the right to pass the Straits if Turkey was not at war. But the Turkish authorities had the right of "sanitary inspection" at several points along the passage, where they could stop vessels to determine whether they were carrying heavy armaments. Both Allied and Nazi ships had carried some artillery since the outbreak of war, but, under the Montreux Convention, it was the sole privilege of the Turks to decide whether the number and caliber were sufficient to change the classification of the ships from merchant to military. Warships were unequivocally barred from the Straits, but the Turks were very lenient about letting through some whose equipment qualified them as "auxiliary vessels of war." Generous exemptions had previously been made in favor of the British navy, so Knatchbull-Hugessen, though he criticized Turkish administration of the Straits from time to time, never really insisted that the Montreux Convention be meticulously interpreted to the disadvantage of the Germans. About 7 June 1944, British intelligence alerted the ambassador that the German war transport, *Kassel*, carrying grain and oil from

Black Sea ports to İstanbul, was about to enter the Straits. Since the *Kassel* was heavily armed and its cargo likely to make the Allied blockade of Turkey less effective, Knatchbull-Hugessen demanded of Menemencioğlu that it be stopped and searched. His protest was almost perfunctory, and he never expected either a swift or compliant reaction.

But on this occasion, transit was not only denied the German vessel, but its very presence became the subject of a stormy debate in the Turkish cabinet. Prime Minister Saracoğlu and the minister for public instruction, both backed by President İnönü, led the attack on Menemencioğlu for his pro-German policies. Though the foreign minister defended himself strenuously, his colleagues voted to impound the *Kassel* and to exclude all German war transports from the Straits in the future. Menemencioğlu correctly observed that this kind of comprehensive exclusion was tantamount to the cancellation of Turkish governance at the Straits. He wanted the passage of each ship, whatever its registry, to be judged on its merits. If the Republic yielded to foreign pressure, he contended, a precedent would be set that the Soviet Union would be the first to exploit. The Kremlin would charge that Turkey was not strong enough to cope with Great Power intimidation and then use this pretext to land a "protective" Red Army force at the Straits. Nevertheless, İnönü dismissed this forecast as too pessimistic and accepted Menemencioğlu's resignation.[60]

The cabinet debate took place on 12 June, and the foreign minister left office on 16 June. In a few days, the British achieved what had eluded them for years. Their old enemy passed so quickly from the scene that they were stunned. They had no convincing explanation for Menemencioğlu's fall, nor at first did anyone else. The least discriminating newspapers charged that the foreign minister had been dropped for malfeasance and graft. Papen was supposed to have bribed him with money that he then invested in an Ankara nightclub that monopolized the entertainment of visiting foreign dignitaries.[61] An editorial in the better in-

---

60. Knatchbull-Hugessen to Foreign Office, 15 June 1944, P.R.O., F.O. 371/R9494/789/44, and 16 June 1944, P.R.O., F.O. 371/R9573/7/44; Knatchbull-Hugessen to Eden, 20 June 1944, P.R.O., F.O. 371/R10541/789/44.
61. Nimet Arzık, *Bitmeyen Kavga: İsmet İnönü*, pp. 82–83, 113–15.

formed journal *Yeni Sabah* stated that Turkish foreign policy had made a "neat turn of the rudder" and Menemencioğlu, for all his qualities, was not flexible enough to turn with it.[62] Why the rudder turned, the editorialist did not say, though the disappearance of all prospects for Turkish expansion into Bulgaria seems a reasonable conjecture. There was now nothing more to be gained from the Germans, and so İsmet İnönü complied with the Allies. But the British did not expect this compliance to be long-lasting or Menemencioğlu to be long undone. As the Foreign Office counselor G. L. McDermott wrote:

> Numan has for years been a sort of central authority or unofficial adviser not only for foreign but also for various home affairs, finance etc. He was, however, never in with the Party, and I don't think his style would ever be likely to please them much. Still, he will be hard at work behind the scenes, and neither now nor when he returns to power will he be friendly to us.[63]

Most of the Turkish diplomatic corps felt that the foreign minister's legal position had been entirely correct, and Essad Aluner, the Turkish ambassador to Spain, wanted to organize his colleagues to demand that President İnönü recall Menemencioğlu. However, the Wilhelmstrasse gave no encouragement to this gambit, nor to another proposal, brought to it by Col. Refik Ahmed, nephew of the previous Turkish prime minister, who offered to set up a kind of government-in-exile, which would charge İnönü and Saracoğlu with taking British bribes and so attempt to bring them down. Instead, Berlin rather maladroitly began to intern Turkish Jews living in various occupied European countries. This caused criticism of Papen in the Turkish press and beclouded the legal merits of the Montreux dispute. Yet Menemencioğlu's dismissal elicited a great deal of popular sympathy on his behalf. Though the foreign minister epitomized a policy of expansion, for which the common people were supposedly not prepared, they rioted in his behalf at Adana, Ankara, and Mersin. In İstanbul, on the other hand, the inhabitants were indifferent, though Mene-

62. Bennett, Ankara, to Sargent, 19 June 1944, P.R.O., F.O. 371/R10200/789/44.

63. Memorandum by McDermott, 18 July 1944, on Knatchbull-Hugessen to Eden, 20 June 1944, P.R.O., F.O. 371/R10541/789/44.

mencioğlu was a parliamentary deputy for the city. In the old Ottoman capital, there were many merchants and traders. They wanted not belligerence, but business as usual.[64]

Papen obtained the release of the Turkish Jews, but this did not prevent the İnönü government from presenting him with his passports. Turkey severed diplomatic relations with Germany on 2 August 1944. Though this was a direction in which the British had long pointed them, the Turks again caught Knatchbull-Hugessen's people by surprise. They also caused the British considerable embarrassment with the Russians. Since the Moscow Conference, Stalin had changed his mind and now did not want Ankara's participation for fear the British would use Turkish troops against the Red Army. Of Vinogradov, the Soviet ambassador in Ankara, Knatchbull-Hugessen wrote:

> He is clearly puzzled as to the real reason the Turks broke off relations with Germany. He does not consider the superficial results, namely cessation of trade and the moral effect in Germany and among the satellites to be a sufficient explanation. He suspects that the underlying motive is to revitalize the Anglo-Turkish Alliance with a view to future possibilities in Anglo-Russian relations. That is putting it rather more strongly than is called for, but Monsieur Vinogradov practically hinted to me that there must be an ulterior motive in the recent démarche here. . . . He raised again the question why we had not gone the whole hog . . . at Moscow and Tehran. I again explained that we had tried and failed and that the situation now was different. . . . Monsieur Vinogradov did not dispute this but he is clearly not satisfied.[65]

But the Soviet diplomat's qualms were nothing compared to Papen's. The German ambassador thought he was returning to a gallows in Berlin. The British embassy described him during his last days in Ankara as fearful of execution, highly nervous, and largely incoherent. President İnönü at first declined to meet him for a last farewell, and it was to Saracoğlu that Papen complained about being "turned out like a thief." But in this interview, he was still sufficiently composed to warn that Turkey, in severing relations with

64. Abetz to Foreign Ministry, 5 August 1944, A.A. 745/3788. Knatchbull-Hugessen to Foreign Office, 26 June 1944, P.R.O., F.O. 371/R10542/789/44.
65. Knatchbull-Hugessen to Sargent, 6 August 1944, P.R.O., F.O. 371/R12731/7/44.

Germany, had isolated herself and was about "to become like the Poles." This allusion agitated an old Turkish fear and, the British thought, won Papen an interview with İsmet İnönü. It was curt but correct.[66] It may have enhanced the diplomat's stature in Hitler's eyes.

When Papen and the Führer met in Berlin, their conversation was surprisingly calm and congenial. Hitler thanked the ambassador for all his services to Germany, said that the end of his mission was not his fault, and finally presented him with a medal for merit. The diplomat then retired to Westphalia and lived with relatives or friends until the advancing Americans took him into custody in April 1945. The following November, he was tried at Nuremberg, not for war crimes but for criminally conspiring at the Anschluss of Austria. The prosecution was unable to prove the charge, and Papen was acquitted. The record of his Turkish service played little part in the Nuremberg proceedings, and to the end of his life the ambassador refused to talk about the Turks. To all inquiries, he only remarked that the Turks were his "friends."[67] But that simple word was the bitter measure of his failure, for he was never able to call them comrades-in-arms.

66. Kerr, Moscow, to Foreign Office, 5 August 1944, P.R.O., F.O. 371/R12939/7/44. Franz von Papen, *Memoirs*, trans. Brian Connell, p. 528.

67. Papen, *Memoirs*, pp. 532, 535, 561, 569. Edward Weisband, *Turkish Foreign Policy, 1943–1945: Small State Diplomacy and Great Power Politics*, p. 82.

Summary and Conclusions

At the two ends of the Mediterranean stand Spain and Turkey. Throughout the Second World War, Spain was neutral though openly benevolent toward the Axis. On the other hand, Turkey, though bound to Britain and France in a mutual assistance treaty since October 1939, broke her pledge to them on numerous occasions and declared war against Germany and Italy only in February 1945, when the fighting was all but over.

To this day, the Spanish government has not lived down the stigma of its association with Hitler and Mussolini. But Turkey, despite her flagrant bad faith toward the Allies, has become a member in good standing of the United Nations, a participant in the North Atlantic Treaty Organization, and the recipient, beginning in 1947, of hundreds of millions of dollars in American equipment and aid. Westerners have tended to forget Ankara's ambiguous foreign policy during the Second World War, and, as if by international agreement, the true story of Turkey's wartime diplomacy has been left deliberately obscure. Only with the rise of Turkish demands for a federally constituted Cyprus, affording Turkish Cypriots local political autonomy, followed by the Turkish invasion of the island, has there been a tendency to examine the past in a harsher light.

The Turks owe their good international press, which they have enjoyed until very recently, to two factors. Their country is undeniably a bedrock of Western defenses against Soviet Russia. The Turks' anti-Communism has never been variable or in doubt. During the Korean War, Turkish troops under United Nations' command fought valiantly and to international acclaim against North Korean aggression inspired by Moscow. Furthermore, Turkish history and culture are still dominated by the overwhelming figure of Kemal Atatürk, founder of the modern republic. As a statesman, Atatürk repudiated adventurism and irredentism. Nonaggression was a cornerstone of the republic that he raised out of the debacle of the Ottoman defeat in the First World War. He used to say, "I am a Macedonian, but I have no territorial ambitions." This meant that Atatürk was publicly reconciled to the loss of the Arab provinces of the old

Ottoman Empire and even to the surrender of the offshore islands of the Anatolian coast, though a foreigner in possession of these islands could disrupt Turkey's peacetime commerce and ruin her wartime defenses. Atatürk was not blind to these realities; however, he had no choice but to leave them to worry his successor. He had just barely cleared a Greek army, sponsored by Lloyd George's hostile ministry, out of Anatolia. For one life, he had seen enough exertions in the field and spent his later years building up the new Turkey internally.

His successor as president, Gen. İsmet İnönü, had more reason to prosecute a dynamic foreign policy. As chief Turkish negotiator at the Lausanne Conference of 1923, which presided over the dismemberment of the Ottoman Empire, İnönü had to let most of the protests raised by extreme Turkish nationalists against this treaty fall on his slender shoulders. İnönü was not popular with many of the Turkish army generals or deputies of the Grand National Assembly. He wanted to redeem himself, and he attempted to do so by gaining territory for Turkey. His choice of path to redemption was logical in a Europe where Hitler and Mussolini were changing boundaries with unparalleled arrogance and lightning rapidity. Like any leader worth the name, İnönü knew that effective diplomacy is made of pragmatism and opportunity, not of dictums and principles, even those made semi-sacred by the memory of Kemal Atatürk.

It may be objected that İnönü had little reason to hope for success. The Turkish army fully mobilized was only two hundred thousand men. The Turks had no first-rate anti-aircraft or antitank equipment. And, as İnönü and his ministers so frequently pointed out, İstanbul was a firetrap without defenses against aerial bombardment. Such slender resources, it would seem, could hardly sustain a healthy national policy, as Atatürk had taught, much less the bristling diplomacy of annexation. But though Turkey was weak in modern weaponry, she had the great natural fortress of Anatolia itself. Though İstanbul might be reduced to blackened timbers, and Ankara, the capital, taken by an invader, the Turks could retreat into their mountain fastnesses and decimate the enemy who tried to follow them into the narrow Anatolian defiles. Their rudimentary railways, which were the butt of foreigners' jokes, could become a distinct asset in war. Under these conditions, a highly mechanized army could not maintain its communications and supplies, while the Turks, used to little, were superb partisan combatants.

The Germans realized this and therefore tolerated almost every variety of Turkish obstreperousness and blackmail. The German Army High Command and the foreign ministry both confidentially admitted the Wehrmacht could either not conquer Turkey or could do so only at a cost too heavy to be acceptable. Stalin shunned combat with the Turks on their own ground even in the aftermath of his great victory at Stalingrad. For much the same reasons, the British, however unendurably frustrated they felt, found it impossible to coerce the Turks into entering the war under the terms of the alliance treaty of 1939. Additionally, the British, still in possession of their vast empire, had to reckon with Turkey's wide ideological sway over the Muslim world. Atatürk had abolished the caliphate and secularized the Republic, but the British feared Muslims might still take a lead from the country that had once been first in Islam. Ambassador Knatchbull-Hugessen told Serge Vinogradov that "Turkey still held a predominantly influential position vis-a-vis the Moslem [*sic*] world. The Anglo-Turkish connection was important for us from that point of view and it helped us in Iraq, Persia, Afghanistan and even India. A hostile Turkey could be a great nuisance to us in that sphere." Monsieur Vinogradov, he added, saw the point of this. Anthony Eden endorsed this position and commented further on this dispatch that Turkey would always have to be placated beyond her due to preclude an outbreak of her aggressive tendencies. "This may seem far-fetched," he wrote, "but I know that all the Iraqis have it at the back of their minds that Turkey might well descend on the Mosul oilfields if for example we should be embroiled with the Arab world over the question of a Jewish State in Palestine."[1]

Therefore it is no wonder that the Turks showed themselves self-confident and bold negotiators during the Second World War. They had real advantages on their side. They were heirs of the wily traditions of the Sublime Porte, and to the methods of the old viziers, they brought the pluck and nerve of the modern gambler. First, they used Italian aggres-

---

1. Knatchbull-Hugessen to Sargent, 6 August 1944, and Minute by Eden, 9 September 1944, P.R.O., F.O. 371/R12731/7/44.

sion in Abyssinia as an excuse to reconsider the regulation of the Straits. At Lausanne, Turkey was deprived of any control over traffic through the narrow body of water. But by 1936, the Powers were ready to allow the Turks to turn back warships at their discretion. Neither Britain, France, nor the Soviet Union wanted to dicker with Ankara when they were already having so much trouble with Rome and Berlin. Thus the restoration of Turkish sovereignty over the Straits at the Montreux Conference became a foregone conclusion. The Turks next demanded a province of northern Syria, the old sanjak of Alexandretta, where many of their countrymen lived under a French mandate that had been conferred by the League of Nations. But with France menaced by a remilitarized Germany, there was never any question that she would yield Alexandretta unilaterally to the Turks, especially since no support was forthcoming from London.

During the Alexandretta crisis, the Turks made their first bid for German support. They did so because in Syria they were confronted not only by French opposition, but also by an unexpectedly vitriolic Arab resistance. From Damascus, Beirut, Riyadh, and Baghdad came denunciations of the new "Kemalist imperialism." To counter these, Numan Menemencioğlu, first secretary of the Turkish foreign ministry, offered a friendship pact to the German foreign minister, Joachim von Ribbentrop, in 1938. Ribbentrop did not seal any bargain at that time because he was afraid of simultaneously alienating the Arabs, among whom he was trying to expand and deepen Germany's contacts. Ribbentrop's decision was probably incorrect, but it must be admitted that he had struck, for the first of many times, the key dilemma of Nazi Middle Eastern policy. He could not concurrently befriend Turks and Arabs. Their cultural differences were incompatible, and their imperial drives irreconcilable. The Turks opposed unification of the Arab Middle East, and the Arabs feared Turkish claims on Syria, Iraq, and even Egypt. The Germans realized that if they signed with the Turks, they had a better chance of keeping the Soviet Union out of the war or, if she came in, of defeating her by encirclement in a giant pincer movement. But a Turco-German treaty would leave the Arab leaders sulking and ranged immutably on Britain's side. Many German strategists felt this could not be allowed to happen, for only with Arab cooperation, they thought, could Germany cut the vital Transjordanian-Iraqi land passage over which the British imperial general staff shifted its forces between the Mediterranean Sea and the Indian Ocean.

The misfortune of German Middle Eastern policy was that it wavered between favoring Turks and Arabs throughout the war. Within the German government, only one man, Franz von Papen, Hitler's wartime envoy to Ankara, had no difficulty in assigning priority to the Turks. Papen worked for a Turkish alliance with persistence and dedication. He believed Germany's ultimate confrontation would come with the Soviet Union. The Red Army, he argued, could be destroyed only in a great flanking movement, whose southern arm would be closed by an allied Turkey. From Turkish bases, the Luftwaffe could bomb the oil installations of Baku and Batum, and also British airfields and troop sites in the Transjordanian-Iraqi "imperial corridor." The Arab states, Papen felt, could not serve any of these goals as well. Arab troops were too undisciplined, their governments too saturated with British influence, and their leaders too numerous, petty, and at odds with one another. In early 1939, Papen urged Berlin to make an immediate alliance with Ankara, before war broke out and the Turks were tempted to raise the price of their support to exorbitant levels. For the cession of the Dodecanese islands by Italy to Turkey, Papen thought Ankara's adherence to the Axis could be bought. But Ribbentrop would not pursue this scheme. He was loathe to pressure Mussolini, though Germany later was increasingly to disregard Il Duce; he also disliked Papen and underrated his judgment. Ironically, Papen's opponent in Ankara, the British ambassador, Knatchbull-Hugessen, held his talents in much greater esteem. In a dispatch to London, Knatchbull-Hugessen commended the German diplomat's excellent feeling for the Turkish psychology and warned that no man was better endowed to make an alliance with İnönü's regime. In fact, for professional competence, Knatchbull-Hugessen rated Papen much more highly than he did Lawrence Steinhardt, the American ambassador to Turkey, whom the Englishman found unmannerly and uninformed.[2]

Certainly Papen correctly predicted the course of Turkey's growing territorial cupidity. Once the war broke out, the

2. Knatchbull-Hugessen to Eden, "Reports on the heads of Foreign Missions in Turkey," 16 July 1943, P.R.O., F.O. 371/R7169/265/44.

Turks were no longer willing to bargain merely for a few islands. They successively demanded a quasi-protectorate over Albania, a rectification of their frontier with Bulgaria, and finally the annexation of Iraq in return for their help. But the Iraqis forestalled the Turks. In 1941, the Iraqi army attacked British troops stationed near Baghdad. They hoped to eject the British from their country and to turn it into a nonbelligerent zone free of British tutelage but secure also against Turkish encroachment sponsored by Germany. Even if their assault on British emplacements failed, the Iraqis could reasonably expect German material assistance and perhaps a larger commitment to the goals of Arab nationalism. However, their timetable caught Hitler unawares, befuddled his generals, and enraged the Turks. Largely because of Turkey's attitude and the necessity of keeping her friendship in the face of the impending invasion of Soviet Russia, Hitler made only a small allocation of arms and aircraft to Iraq. A German military mission accompanied it but was able to hold its position at Baghdad for barely a month. Their hasty retreat from the area permanently destroyed Germany's prestige in the Middle East. It also discouraged further Arab attempts to assist the Axis. And it deprived Hitler of his most compelling inducement to bring Turkey into the war.

During the Russian campaign, the Turks offered to collaborate with the Wehrmacht by occupying the Crimea and Transcaucasia as an "antiCommunist and nonaligned peacekeeping force." But the Germans could not have accepted this offer even if they had wished to. The Wilhelmstrasse quickly found out that the pious Muslims of Crimea, Georgia, and Azerbaijan detested the secularized Turks almost as much as they did the atheistic Soviets. The rule of Turkey in southern Russia would not have been long tenable.

In short, for a variety of reasons, Papen's mission failed. He never achieved his Turkish alliance. Yet Knatchbull-Hugessen and the British could claim no greater success. They could have secured Turkish participation earlier in the war by espousing Ankara's claims to the Dodecanese islands. But they realized that any encouragement for this claim would elicit another, for Cyprus, a British crown colony. Churchill would condone no such negotiations and did not succeed in getting Turkey into the war until it was almost over. Before he left Ankara, Knatchbull-Hugessen confessed that the long delay had daunted more than his patience. He was afraid it had permanently damaged Britain's credibility as a Great Power. He predicted that the British would have to resign their traditional ascendency in the Middle East to either the Americans or the Russians.[3]

Throughout the Second World War, Turkey was a non-belligerent but not an ineffective bystander. By diplomacy alone, she maintained her territorial integrity against both Nazi Germany and the Soviet Union. She took expensive lend-lease equipment from Britain and gave only over-priced commodities in return. She deprived Germany of an Arab alliance and withheld her own alliance for the highest price. She emerged from the war with her land unscathed and her Kemalist heritage intact.

Turkish diplomacy during the war was a brilliant accomplishment by all standards except those of honesty and integrity. Only thirty years later, when they invaded Cyprus, did the Turks reveal that, after all, they had been dissatisfied with what that diplomacy had gained for them.

3. Knatchbull-Hugessen to Foreign Office, 29 July 1944, P.R.O., F.O. 371/R12534/1321/44.

Bibliography

Unpublished Materials

Most of this book is based on unpublished correspondence from the German and British foreign ministries. The German material is on microfilm reels at the National Archives, Washington, D.C. In the notes to this book, the German dispatches are designated by the capital letters A.A., that is, *Auswärtiges Amt* (the German Foreign Ministry) followed by a multidigit number. The digits before the diagonal bar identify the appropriate reel; the digits after the bar designate the individual document cited. A list of the German Foreign Ministry files consulted is given below.

The Foreign Office papers are not on microfilm as yet. Unlike the German correspondence, the Foreign Office papers are not organized under country designations but under topical headings, for instance, Turkish statesmen; relations with Bulgaria; foreign trade. The number and variety of these topical headings are almost infinite, and it would be impossible to list here all the headings from which I have taken British dispatches. However, each British paper is identified by its individual call number. Readers wishing to be acquainted with all the topical divisions relating to Turkey and her neighbors must consult Great Britain, Foreign Office, *Index to the Correspondence of the Foreign Office*.

The German Foreign Ministry Files:

Akten
"Politische Beziehungen der Türkei zu Deutschland," vol. 2.

Clodius, Handakten
Vols. 15/1; 54; 55/4–5.

Deutsche Botschaft Rom
"Politik Italien-Türkei," vol. 3.
"Türkei," vols. 4–6.

Abbreviations Used in this Volume

P.R.O., F.O.——Public Record Office, Foreign Office
A.A.——Auswärtiges Amt (German Foreign Ministry)
DGFP——*Documents on German Foreign Policy, 1918–1945*
FRUS——*Foreign Relations of the United States: Diplomatic Papers*

Deutsche Botschaft in der Türkei
 "Aegypten," vol. 142/2.
 "Arabien," vol. 141/3.
 "Besuche führender Staatsmänner," vol. 139/2.
 "Deutsche Innenpolitik: Auslandsorganisation," vols. 154–55.
 "England," vol. 142/3–4.
 "Geheime Erlasse," vols. 149/1–5; 150/1–4, 10–12; 151/1–2, 14–
  15; 152/1–2, 4, 16–19; 153/1–2, 4–5, 20–24; 154/1–5, 28–29;
  203/4.
 "Geheime Reichssachen," vol. 152/19.
 "Irak," vols. 142/7–7a.
 "Judentum," vol. 146/1.
 "Kulturreferent: Geheim," vol. 211/3.
 "Marine-Militär," vols. 131/5; 147/1–3.
 "Palästina," vol. 143/7.
 "Persien," vol. 143/8.
 "Politik Italien-Türkei," vol. 1.
 "Politik Türkei," vols. 4–6.
 "Politische Übersichten," vol. 131.
 "Presse," vol. 202/2.
 "Propaganda," vols. 202/3; 212.
 "Rüstungsindustrie," vol. 166/1–2.
 "Syrien," vols. 138; 144/7.
 "Syrien: Italienische Waffenstillstandskommission," vol. 138.
 "Syrien: Presse-Propaganda," vols. 210/1–6.
 "Wirtschaftliche Beziehungen zwischen Deutschland und die
  Türkei: Verträge," vols. 157–58.
 "Wirtschaftsverhandlungen," vol. 157/1–4.

Ettel, Gesandter
 "Aegypten," vol. 2.
 "Iran," vol. 2/5.
 "Kaukasus-Land," vol. 1.
 "König Faruk von Aegypten," vol. 2.

Ha Pol VII
 "Akten betreffend Chromerz," vols. 6/5–8; 7.

Ha Pol Wiehl
 "Türkei," vol. 44/2, 7.

Inland II
 "Geheime Reichssache," vols. 15; 25.
 "Handakten Bobrick."

"Juden in Frankreich," vol. 55/4.

Partei Dienststellen
"Politische Berichte," vol. 6.

Politische Abteilung
"Allgemeine auswärtige Politik," vol. 231/1.
"Arabien," vol. 2.
"Beziehungen Palästinas zu Deutschland," vol. 2.
"Beziehungen zwischen Rumanian und Russland," vol. 2.
"Beziehungen zwischen Russland und der Türkei," vol. 42/6.
"Beziehungen der Türkei zu Deutschland," vol. 1.
"Saudisch-Arabien," vol. 1.
"Türkei: Allgemeine auswärtige Politik," vol. 4.
"Zwischenstaatliche Probleme: Dardanellenfragen," vol. 1.
"Zwischenstaatliche Probleme: Meerengenkonferenz Montreux," vol. 1.

Ritter, Botschafter
"Afghanistan," vol. 1.
"Bulgarien," vol. 3.
"Türkei," vol. 105.

Staatssekretärs, Büro des
"Aegypten," vol. 1.
"Arabien," vols. 1–2.
"Arabien-Syrien-Iraq," vol. 1.
"Bulgarien," vol. 6.
"Diplomatische Besuche," vol. 2.
"Syrien," vols. 1–2.
"Türkei," vols. 1–9.

Stabsamt des Ministerpräsidenten Generalfeldmarschall Goering
"Auslandsberichte," vol. 150.

Unterstaatssekretär, Büro des
"Abwehr: Afghanistan," vols. 4–5.
"Aegypten," vol. 9.
"Irak," vols. 2–4.
"Panturan," vol. 24.
"Rahn Erlasse," vol. 1.
"Syrien," vol. 2.

Verträge
"Türkei," vols. 1–2.

Official Documentary Collections:

Great Britain, Foreign Office. *Index to the Correspondence of the Foreign Office: Now Preserved in the Public Record Office, London.* Nendeln, Liechtenstein, 1972.

U.S., Department of State. *Documents on German Foreign Policy, 1918–1945.* Series D, vols. 5–11. Washington, D.C. 1949–1964.

U.S., Department of State. *Foreign Relations of the United States: Diplomatic Papers, 1940.* Vol. 3, *The British Commonwealth, the Soviet Union, the Near East, and Africa.* Washington, D.C., 1958.

U.S., Department of State. *Foreign Relations of the United States: Diplomatic Papers, 1942.* Vol. 4, *The Near East and Africa.* Washington, D.C., 1963.

U.S., Department of State. *Foreign Relations of the United States: Diplomatic Papers, 1943.* Vol. 4, *The Near East and Africa.* Washington, D.C., 1964.

U.S., Department of State. *Foreign Relations of the United States: Diplomatic Papers. The Conferences at Cairo and Tehran, 1943.* Washington, D.C., 1961.

Memoirs:

Abdullah ibn-Husein. *Memoirs of King Abdullah of Transjordan.* Edited by Philip P. Graves. London, 1950.

———. *My Memoirs Completed.* Washington, D.C., 1954.

Abetz, Otto. *Das offene Problem: ein Rückblick auf zwei Jahrzehnte deutscher Frankreichpolitik.* Cologne, 1951.

Alexander, Harold. *The Alexander Memoirs, 1940–1945.* Edited by John North. London, 1962.

Archer, Laird. *Balkan Journal.* New York, 1944.

Badoglio, Pietro. *Italy in the Second World War: Memories and Documents.* Translated by Muriel Currey. London, 1948.

Beloff, Max. *The Foreign Policy of Soviet Russia, 1929–1941.* 2 vols. London, 1956.

Belot, Raymond de. *The Struggle for the Mediterranean, 1939–1945.* Translated by James A. Field, Jr. Princeton, 1951.

Butcher, H. C. *My Three Years with Eisenhower.* New York, 1946.

Catroux, Georges. *Dans la Bataille de Méditerranée: Égypte, Levant, Afrique du Nord, 1940–1944.* Paris, 1949.

Cebesoy, Ali Fuat. *Ali Fuat Cebesoy'un Siyasî Hatıraları.* İstanbul, 1957.

Churchill, Winston S. *Blood, Sweat, and Tears.* New York, 1941.

―――. *The Second World War.* Vol. 3, *The Grand Alliance;* vol. 4, *The Hinge of Fate.* Boston, 1950.

Ciano, Galeazzo. *Ciano's Diplomatic Papers.* Edited by Malcolm Muggeridge. Translated by Stuart Hood. London, 1948.

Cunningham, Andrew B. *A Sailor's Odyssey: The Autobiography of Admiral of the Fleet, Viscount Cunningham of Hyndhope.* New York, 1951.

Dalton, Hugh. *The Fateful Years: Memoirs, 1931–1945.* London, 1957.

De Chair, Somerset. *The Golden Carpet.* London, 1944.

De Gaulle, Charles. *War Memoirs.* Vol. 2, *Unity, 1942–1944.* Translated by Richard Howard. New York, 1959.

Douglas, William Sholto. *Combat and Command: The Story of an Airman in Two World Wars.* New York, 1963.

Eden, Anthony. *Facing the Dictators: The Memoirs of Anthony Eden, Earl of Avon.* Boston, 1962.

―――. *The Reckoning: The Memoirs of Anthony Eden, Earl of Avon.* Boston, 1965.

Evans, Trefor E., ed. *The Killearn Diaries, 1934–1946.* London, 1972.

Gafencu, Grigore. *Last Days of Europe: A Diplomatic Journey in 1939.* Translated by E. Fletcher-Allen. New Haven, 1948.

―――. *Prelude to the Russian Campaign: From the Moscow Pact to the Opening of Hostilities in Russia.* Translated by E. Fletcher-Allen. London, 1945.

Grew, Joseph C. *Turbulent Era: A Diplomatic Record of Forty Years, 1904–1945.* Edited by Walter Johnson. Boston, 1952.

Grobba, Fritz. *Männer und Mächte im Orient.* Göttingen, 1967.

Halder, Franz. *Kriegstagebuch: tägliche Aufzeichnungen des Chefs des Generalstabes des Heeres, 1939–1942.* Vols. 1–2. Stuttgart, 1962–1963.

Hassell, Ulrich von. *The von Hassell Diaries, 1938–1944: The Story of the Forces Against Hitler Inside Germany. . . .* Garden City, N.Y., 1947.

Hayes, Carlton J. H. *Wartime Mission in Spain, 1942–1945.* New York, 1946.

Hentig, Werner Otto von. *Mein Leben: Eine Dienstreise.* Göttingen, 1962.

Hitler, Adolf. *Hitler's Table Talk, 1941–1944.* Translated by Norman Cameron and R. H. Stevens. London, 1953.

Hull, Cordell. *The Memoirs of Cordell Hull.* 2 vols. New York, 1948.

Kállay, Nicholas. *Hungarian Premier: A Personal Account of a Nation's Struggle in the Second World War.* New York, 1954.

Kesselring, Albert. *Kesselring: A Soldier's Record.* 1954. Reprint. Westport, Conn., 1970.

Kirkbride, Alec S. *A Crackle of Thorns: Experiences in the Middle East.* London, 1956.

Knatchbull-Hugessen, Hughe. "Ambassador in Turkey." *The Fortnightly* 165 (April 1949): 228–35.

———. *Diplomat in Peace and War.* London, 1949.

Leahy, William D. *I Was There: The Personal Story of the Chief of Staff to Presidents Roosevelt and Truman. . . .* New York, 1950.

Lyttelton, Oliver [1st Viscount Chandos]. *The Memoirs of Lord Chandos.* London, 1962.

Mackenzie, Compton. *Eastern Epic.* London, 1951.

Maclean, Fitzroy. *Eastern Approaches.* London, 1949.

Macready, Gordon. *In the Wake of the Great.* London, 1965.

Massigli, René L. *La Turquie devant la Guerre: Mission à Ankara, 1939–1940.* Paris, 1964.

Meinertzhagen, Richard. *Middle East Diary, 1917–1956.* London, 1959.

Montgomery, Bernard. *The Memoirs of Field-Marshal Montgomery of Alamein.* London, 1958.

Murphy, Robert D. *Diplomat Among Warriors.* Garden City, N.Y., 1964.

Papen, Franz von. *Memoirs.* Translated by Brian Connell. London, 1952.

Pearse, Richard. *Three Years in the Levant.* London, 1949.

Peterson, Maurice D. *Both Sides of the Curtain: An Autobiography.* London, 1950.

Rahn, Rudolf. *Ruheloses Leben: Aufzeichnungen und Erinnerungen.* Düsseldorf, 1949.

Reynaud, Paul. *In the Thick of the Fight, 1930–1945.* Translated by James D. Lambert. New York, 1955.

Ribbentrop, Joachim von. *The Ribbentrop Memoirs.* Translated by Oliver Watson. London, 1954.

Rintelen, Enno von. *Mussolini als Bundesgenosse: Erinnerun-*

gen des deutschen Militärattachés in Rom, 1936–1945. Tübingen, 1951.

Roosevelt, Elliott. *As He Saw It.* New York, 1946.

Russell, Sir Thomas W. *Egyptian Service, 1902–1946.* London, 1949.

Schmidt, Heinz Werner. *With Rommel in the Desert.* London, 1951.

Stark, Freya. *The Arab Island: The Middle East, 1939–1943.* New York, 1945.

———. *Dust in the Lion's Paw: Autobiography, 1939–1946.* New York, 1961.

———. *Letters from Syria.* London, 1942.

Stimson, Henry L., and Bundy, McGeorge. *On Active Service in Peace and War.* London, 1948.

Weizsäcker, Ernst von. *Memoirs.* Translated by John Andrews. London, 1951.

Welles, Sumner. *We Need Not Fail.* Boston, 1948.

Weygand, Maxime. *Mémoires.* Vol. 3, *Rappelé au Service.* Paris, 1950.

Wilson, Henry Maitland. *Eight Years Overseas, 1939–1947.* London, 1949.

Yalman, Ahmet E. *Turkey in My Time.* Norman, Okla., 1956.

Secondary Sources: Books, Monographs, and Articles.

Abshagen, Karl Heinz. *Canaris: Patriot und Weltbürger.* Stuttgart, 1949.

Addington, Larry H. *The Blitzkrieg Era and the German General Staff, 1865–1941.* New Brunswick, N.J., 1971.

Allen, Henry E. *The Turkish Transformation: A Study in Social and Religious Development.* Chicago, 1935.

Arzık, Nimet. *Bitmeyen Kavga: İsmet İnönü.* Ankara, 1966.

Arsenian, Seth. "Wartime Propaganda in the Middle East." *The Middle East Journal* 2 (October 1948):417–29.

Assmann, Kurt. *Deutsche Schicksalsjahre: historische Bilder aus dem Zweiten Weltkrieg und seiner Vorgeschichte.* Wiesbaden, 1950.

Ataöv, Türkkaya. *Turkish Foreign Policy, 1939–1945.* Ankara, 1965.

Aydemir, Şevket S. *İkinci Adam: İsmet İnönü.* 3 vols. İstanbul, 1966–1968.

Barnett, Correlli. *The Desert Generals.* 2d ed. London, 1960.

Birdwood, Lord. *Nuri as-Said: A Study in Arab Leadership.* London, 1959.

Brodrick, Alan H. *Near to Greatness: A Life of the Sixth Earl Winterton.* London, 1965.

Bryant, Arthur. *The Turn of the Tide: A History of the War Years Based on the Diaries of Field-Marshal Lord Alanbrooke, Chief of the General Staff.* New York, 1957.

Buckley, Christopher. *Five Ventures: Iraq, Syria, Persia, Madagascar, Dodecanese.* London, 1954.

Bullard, Reader. *Britain and the Middle East from the Earliest Times to 1950.* London, 1951.

————. *The Camels Must Go: An Autobiography.* London, 1961.

Davison, Roderic H. *Turkey.* Englewood Cliffs, N.J., 1968.

Edwards, A. C. "The Impact of the War on Turkey." *International Affairs* 22 (July 1946):389–400.

Elath, Eliahu. *Haj Amin al-Husseini: Mufti of Jerusalem.* Jerusalem, 1968.

Farmer, Paul. *Vichy Political Dilemma.* New York, 1955.

Feis, Herbert. *Churchill, Roosevelt, Stalin: The War They Waged and the Peace They Sought.* 2d ed. Princeton, 1967.

Fergusson, Bernard E. "Turkey in 1941: Reminiscences." *Journal of the Middle East Society* 1 (Autumn 1947):55–59.

Fisher, Sydney N. *The Middle East: A History.* London, 1959.

Frey, Frederick W. *The Turkish Political Elite.* Cambridge, Mass., 1965.

Galatoli, Anthony. *Egypt in Midpassage.* Cairo, 1950.

Gallman, Waldemar J. *Iraq under General Nuri.* Baltimore, 1964.

Glubb, John B. *The Story of the Arab Legion.* London, 1948.

Gordon, David L., and Dangerfield, Royden. *The Hidden Weapon: The Story of Economic Warfare.* New York, 1947.

Görlitz, Walter. *Der Zweite Weltkrieg, 1939–1945.* 2 vols. Stuttgart, 1951–1952.

Grobba, Fritz. *Irak.* 2d ed. Berlin, 1943.

Hart, Liddell. *History of the Second World War.* New York, 1971.

————. *The Other Side of the Hill: Germany's Generals, Their Rise and Fall. . . .* London, 1948.

Hartmann, Hans W. *Die Auswärtige Politik der Türkei, 1923–1940.* Zurich, 1941.

Heyworth-Dunne, James. *Religious and Political Trends in Modern Egypt*. Washington, D.C., 1950.

Higgins, Trumbull. *Soft Underbelly: The Anglo-American Controversy over the Italian Campaign, 1939–1945*. New York, 1968.

———. *Winston Churchill and the Second Front, 1940–1943*. New York, 1957.

Hildebrand, Klaus. *Vom Reich zum Weltreich: Hitler, NSDAP und koloniale Frage, 1919–1945*. Munich, 1969.

Hinsley, F. H. *Hitler's Strategy*. Cambridge, 1951.

Hirszowicz, Łukasz. *The Third Reich and the Arab East*. Translated from the Polish. London, 1966.

Hostler, Charles Warren. *Turkism and the Soviets: The Turks of the World and their Political Objectives*. London, 1957.

Howard, Harry N. "Germany, the Soviet Union and Turkey during World War II," *Department of State Bulletin*, 19:63–73.

Howard, Michael E. *The Mediterranean Strategy in the Second World War*. London, 1968.

Hourani, Albert H. *Syria and Lebanon: A Political Essay*. London, 1946.

Hüber, Reinhardt. *Deutschland und der Wirtschaftsaufbau des Vorderen Orients (Türkei, Ägypten, Iran, Irak, Syrien-Libanon, Palästina)*. Stuttgart, 1937.

Hussein, Ahmad. *Egypt's War Effort: A Reply to the Charges of the American Christian Palestine Committee*. New York, 1947.

Issawi, Charles. *Egypt at Mid-Century: An Economic Survey*. Rev. ed. London, 1954.

Jacobsen, Hans-Adolf, ed. *Entscheidungsschlachten des Zweiten Weltkrieges*. Frankfurt, 1960.

Karpat, Kemal H. *Turkey's Politics: The Transition to a Multi-Party System*. Princeton, 1959.

Kedourie, Elie. *The Chatham House Version and Other Middle Eastern Studies*. New York, 1970.

———. *England and the Middle East: The Destruction of the Ottoman Empire*. London, 1956.

———. "Wavell and Iraq, April-May, 1941." *Middle Eastern Studies* 2 (July 1966):373–86.

Khadduri, Majid. "General Nuri's Flirtations with the Axis Powers." *Middle East Journal* 16 (1962):328–36.

———. *Independent Iraq, 1932–1958: A Study in Iraqi Politics*. 2d ed. London, 1960.

Kinross, John Patrick, Lord. *Atatürk: The Rebirth of a Nation.* London, 1964.

Kirk, George. *The Middle East in the War. Survey of International Affairs,* vol. 2. London, 1953.

Kocaeli, Nikat. "The Development of the Anglo-Turkish Alliance," *Asiatic Review* (October 1946):347–51.

Koeves, Tibor. *Satan in Top Hat: The Biography of Franz von Papen.* New York, 1941.

Krecker, Lothar. *Deutschland und die Türkei im Zweiten Weltkrieg.* Frankfurt, 1964.

Külçe, Süleyman. *Mareşal Fevzi Çakmak.* 2 vols. İstanbul, 1953.

Langer, William L. *Our Vichy Gamble.* New York, 1947.

Leverkühn, Paul. *Der Geheime Nachrichtendienst der deutschen Wehrmacht im Kriege.* Frankfurt, 1957.

Lewis, Geoffrey. *Turkey.* New York, 1955.

Long, George. *Greece, Crete, and Syria.* Canberra, 1953.

Longrigg, S. H. *Syria and Lebanon Under the French Mandate.* London, 1958.

Lugol, Jean. *L'Égypte et la Deuxième Guerre Mondiale.* Cairo, 1945.

Luke, H. C. *The Making of Modern Turkey: From Byzantium to Angora.* London, 1936.

Macintyre, Donald G. *The Battle for the Mediterranean.* London, 1964.

Mardor, Munya M. *Strictly Illegal.* London, 1957.

Marlowe, John. *Anglo-Egyptian Relations, 1800–1953.* London, 1954.

Marston, Elsa. "Fascist Tendencies in Pre-War Arab Politics." *Middle East Forum* 35 (May 1959): 19–22.

Marzari, Frank. "Western-Soviet Rivalry in Turkey, 1939." *Middle Eastern Studies* 7 (1971):63–77, 201–20.

Michie, Allan A. *Retreat to Victory.* Chicago, 1942.

Middlemas, Keith. *Diplomacy of Illusion: The British Government and Germany, 1937–1939.* London, 1972.

Mikusch, Dagobert von. *Mustapha Kemal: Between Europe and Asia.* Translated by John Linton. London, 1931.

Monroe, Elizabeth. *Britain's Moment in the Middle East, 1914–1956.* Baltimore, 1963.

———. *The Mediterranean in Politics.* London, 1938.

Moorehead, Alan. *African Trilogy.* London, 1965.

Morgan, Frederick E. *Overture to Overlord.* Garden City, N.Y., 1950.

Morris, Robert. *The Hashemite Kings*. New York, 1959.

Mosley, Leonard. *The Cat and the Mice*. New York, 1958.

Moyzisch, L. C. *Operation Cicero*. Translated by Constantine Fitzgibbon and Heinrich Fraenkel. With a postscript by Franz von Papen. New York, 1950.

Orga, Irfan. *Phoenix Ascendant: The Rise of Modern Turkey*. London, 1958.

Ostroróg, Leon. *The Angora Reform*. London, 1927.

Paxton, Robert O. *Vichy France: Old Guard and New Order, 1940–1944*. New York, 1972.

Philby, Harry. *Sa'udi Arabia*. London, 1955.

Playfair, Ian S. *The Mediterranean and the Middle East*. 2 vols. London, 1956.

Porath, Yehoshua. *The Emergence of the Palestinian-Arab National Movement, 1918–1929*. London, 1974.

Raswan, Carl R. *Escape from Baghdad*. London, 1938.

Rustow, Dankwart A. "Politics and Islam in Turkey, 1920–1955." In *Islam and the West: Proceedings of the Harvard Summer School Conference on the Middle East, July 25–27, 1955*, edited by Richard N. Frye, pp. 69–107. The Hague, 1957.

Said, Nuri as-. *Arab Independence and Unity*. Baghdad, 1943.

Schechtman, Joseph B. *The Mufti and the Fuehrer: The Rise and Fall of Haj Amin el-Husseini*. New York, 1965.

Schmidt, H. B. "The Nazi Party in Palestine and the Levant, 1932–1939," *International Affairs* 28 (October 1952):460–69.

Sherwood, Robert E. *Roosevelt and Hopkins: An Intimate History*. New York, 1948.

Sonyel, Salahi Ramsdan. *Turkish Diplomacy, 1918–1923: Mustafa Kemal and the Turkish National Movement*. Beverly Hills, Calif., 1975.

Tillman, Heinz. *Deutschlands Araberpolitik im II Weltkrieg*. East Berlin, 1945.

Toynbee, Arnold J., and Toynbee, V. M., eds. *The War and the Neutrals*. London, 1956.

Twitchell, Karl S. *Saudi Arabia*. 2d ed. Princeton, 1953.

Váli, Ferenc A. *Bridge Across the Bosporus: The Foreign Policy of Turkey*. Baltimore, 1971.

Vere-Hodge, Edward. *Turkish Foreign Policy, 1918–1948*. Ambouilly-Annemasse, Switzerland, 1950.

Vernier, Bernard. *La Politique Islamique de l'Allemagne*. Paris, 1939.

Viénot, Pierre. *Le Traité Franco-Syrien*. Paris, 1939.

Wavell, Archibald. *Soldiers and Soldiering*. London, 1953.

Webster, Donald E. *The Turkey of Atatürk: Social Process in the Turkish Reformation*. Philadelphia, 1939.

Weisband, Edward. *Turkish Foreign Policy, 1943–1945: Small State Diplomacy and Great Power Politics*. Princeton, 1973.

Woodward, Sir Ernest Llewellyn. *British Foreign Policy in the Second World War*. 3 vols. London, 1970–1971.

Woollcombe, Robert. *The Campaigns of Wavell, 1939–1943*. London, 1959.

Yisraeli, David. "The Third Reich and Palestine." *Middle Eastern Studies* 7 (October 1971):343–53.

Index

A

Abdullah, King, 15, 24

Abwehr, 199, 200

Abyssinia: Turkey and, 8 and
n, 215–16

Accord(s), Turkish: with France,
10; with Britain and France,
32, 33; with Russia, 61. *See
also* Agreement(s), Turkish;
Alliance, Turkish; Pact(s),
Turkish; Treaty(ies), Turkish

Adana meeting, 162–64, 165–66

Afghanistan, 76–77, 160

Agreement(s), Turkish: with
Italy, 9; with Germany, 15,
19, 120; with Britain, 129,
131. *See also* Accord(s),
Turkish; Alliance, Turkish;
Pact(s), Turkish; Treaty(ies),
Turkish

Aid: from Britain, 195; from
United States, 213. *See also*
Lend-lease materials

Airbases, Turkish: lease of, to
Allies, 188, 189, 195, 204

Airfields, Turkish, 192–93

Albania: Turkey and, 30, 31, 33,
43, 52, 60, 63, 64, 69, 127,
128, 134; and Balkan Federation, 178; mentioned, 59, 69,
71. *See also* "Cicero"

Aleppo: Turkey and, 32

Alexandretta: Turkish recovery
of, 10–18 *passim*, 20

Ali Çetinkaya. *See* Çetinkaya,
Ali

Ali Fuad Erden. *See* Erden, Ali
Fuad

Alliance, Turkish: with Britain,
vii, viii, 5–6, 30, 38, 40–45
passim, 48, 52, 59–60, 61, 69,
94, 95, 165, 179, 205; with
Germany, vii, 24, 25–28 *passim*, 34, 35, 48–49, 52, 61–63
passim, 75, 80n, 81, 93–96,
97, 98, 117, 131, 139–40, 147,
196, 217, 218, 219; with
France, vii, 29, 38; with
Britain and France, vii, 29, 38,
40–45 *passim*, 52, 59; basis
of, 20; with Italy, 52; with
Rumania, 167, 169, 170–71;
with Bulgaria, 167, 170; with
Hungary, 167, 170, 171. *See
also* Accord(s), Turkish;
Agreement(s), Turkish;
Pact(s), Turkish; Treaty(ies),
Turkish

Allies, Turkish relations with:
regarding chromite, 150; regarding war entry, Turkish,
177; regarding Cairo meeting,
first, 188–90; regarding airbases, Turkish, 188, 189, 195,
204; regarding Cairo meeting,
second, 188, 191–94 *passim*;
regarding lend-lease ma-
terials, 205

Anatolia, 214

Annexation, Turkey and: of
Alexandretta, 18; of Iraq,
89, 105, 218; of contiguous
territory, 107; beyond Ottoman Empire, 107; of Dode-
canese islands, 164; diplomacy
of, 214. *See also* Territorial
aspirations, Turkish

Anti-Communism: Turkish,
103, 167, 169, 180, 213, 218

Anti-Semitism: Ottoman Empire and Turkish, 22

Arab independence: Italy and,
53, 58; Germany and, 53–57
passim, 70, 74–77 *passim*, 78–
80 *passim*, 104, 153–56, 218

Arabs: Germany and, viii, 15–
18, 52–58 *passim*, 69, 74–77
passim, 78–80 *passim*, 103,
104, 153–56, 218; Turkey and,
12, 15, 37, 39, 70, 109, 112,

DATE DUE

GAYLORD

PRINTED IN U.S.A.